Life List

Life List
A Birder's Spiritual Awakening

Chris Dunford
illustrations by Robin Mouat

NOVALIS

© 2006 Novalis, Saint Paul University, Ottawa, Canada

Cover images: © Guy Langevin 2005 (Yellow Warbler); © Bill Wittman (Stones)
Interior illustrations: Robin Mouat
Layout: Pascale Turmel

Business Office:
Novalis
10 Lower Spadina Avenue
4th Floor
Toronto, ON
M5V 2Z2

Phone: 1-800-387-7164
Fax: 1-800-204-4140
E-mail: cservice@novalis-inc.com
www.novalis.ca

Library and Archives Canada Cataloguing in Publication

Dunford, Chris, 1948-
  Life list : a birder's spiritual awakening / Chris Dunford.

ISBN 2-89507-713-4

  1. Dunford, Chris, 1948-. 2. Bird watching--Religious aspects--Christianity.
3. Bird watching--Manitoba--Churchill Region. 4. Bird watchers--United States--Biography.
I. Title.

BV4596.B57D85 2006   598'.092   C2005-907665-8

Printed in Canada.

All rights reserved. No part of this publication may be reproduced, stored in a retrieval system, or transmitted in any form, or by any means, electronic, mechanical, photocopying, recording, or otherwise, without the written permission of the publisher.

We acknowledge the financial support of the Government of Canada through the Book Publishing Industry Development Program (BPIDP) for our publishing activities.

5   4   3   2   1   10   09   08   07   06

To Chris and Jeremy

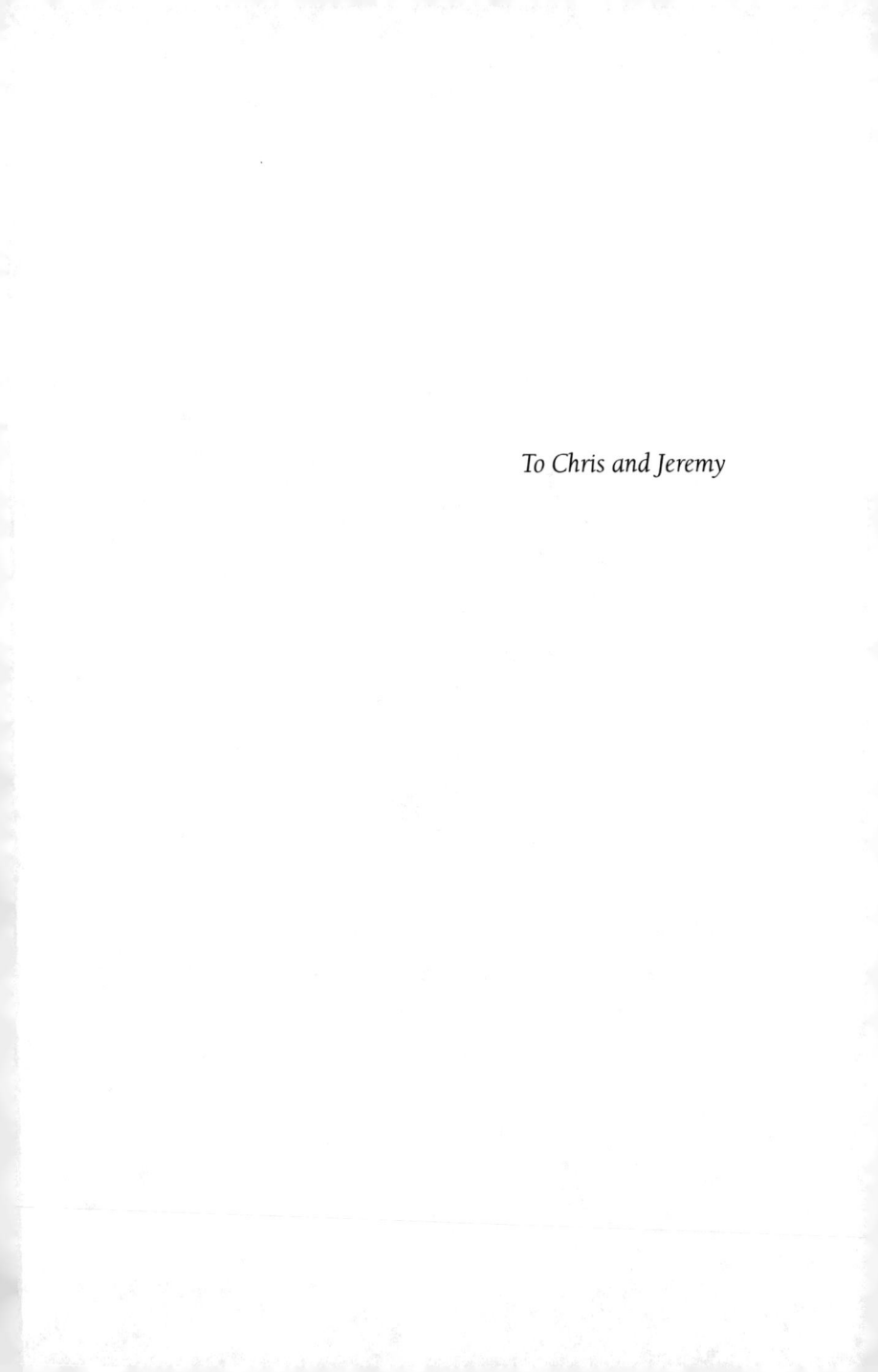

Contents

1. A Private Lunacy 9
2. The Wilderness Train 35
3. The Real Adventure 59
4. The Big Day 87
5. The Boreal Forest 133
6. The Day Off 177
7. On the Water 235
8. "A Waxwing!" 287

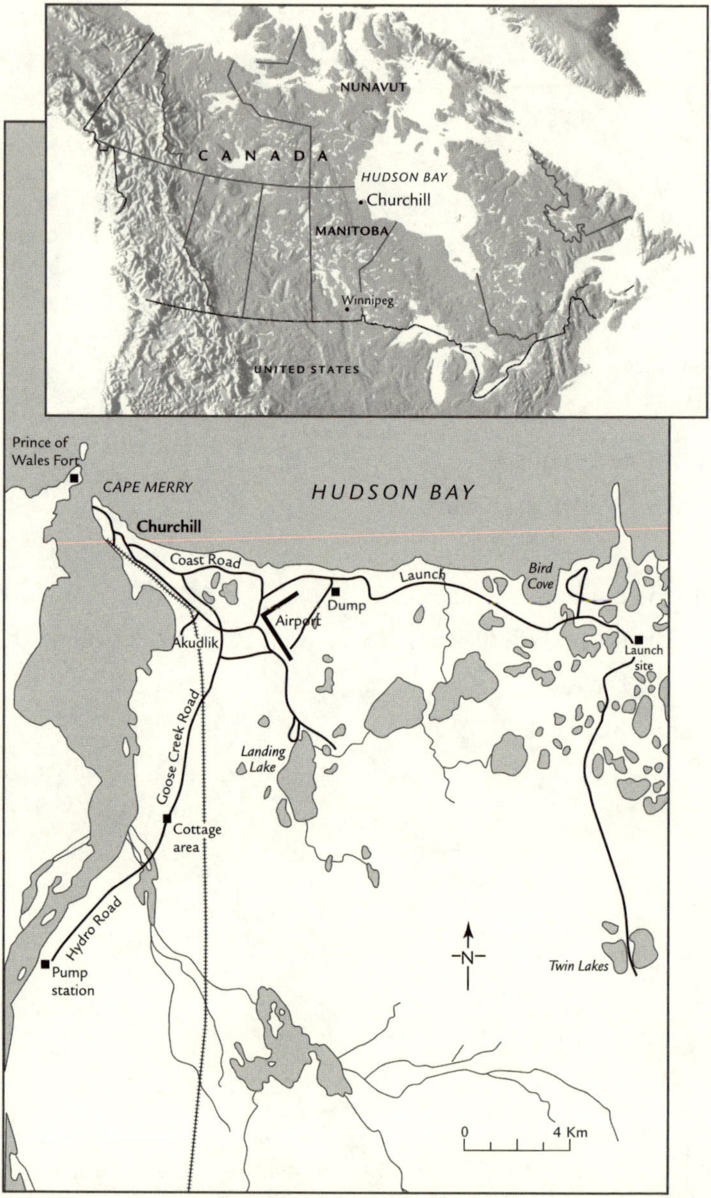
NUNAVUT
C A N A D A
HUDSON BAY
Churchill
MANITOBA
Winnipeg
UNITED STATES
Prince of Wales Fort
CAPE MERRY
HUDSON BAY
Churchill
Coast Road
Launch
Bird Cove
Dump
Airport
Akudlik
Launch site
Goose Creek Road
Landing Lake
Cottage area
Hydro Road
Pump station
N
Twin Lakes
0
4 Km

1

A Private Lunacy

Ruby-crowned Kinglet

The crunching chatter of wheels on gravel was suddenly silent. Buoyed upward like a butterfly on a relentless breeze, I was launched over the tundra with the roar of turboprops. The plane banked toward Winnipeg; there below was my whole week in new perspective, a quilted texture of pastel greens and yellows, browns and grays, and silver pools laid out below, intimately known close up, better understood from above.

The plane straightened and climbed. Now I could see the wide blue ribbon of the Churchill River. I looked back through the oval window, and there it was – the dazzling white of sea ice, spread across Hudson Bay to the smooth line of the northern horizon.

Again I studied the tundra quilt, but greater fascination drew my eyes over and over to the white sheet, receding into my past. I watched as long as I could, trying to hold on to the feeling, knowing I could return, but convinced I would not. Then the white was gone, extinguished like a sunset.

I relaxed into my seat with a smile – and started to write this book. When you travel for days to reach a tiny, lonely town at the Arctic frontier, you must explain why. Some reasonably sane, short answer will do for public consumption. I told friends and co-workers, "I'm going birding." I wasn't inventing a clever cover story. I sought out, identified, and, given the chance, really watched birds. But that is not the only reason, not the deeper reason for this journey.

I tried to imagine what my wife of 14 years and my nearly seven-year-old son were doing at this moment at home in California. Probably getting ready to go to his "farm league" baseball game. They would be wishing I was there to help, then to watch him play. My son thinks nothing in life could be better than the "plink" of an aluminum bat making solid contact with a baseball. When he is the one swinging the bat, my wife and I have to agree. I should be there.

It's difficult to explain – even to myself, much more so to my wife and son – a solitary trip to Churchill, Manitoba. For all three of us, there would have to be a fuller accounting. Given who I am, it couldn't be a verbal tale. I would have to write it – to explain to the two most important people in my world the need I have to follow the urging of the spirit. If my explanation speaks to others as well, then more is the benefit, fruit of a journey that is as much about searching as it is about identifying and recording.

As the plane droned toward Winnipeg, defying the silence of the Canadian wilderness, the enormity of my task came slowly into focus. What I wrote would have to be intensely first person, because this was a journey of body, mind and spirit, as any worthwhile journey must be. Not just anybody's journey – mine. The journey of the body must be in the style of a travelogue – where I went, what I saw, what I did, even what I ate and where I slept. Overlying the physical journey would be that of the mind, restlessly observing, comparing, questioning, tentatively answering, in the style of the old natural historians. I'd have to put a reasonable check on my lifelong enthusiasm for birds, lest I lose the interest of my family in a blur of feathery details. Yet this record of a journey would be my opportunity to explain to them the art and culture of birdwatching, and to share my enthusiasm for nature – especially with my wife and son, but also with anyone who might pick up this book.

At first I thought body and mind would be the whole story. Then I understood that I could not convey my enthusiasm without reckoning with the journey of the spirit. I would have to reveal the meaning birds hold for me. They are treasured keys that open a door to a world beyond my "life list," my science and myself. I would have to tell my family about that world beyond – with words and metaphors I had yet to discover. Even if I was successful, my son would be many years older before he could understand this deeper meaning.

My will to continue almost failed at this point. If I could summon and maintain the conviction that I have something worthy of sharing at the level of the spirit, how would I tell a story I did not yet know?

I supposed I could do no better than retrace the physical journey in my mind, let the remembered events jog recollection of the mental journey, and watch carefully for the openings to the spiritual. I knew the openings were there during the real journey. I remembered feeling them, with joy and wonder and concern and even a tinge of fear. Rediscovering these openings, I would then have to plunge through them, like Alice through the looking glass, in hope of returning with images and feelings I could put to paper in coherent thoughts. It would make a choppy narrative, jumping back and forth between the three levels of the journey: from the mundane to the sublime and back and forth – mostly mundane, but all real.

Still in the air over Manitoba, I was ready to write. But I couldn't get started without recounting antecedents to explain why Churchill, of all places, should be the destination for this three-layered journey.

On the surface it made no sense. I could have seen as many species of birds by spending a week at Bodega Bay (near my northern California home) at the right time of year. I've been to Bodega Bay more than 50 times at all times of year, often on my own, sometimes with my wife before our son was born, then with both, and a few times just as father and son. There I know the birds and their habitats like old friends. Yet I still find a surprise or two on each visit. Why not just go to Bodega Bay for a few days and save a bundle of money?

The obvious response is that "I wanted to see some *new* bird species." Around Churchill, there are birds that rarely leave subarctic Canada or that confine their movements to the centre of North America, which is nearly unknown to me. That sounds credible to sympathetic listeners. In fact, I did see 14 species that were new to me, and many others I had hardly known or hadn't seen in decades.

Yet on a recent business trip to Uganda I saw even more new and near-new birds during stolen moments from work and a couple of free mornings at the Entebbe Botanical Gardens. The birds of Africa are so much more diverse – and colourful! – than the birds of North America, much less central Canada. I love the natural areas of East Africa. I've come to know many of them, their birds, and, even more, their amazing large mammals. Why not a safari to East Africa? I lived and worked in Kenya and Tanzania in the 1970s and routinely went on safari. My wife joined me there for several weeks in 1980. We dream of going again, all three of us. If a safari for myself alone is too much of an indulgence, wouldn't a trip to Churchill be equally indulgent? Why are the cost and time away from family more justified? Why this attraction to birds, to nature, to the North?

A Private Lunacy

I'd been struggling with these questions since the idea of going to Churchill occurred to me in April 1992. I had attended a meeting in Rhode Island and afterward saw the chance for a day of birdwatching at Plum Island on the shore north of Boston, a sandy barrier beach where I birded as a teenager a few times. It has the simple, stark beauty of open space – ocean blunted by a long, thin island of sand, protecting a vast salt marsh that cushions the coast of Massachusetts. Elfin trees and fruiting shrubs hang on to life in the dunes, cringing from the salty, cold ocean winds. Little birds in migration cling to these patches of life, resting a bit until their own energy and the weather permit them to push on. Large birds – ducks, geese, gulls and sandpipers – seek the salt marsh and its invertebrate life in the ooze, or the fish that thrive in the more open water of the marsh. They, too, are fuelling up before pushing on. The scene of sea, sand and mud is so simple, severely elemental, yet here are all these beautiful creatures. Plum Island is a key way station for one of earth's most compelling phenomena – the biannual migration of birds betting their lives on reaching distant destinations. My impromptu visit rekindled a passion I thought had been tamed decades before.

Witnessing the pageant of migration in my early years excited my fascination for "wild" life – birds being the most visible wildlife in Connecticut – and my imagination of life in exotic lands to the north and the south. Bird books revealed that every species has a special story, sometimes connecting the Arctic to the Tropics and back. I'd look at a tiny warbler flitting through the new May foliage and marvel at its beautiful patterns of colour and song and picture in my mind its destination. The book said it would nest in dwarf spruce trees on the edge of the tundra. "What is tundra?" I wanted know. What would it be like to stand there and watch this very bird singing from the top of a stunted tree to stake its territory, where it would re-enact the life story of its species?

This image of the North became layered with images from television – *The Wonderful World of Disney* and *Wild Kingdom* – of migrating herds of caribou shadowed by packs of wolves, and hunter-trappers living off the wilderness and its many mammals, such as moose, beaver, bear, mink, marten and wolverine. In high-school biology, my imagination was captured by the boom-bust cycles of lemmings – how busts would drive the Snowy Owls far to the south, even as far as the northern United States, and how the fate of the lynx population was geared to that of the hares (recorded for decades in the sales of lynx and hare pelts to the Hudson's Bay Company).

In those days, the 1960s, it seemed that "North" and "wild" were synonymous, like "Africa" and "wild." There didn't seem to be much information about the tropical American destinations of the migratory songbirds, or if there was, it just didn't grab my attention. So the story of these birds seemed more about the North than the South. As fascinating as Africa seemed, it was too far away, too exotic and inaccessible. I didn't know any people – or birds – who had ever been there.

My first taste of the North was Monhegan Island, 10 miles off the coast of Maine. This square-mile chunk of granite covered by boreal (northern coniferous) forest is surrounded by the open Atlantic. It was a taste of the North, bringing it more into focus. The dominant feature was the ocean. This experience launched a deep attraction to boats and other things marine. That is another story in itself, but there were land and sea birds on and around Monhegan that summered and bred that far but no farther south. I was perched on the edge of a world that spread out before me to the North.

Then I got a chance to visit that world. My math teacher in my junior year of high school also ran a canoe camp in the summers up north in central Québec. It was *far* from civilization. We would be in the wilderness, canoeing and camping for a month. I signed up for August 1965. My imagination went to work, setting me up for one of my life's early reality checks.

Getting a group of 16 canoe campers into the wilderness automatically means that compromises must be made, although not many in this case. A purist would say that a true wilderness would not have been worked over for centuries by Algonquin and Cree hunter-trappers and, more recently, by fishermen coming up from the States for a week or two without having to shave. It also would not have a railroad running through it or logging trucks rolling down long gravel roads to unknown destinations. It would not have occasional Aboriginal communities each with its tiny Hudson's Bay Company store, or a gold-and-copper-mining town called Chibougamau. And we would barely cross the 50°N latitude. This was not the wilderness mourned by John Muir or Aldo Leopold.

Still, it *was* wilderness – for me, at age 17. The journey started when I boarded an overnight train in Montréal. Amid the anticipation of entering a new world, I didn't fall asleep until after the long midnight halt at provincial La Tuque. When I woke at first light, I looked out at a very different scene – spruces and water, water and spruces, even a moose splashing away from the train. No people, nothing of civilization other than the rail line itself. Even now, the thought of this train rolling away from civilization into the nighttime wilderness thrills me with a slightly haunted feeling.

Then the train stopped. The canoe campers stepped down with their gear and found two trucks and a kind of shelter by the rail line. That was it: a clearing among the stunted spruces and a vehicle track heading off into the bush. The romance of the North Woods soon gave way to the reality of the Canadian bush: low rainy clouds, temperatures barely breaking 50°F, biting insects in the thousands, and sodden ground underfoot. After a few weeks and hundreds (well ... tens) of portages from lake to lake, I began to get used to it all – canoeing, portaging, making and breaking camp while frozen or wet or both. I knew then what the army would be like and vowed to shun it. My tent mates and I kept reminding ourselves in private to remember forever how bad it was and thereby not come again. We were simply recognizing the power of the ideal of the North Woods, its call upon our romantic, forgetful minds.

There were moments when the ideal became real. As when the sun had just set on the far side of a silent lake, silhouetting jagged spikes of distant spruces against crimson and purple sky, and I squatted on the gravelly shoreline to dip a toothbrush into water the colour of weak tea yet so clear I could see the bottom slope below the surface at least 20 feet before it disappeared into unknown depth, and suddenly the heart-stopping, ghostly yodel of a unseen loon challenged the dusk. There were many magic moments.

But I had expected more. I thought the wilderness would be crawling with creatures. I was surprised by the scarcity of birds and mammals. Because it is a monotonous patchwork of spruces and water, there *naturally* was not a diverse fauna, I now know. I also have learned that August is a post-breeding, pre-migration quiet time in most places, when animals tend to be more secretive and generally harder to find. Profoundly disappointed to see few big animals, I withdrew from the ideal of the North. Its charm paled by comparison to its cold, its wet, its monotony, its lack of the animals I wanted to see – and its mosquitoes and blackflies!

But that train rolling through the wilderness haunted me still – I knew it had not taken me far enough.

My fascination and my career were later drawn to warmer, drier places – Arizona, Australia, Africa. But Plum Island drew me back into that northern frame of mind. The day before I went there in

1992, a friend told me that a Snowy Owl had been wintering there and had been seen recently. That news raised a hope I had not felt since a snowy day at Cornell University in 1967 when Charlie Leck, my ornithology graduate-student friend, invited me to drive up to the Syracuse airport to look for the Snowy Owl that had been reported there. Such a rare sighting and such a magnificent bird from the far North – that deserved a special trip, in Charlie's world view. He didn't have it on his life list. Neither did I.

(Despite much effort and disappointment, we never found the owl. But Charlie did introduce me to my first-ever McDonald's hamburger.)

My parents introduced me to the keeping of a life list of birds. Charlie was the one who taught me, by his own example, what it means to be a "birder" as contrasted with a "birdwatcher." A birder is a life lister, a hunter whose belly is never full. Charlie was a fanatic before birding crossed the line from pastime to industry. Nowadays, tour companies specialize in birding trips to odd places guaranteed to build your life list. Birding hotlines and websites cater to those ready to jump on a plane to Brownsville, Texas, to make a confirmed sighting of a Mexican species seldom seen in the United States (even if fairly easy to find farther south). Birding has turned into yet another sanctioned lunacy. But Charlie's form of fanaticism was fun, and he infected me with it.

He would get to know local hot spots for birds – dumps, sewage treatment plants, even a beet sugar refinery with stinky waste ponds; you wouldn't believe what variety of gulls and shorebirds favour these nasty places! A birding trip with Charlie was a scavenger hunt, a game. He was scoring points, trying to beat the record and the clock. My father and mother had earlier introduced me to the "Big Day," which is when you carefully choose a day in May to catch spring migration at its peak (always a guess) and then blast away dawn to midnight (listening for owls) to see how many birds you can identify in one day. No one could do a "Big Day" like Charlie. He invited me on one in May 1968. I still have the list of species seen – 113 in all – as we covered a broad swath of central upstate New York. It was fun, a game for people to enjoy together.

For me, however, birding has been mostly a game of solitaire. With the pleasant exception of my few years with Charlie, brief trips with others, and in my father's company at Bodega Bay around Christmastime in the 1990s, I've played alone. Listing birds seen in a certain time period becomes meaningless very quickly without the goad of a fellow lunatic. Practised alone, the listing is simply lunacy, even if enjoyable.

To rationalize my private lunacy, I made myself into a wildlife ecologist. An early university mentor persuaded me to study members of the squirrel family – chipmunks and ground squirrels – rather than birds. That became my job, a wonderful job, throughout my university years. I was even rewarded for the effort with a Ph.D. from the University of Arizona in Tucson. I was at heart a backyard biologist, content to let the glory go either to those who could master the mathematics of theoretical modelling or to those willing to travel far, suffer the hardships and danger in the wilderness, and be patient and resourceful enough to observe elusive yet well-known birds and mammals. My fieldwork built on and reinforced a simple inclination to make a list of what I saw outdoors, hoping to make sense of it. I was, and am still, trying to give meaning to solitary watching. In my relaxed moments outdoors, the animals most likely to present themselves for watching are birds.

∞

Fascinated by the chickadees and nuthatches coming to a window feeder outside my Connecticut home, I was taught by age six how to use a pair of binoculars ("a binocular," the purist would insist) and a bird book to identify the birds at the feeder. From age seven, I have a remarkably distinct memory of a crisp autumn day, sitting alone in an old orchard, watching a Ruby-crowned Kinglet.* I'd never seen one before.

But something more was at work that lovely day, one of those last warm-in-the-sun days of October. Dusky golden light slanted through the old apple trees, whose twisting branches still clutched a few yellowing leaves, momentarily to fall into the mass of spent goldenrod and asters below. The thick, still light seemed to carry the odour of sun-cured weeds, overripe apples, and distant leaf burning by neighbours down the hill. Even a seven-year-old boy could appreciate the gentle warmth and still-life beauty of this remainder of summer taking its last stand against the skeletal grays and white of winter.

The orchard was silent, and I was daydreaming – until a staccato, rapid *chit-it-chit* call drew my eyes to an apple branch above my right shoulder. There was a bird, bouncing from twig to twig like an olive-gray ping-pong ball, hardly bigger than a hummingbird, with short tail and short needle bill and proportionally huge black eyes bracketed by white parentheses, just failing to meet each other atop and below the eye. It snapped its wings open-shut every few seconds while clutching a tiny twig and surveying its next perch, not staying more than a split moment in any spot, darting,

---

* It is a convention to capitalize the common (or English) names of bird species. Each and every species of plant and animal has a unique scientific (or Latin) name, such as *Regulus calendula* for the Ruby-crowned Kinglet. However, the common names of birds are so widely used in speech and literature, and in the past there was often such confusion among two or more competing common names, that the American Ornithologists' Union adopted a unique common name to go with the scientific name of each distinct bird species. Capitalizing the common name indicates that this is the official name of this one species, not just a descriptive name or a generic name that might be used to refer to any of several species.

looking, hovering, snatching at some invisible insect where a leaf joined a twig, then darting again to another twig and another tiny insect. "Intense" is the synonym for "kinglet." It makes almost any other bird seem relaxed. Its tiny fearlessness must be the root of its name.

For all its intense, constant activity, this was no automaton. I had a keen sense of being examined by the kinglet. It had come to me for a good look. Despite its compulsive darting and snacking, its big, black eyes were fixed on me for what must have been long moments of kinglet time. And I looked back with equal intensity. Our eyes met. Contact was made. Then the kinglet moved hurriedly on to try its luck in another apple tree. And I hurried home to look in my father's book, and there it was, the tiny olive-gray bird with big black eyes bracketed by white parentheses, staring at me again from the page, with the name Ruby-crowned Kinglet underneath. That name would be forever joined in my mind with that silent, riveting moment of direct contact in the orchard.

I would be a birdwatcher for the rest of my life.

My interest in birds waxed and waned as opportunities to see new species came and went. I was interested, but with the easily distracted mind of a kid. It was a passion that ebbed and flowed as other passions swept over me like changes of the weather and the seasons. Then came another, even more profoundly life-changing sighting of a bird.

My mother and father had loved the week on Monhegan in 1957 and, even more, the two weeks in 1960. I did, too. I remember being thrilled by my mother's decision to rent a house on the island for the month of July 1963 (my father continued to work during the weekdays and came out to the island for long weekends). It was a challenge for a homemaker – wood fire for heat, no electricity, only bottled gas for cooking and lights (lighting each gas lamp with a match was a treasured task for a boy), and groceries had to be bought on the mainland and brought out by boat to the island. Though about to turn 15, I was barely aware of my mother's efforts to turn a cold cottage into a summer home. I was alone and a bit bored, but not as much as some would have been. My brother had already gone off to college, and the last place a college kid wanted to spend his summer was with his parents on a remote island. At first, however, I was entertained by the rhythms of the island, defined by the sun and the boats.

The mail boat *Laura B* came year-round from Port Clyde, daily in the summer months. It was always a good diversion to go down to the wharf and catch the rope thrown by the deckhand and loop it over a piling to halt the forward motion of the little ship. And then to see who and what was coming and going that day. The *Balmy Days* was a summer-only tourist boat that also came daily, from Booth Bay Harbor. It yielded mainly day-visitors rather than the more serious folks who lived for days to years on the island. As renters, my family ranked in islander status below the resident lobstermen and their families and the summer-home owners, but clearly above the guests at the three little hotels, and way above the day-visitors. The *Balmy Days* also offered a daily round-the-island excursion, which my mother and I enjoyed several times that month.

Still, island life was very slow, and as an energetic teenager, I had to work hard at entertaining myself. My mother taught me to play cribbage, and every evening we played after the lighting of the gaslights. During the day, she read and wrote and was glad to have me out of the house. So I was outdoors and free to roam the square-mile island. I explored the inter-tidal zone along the shore and prowled the dark spruce forest that spread across most of the island interior. I would emerge from the forest onto the tops of the dramatic cliffs of the island's uninhabited side and imagine myself wandering lost in the wilderness and then "discovering" the great expanse of the Atlantic Ocean, stretching beyond the horizon toward Nova Scotia and then Europe.

I often lurked in a part of the forest called Cathedral Woods, hoping to see the hidden singer of an ethereal melody. Starting as an outburst of excited stuttering in low, sweet notes, emanating unseen from somewhere amid the moss-covered jumble of storm-felled trunks and upturned roots, the song would rise to a tinkling trill that seemed to hover in the few dusty sunbeams allowed through the solid canopy of needles high above. Tumbling back to earth in a tangle of argumentative chatter, the song would then vault to an impossibly high-pitched trill, an audible mist in the crowns of the spruces and fir trees, held aloft by timber columns that inspired dark Gothic comparisons. Without pause the hidden singer would repeat the sequence once more, then suddenly the forest was breathlessly still.

That whole month, I never did see the singer. I could have concluded I was being teased by a forest sprite. But I had my own bird book by then and searched it thoroughly, finally deciding the melody had to come from a Winter Wren. This tiny brown bird is about as close to a forest sprite as there is, with the scientific name *Troglodytes troglodytes*, the same as Europe's only wren, the original forest troglodyte.

This and other identifications led me to create my first bird list for a particular place and month. I suppose I thought this was the least I could do to capture the essence of Monhegan on paper. After all, my mother was a writer, so I had to write something, too.

She introduced me to many books and encouraged my natural explorations, if not my mental journeys to far-off lands I found in the atlas. She was taking a correspondence course from Professor Huston Smith of the Massachusetts Institute of Technology, which was also where my brother attended college. My curiosity and boredom led me to try reading the course text by Prof. Smith, *The*

Religions of Man (retitled in later editions *The World's Religions*). It was like an atlas of religions, Western and Eastern. Questions beginning to interest me were addressed from a fascinating variety of angles. My perennial question for the atlas was "Where will I live when I grow up?" (which I allowed could be anywhere on earth). *The Religions of Man* let me explore the question "What will I believe when I grow up?" My mother seemed to encourage freedom of choice in that matter.

She and my father were both raised as Roman Catholics, but together abandoned that faith in favour of Congregationalism. My mother's only book, published in the early 1950s, was about her spiritual search. Curiously, I was encouraged to do my own search, but was given no religious education, no baseline to work from. I was both liberated from the Christian perspective and disconnected from the centuries of intellectual and spiritual achievement that still underpins our post-Christian culture. Left to my adolescent interpretations of what I read, I gravitated to the Eastern religions as Prof. Smith described them, perhaps because they seemed free of oppressive focus on sin. I was particularly drawn to Taoism, because it seemed to honour Nature as the spiritual force of the universe, to which we humans should be tuned like the other species of the earth, if we would live good lives. Nature was sufficient explanation and guidance, I thought.

It was about that time, on July 18 by a notation in the bird book, that mother and son took one of the round-the-island trips on the *Balmy Days*. It was a dependably dramatic excursion. Leaving the lobster boats at their out-of-season moorings, the *Balmy Days* would sail around the south end of the island, marked by a hidden rock called the Washerwoman, because of the constant pounding of waves that warned skippers to swing wide. In a storm many years before, the captain of the *P.T. Sheridan* had not swung wide enough, and the small freighter was thrown onto the huge boulders of the island's southern extreme. To this day, decades later, the wreck rusts in picturesque, menacing warning that the weather is not always so pleasant. Once past the wreck, passengers could see the headlands of the precipitous eastern shore appear in succession – Burnt Head, White Head, Little White Head, Black Head – rising 100 to 150 feet above the unrestrained assault of the open Atlantic. At this point, the captain would announce solemnly that no person falling into the water on this side of the island had ever been rescued. A predictable chill would sweep the deck clean of happy thoughts, even as all admired the beauty of these cruel cliffs.

The mood would soften as the boat rounded the north end of Monhegan and the several small bird islands off the gentler western shore came into view. On these islets the nesting could occur in safe isolation from the main island – the Herring Gulls whose tenor voices were the official anthem, punctuated by the baritone of Great Black-backed Gulls, with no audible contribution from the Double-crested Cormorants, Black Guillemots, and Common Eiders, who warily protected their eggs and youngsters from the ruthless gulls.

To this point, the July 18 excursion had followed the routine script, until near the Seal Ledges, I pointed out to my mother a dark seabird floating just off the port bow. We could tell this was no gull. It was almost as large, but more streamlined. As the boat closed in, the bird reluctantly lifted off the water and flew stiffly away, giving us a brief but clear view of its peculiarly long, narrow, straight wings, its black cap and its white rump. Back at the cottage that afternoon, I pored over my bird book, hoping to identify this odd bird. And there it was on the page, a Greater Shearwater! How amazing it was to see a bird that lives almost totally at sea, out of sight of land except to breed. Even more amazing to me

A Private Lunacy

was that this bird breeds only on the islands of Tristan da Cunha in the extreme South Atlantic.

This bird had come all the way from Tristan da Cunha!

I shot to the atlas to find this speck of land and discovered it about halfway between the Cape of Good Hope and Cape Horn. Another source told me that a tiny British colony lived there, connected to the outer world only by an annual freighter visit from Cape Town, South Africa (nowadays, surely there is some sort of air service as well). To me, that shearwater was a visitor from an alien world, almost beyond my imagination, but not quite. This intriguing bird, combined with the intrigue of Taoism, seemed to seal a commitment to the study of nature as my form of spiritual search. I must have decided there on Monhegan Island, Maine, with the clarity of a 15-year-old mind, that I would roam the world in search of understanding the spiritual force of the universe. And birds like this shearwater would be my guides.

In August, reluctantly back in my mundane world in Connecticut, I wondered what I could do to prepare myself for this life's work, to keep my resolve alive.

I hit upon the idea of recording the change of seasons by observing the change in birds from month to month, a sort of bird calendar representing the larger seasonal pattern of my natural surroundings. From August 1963 through June 1964, I listed all the bird species I saw in each successive month in the area of home, school and in between. This was surprisingly easy. Usually my sightings were without binoculars, often by ear only, while walking through the woods to and from school.

It was deeply satisfying at several levels. At the surface, the exercise entertained me with a "guess what I am" game as I trudged back and forth. At a deeper level, it gave me a feeling of competence as I got quite good at recognizing birds flying, in silhouette, singing, and even single call notes. Deeper still, I might have recognized that the game kept me tuned in to the natural world around me. It kept me alert for little surprises and reassuring familiarity.

Deeper yet, although I may not have been conscious of this, I think my game was a very satisfying form of meditation. Watching for wild animals focused my brain on the present, the moment in which I was living, instead of previous and future moments, with their regrets and worries.

It works for me still. I feel in touch with the universal forces – with God – when I see a wild animal, which is usually a bird. An animal is living in and driven by the *moment*. At the same time, the animal represents a progression through time, the result of life's underlying process. Observing nature and wild beings is like listening to a language I don't understand. If I concentrate, I hear rhythms and patterns of sounds I know must mean something. It sets me to wondering *what* it means. I also wonder whether my son will hear these rhythms and patterns of nature as I do. It would give us a common bond on which to build a common language of our own. But that is a question for the future, not the present.

∞

As I became a traveller, often to the same exotic places repeatedly, I tried to relate my watching and listing to understanding differences, not only between seasons but also between places. The birds coming forward to be named and recorded became the ambassadors from their world on Monhegan Island or Plum Island or central Québec to my world of questioning and seeking for meaning. Each bird had its story about where it lived, what it ate, its habits, habitat, biological community and physical environment. There wasn't much science in this. Mostly, birdwatching became for me a quick, dependable way to tune into different natural worlds I had the privilege to visit, never to really understand, but always to appreciate, with a schooled intuition for how things work together – birds, mammals, plants, landscapes, climate – and people.

Here I encounter a problem in my rationale for birdwatching. Why, then, would I make a special effort to see a Snowy Owl at the Syracuse airport or on Plum Island? How would seeing such a bird help me to tune into the natural world of upstate New York or coastal Massachusetts? Here the Snowy Owl is a refugee, out of place, almost *un*natural. Would I interview an African refugee newly arrived in Maine in order to understand the people of Maine? It would be a treat to see a bird as magnificent as a Snowy Owl, but seeing magnificent creatures can be achieved rather more dependably at a good zoo than in the wild. So, there is something more at work. Something called a life list.

The life list is what turns a birdwatcher into a birder. What is meaningful about a life list is that it records the bird species of which you have seen at least one individual – naturally, in the wild – well enough to honestly identify it on your own. Then, and only then, that species goes on the life list. No flash of white with someone shouting, "There goes a Snowy Owl!" You have to be properly introduced to claim the acquaintance. Judging when that has happened is a personal call. It requires considerable integrity. Sometimes the primal urge to "list" will overcome even the best in their excitement of discovery. The list-maker must guard against wishful thinking and self-delusion. Bird species can be very hard to identify, and sometimes it requires excruciating self-discipline to consign a sighting to the "unknown" or "not sure" category. It is very frustrating. There is enough of the birder in me to know the feeling well. A few times I've had to remove a species from my life list, when later, upon cooler reflection, I had to admit to myself that I couldn't be sure of my identification.

So I would go out of my way to see a Snowy Owl, even as a winter refugee at Syracuse airport, where I would not otherwise choose to go on a cold January day. Not because I am a birdwatcher, but because I'm a birder as well. I "need" this species for my life list. On the other hand, the birdwatcher in me says a Snowy Owl is more than another "life bird." It is an emissary from the Arctic, as impressive and exotic as any splendid ambassador from a faraway land. Seeing one would be a magic moment. I say "would," because I didn't see one on Plum Island that day in April 1992. After a miserably cold day in the field, I went through my favourite bird book, reviewing what I *had* seen. When I came to the owl section, I checked the range map for the Snowy Owl, just to see where I could reliably see one. It would definitely be better to see one in its home country, where it could help me understand in my small way its own world of the Arctic.

This non-encounter on Plum Island brought two earlier thoughts back into focus. First, while browsing the bird guides to exotic lands at The Naturalist, a lovely store in my hometown, I found one day *The Birder's Guide to Churchill,* by Bonnie Chartier. I was surprised and intrigued – not because I had never heard of Churchill (remember my penchant for atlas browsing). I never thought of Churchill as a special place for birds, worthy of its own bird-finding guide. I was intrigued, too, because of long fascination with outposts of civilization in the midst of or on the edge of wilderness, places where people have to develop a special relationship with their isolation and their vulnerability to a totally natural regime – where people exist in a different perspective. What motivates people to be there and how do they sustain themselves? The question of motivation is more relevant to people from the modern world who have chosen to be there, in contrast to traditional inhabitants of such areas. It is a question relevant to *me* – I could choose to live there. What would my life be like if I did?

This is not an idle thought in my case. My visits to Monhegan Island got the ball rolling, especially when compounded by the

Greater Shearwater drawing my imagination to Tristan da Cunha. In 1974, I visited and very nearly settled in Alice Springs, Australia. Later that same year, I thought very seriously about taking a position offered to me by the Peace Corps in Punta Arenas, Chile (the "jumping off" point for Antarctica), but turned it down as being too cold for my taste. I've been to French Polynesia three times and each time have extended my length of stay and finally pushed out to the remotest atoll with hotel accommodation (my adventurous nature has well-defined limits since my canoe-camping experience in Québec). I spent a week in Leticia, Colombia, on the banks of the Amazon River, 2,000 miles upriver into the rainforest. I've relished my work opportunities to visit remote outposts in Africa, such as El Fasher in the Sudanese Sahara and Maun, Botswana, beyond the Kalahari. Each time I withdrew from choosing to reside in these remote outposts, but I would still jump at the chance to visit for a few days.

I would not use my own money, my family's money, to go without very compelling reasons. I put the book back on the shelf that time, but Churchill was added to my list of intriguingly remote outposts, even before I realized that by going there I might see a Snowy Owl on its own turf.

The second thought was that the Arctic tundra was the only biome I had never experienced first-hand. A biome is a very broad category of earth's main terrestrial ecosystems – like tropical rainforest, broad-leafed deciduous forest, temperate grassland, semi-desert scrub, and so on. I had travelled through representative examples of each of these terrestrial biomes, with the exception of the Arctic tundra. This is another manifestation of the listing imperative. Add the tundra and my list would be complete. From an ecologist's viewpoint, visiting all the biomes is far more significant than visiting all nations. Somehow my ecological understanding of the earth would be more complete if I could visit the Arctic tundra. I wasn't enthusiastic, however, because of my dislike for cold and for bugs – you get one or the other in the Arctic. But my tolerance for moderate cold seems to have grown in the 1990s, partly because of my enjoyment of Bodega Bay at all seasons. After a bone-chilling day on Plum Island, I was seriously considering a trip to Churchill, Manitoba!

Back in California, I bought Bonnie Chartier's book and read it carefully. She lives in Churchill and runs a nature tour company called Churchill Wilderness Encounter. I called her to get some more logistical details. We had a nice conversation, and she confirmed that mid-June is the prime time for catching the arrival of shorebirds on their tundra breeding grounds, as well as passage migrants heading farther north. But mid-June is a little late to see Snowy Owls and Gyrfalcons – they *winter* in Churchill, which is in the subarctic. Geographically, the Arctic is north of the Arctic Circle at 67°N (Churchill is 59°N), but the tundra extends as far south as Churchill due to the chilling influence of Hudson Bay. One reason the birds and other wildlife are so diverse is that the Churchill area is a boundary or blending zone between the boreal forest (such as I experienced in Québec) and the tundra.

Mid-June is the time to go for birds, when snow should be unlikely and before the mosquitoes come out. The ice on the Churchill River should be mostly gone, but Hudson Bay should still be icebound. Too early for polar bears to come ashore (as long as they can be out on the ice on the Bay, they can feed on seals – they fast when on shore), but you never know. Beluga whales might start to enter the river mouth from the Bay (later in summer there would be around 3,000 of them in the tidal mouth of the river). The possibilities are exciting, but there is no one time when you're guaranteed to see it all.

Churchill exists because a rail line was built in the 1920s to carry wheat from Winnipeg to Hudson Bay, where it is loaded on ships during the ice-free season (late July to mid-October) for shipment to Europe. Churchill became Canada's "Arctic Seaport." A passenger train runs the route three times a week and takes 33 hours (two nights and a day). There is no road in. Bonnie recommends taking the train up from Winnipeg and flying back to Winnipeg.

This all sounded great to the birder in me! But I couldn't give this idea serious thought without my wife's blessing. She is not a birder. In fact, she was not even a birdwatcher when we met in 1980. We started our friendship as regular dance partners in Tucson when that exotic little city was the centre of a country and western swing-dancing craze and many of the ecology graduate students at the University of Arizona were ardent aficionados. But she was neither a grad student nor an ecologist. She was just a lovely, smart, dependable young woman with an unusually positive life attitude who loved to dance. From the first date, we felt deeply at ease with each other. We met as I was returning to Tucson after several years of being a scientific desk-jockey in East Africa. There I had a few good nature-loving friends who regularly joined me on weekend safaris to see the big mammals, but they were casual birdwatchers at best. They appreciated the bigger, more colourful birds, so they were patient with my binocular work, especially because I was often able to point out animals they would not have seen otherwise. I became comfortable with birding on the run and on the sly, so as not to test their forbearance needlessly. Hence, my wife-to-be's initial lack of enthusiasm for birds was not a deal-breaker. She soon learned to be equally forbearing and even developed a discerning appreciation for the more conspicuous local birds. But nature and birds did not hold the meaning for her that they did for me. There were understandable limits to her forbearance.

In 1991, we had a son, and he was still a toddler when the idea of going to Churchill first occurred to me. It soon was evident that the natural world was far less interesting to him than sports involving some sort of ball. The idea of all three of us going to Churchill was preposterous, and even the idea of going by myself seemed so far-fetched that I didn't even bring it up. I put Bonnie's book on my bookshelf along with all the other bird books. Then, a year or more later, my wife said to me one day, when it was clear that my work was draining me dry, that I "deserved" a real break, that I should go do something that I really wanted to do, on my own – like go to the Galapagos Islands! What birder wouldn't want to visit the Galapagos someday? She even proposed that we should set aside some family resources for that purpose – a birding trip for me. I was very pleased that she should think I deserved something so special as that. But, somewhat guiltily, I told her that I might prefer to go to Churchill. Huh? Where's that and why would you want to go there? Obviously, I hadn't been sharing my thoughts with my own wife!

Because it was birding lunacy.

2

The Wilderness Train
June 4–6

Clay-colored Sparrow

It was six years after the visit to Plum Island before I finally made the trip. I drove to San Francisco, flew to Vancouver, British Columbia, spent the night near the airport, then flew on to Winnipeg to catch the train at 10:00 p.m. on June 4, 1998. Actually, I arrived at the Winnipeg train station at 6:00 p.m. and found it empty, except for a ticket agent.

"Going north?" he asked as soon as I approached.

I guessed that few passengers came through here anymore. He was relaxed and friendly. I felt the same as I contemplated a leisurely dinner, a walk along the Red River and then nearly two days on the train.

I was soon off to an auspicious start in my birding. In the park shrubbery at the confluence of the Red and Assiniboine Rivers, a sparrow I'd never seen before popped up next to me so close I could study it with the naked eye. The word "nondescript" comes to mind whenever I see a sparrow without the benefit of binoculars, but this one was close enough for me to see a bridle of stripes forming a triangle on the cheeks behind and below the eye. Its back was also striped, black on beige, but its breast and underparts were unmarked buffy gray. We looked at each other for a long moment before the sparrow dropped back into the shrubbery. Too often sparrows rise from their protective cover long enough to confirm their worst fears, then disappear just as my brain starts to register descriptive details. This one almost lingered in its inspection of the foreign visitor. Its message might have been "Welcome to central Canada. Name me if you can! We're not flashy around here, but we're different. Bye."

I normally don't carry a bird book into the field. I depend on my good memory for images and sounds. Other birders shake their heads in disbelief. But I find it more enjoyable to be a lightweight birder and suffer the risks of missing an identification. The preference was born of an adaptation to travelling with non-birders, who are reluctant to stand around while I check the book and then try to recheck the bird. I may lose details before getting to the book at home or in the car. There is no getting a second look to see whether the bird did or did not have the yellowish spot between the bill and the eye, which I hadn't noticed on first examination and which would mark the difference between two possible species. In this case, I had no second opportunity to see the sparrow, but I did have a bird book in my over-the-shoulder travel bag. I immediately sat on a park bench, opened the book to the sparrows, and found to my great relief that I had seen enough to positively identify my first Clay-colored Sparrow. It is rather more striking than the name suggests (the colour of dirt!), and rather common if you spend time in the Prairie provinces or the Dakotas.

My first life bird of the trip, unexpected in downtown Winnipeg. Seeing a life bird colours any time and place in vivid hues. This could no longer be just an ordinary riverside city park, soon to be forgotten in a blur of travel. This moment would be forever treasured in my memory as the time and place I saw my first Clay-colored Sparrow, no matter how nondescript, even if the colour of dirt. This is the gift that birding sometimes gives to otherwise mundane experience.

It was getting dark as the VIA Rail train slid away from the station at exactly 10:00 p.m. with two locomotives, a baggage car, two coach cars, a dining car, and a sleeper at the end. There were five passengers: a late-middle-aged woman in coach, three young German-speaking men going fishing somewhere, and me, the only one bound for Churchill. I was stunned. This was supposed to be the big season for birders, so I had expected a train full of them. Later I would discover that birders (perhaps appropriately) prefer to fly – or at least board the train farther up the line. I was also a little ahead of the peak season. The sleeping-car attendant assured me, nonetheless, that the train always fills up as they go north.

Assigned to Roomette/Chambrette 8, I was stunned again. It was so small! I had trouble getting my two small bags and myself into the compartment. I spent the first hour settling in, unpacking some stuff, discovering an upper shelf that would take both bags, strategic hooks for jackets and sweater, a tiny shelf for toiletries, a slightly larger one for bird books and binoculars (ready for the next day of watching from the train), and learning how to use the fold-up sink, the toilet, and how to fold down the bed without having to leave the compartment (good thing I'm still fairly thin). By midnight, I was stretched out in bed; well, it was not quite long enough for stretching out. There was more rolling and stuttering motion than I expected, and the track had distinct breaks between rails that gave off a clacketty clatter. I felt some queasiness from the whole effect, which I found alarming. Unlike my wife and son, I tried to persuade myself, I am *not* vulnerable to motion sickness. It was an uncomfortable night. Maybe taking the train was not the best idea? I quickly shrugged off that second thought and found myself waking up at 4:30 a.m. in Canora, Saskatchewan.

To skirt the vast lakes of central Manitoba, the train had gone west from Winnipeg and a short way into Saskatchewan before committing itself to a northerly route that would loop northeast, back into Manitoba and toward Hudson Bay. Wheat fields, aspen woods, grain elevators, plain boxy houses, "prairie pothole" ponds with ducks in silhouette and the distinctive figure of an American Avocet, a coyote pushing the northern limit of its range, and a small wooden church with an onion-dome steeple in the middle of nowhere (reflecting the history of Ukrainian immigration): these were the passing images in the dawn light as I sat up in bed feeling very comfortable and watching.

We rolled into forest country, with occasional rivers and lots of smaller streams turned to ponds and swamps by beaver dams. Now I saw pines, spruces and birches as well as aspens. I sat down to breakfast at 6:45 a.m. and had the undivided attention of the dining-car attendant. He told me I had just missed three big elk. I sat back and watched central Saskatchewan roll at me and away on both sides of the dining car. Having no prospect of anything else for the rest of the day and next night and morning, I had as profound a sense of satisfaction and relaxation as I've ever experienced.

∞

Up to this point, I had been fuelled by a mixture of excitement and apprehension about the possibilities of such a trip into the unknown. I was excited for the obvious reason that the unknown brings possibilities of discovery and surprise. I might find something I never expected, that might forge new understanding, even changing my world view, the way the Greater Shearwater had done 35 years before. I was apprehensive because the unknown brings possibilities of disappointment and even unpleasant surprise.

Experience tells me that satisfaction is inversely related to expectation. I had avoided reading much about Churchill and the vicinity before the trip. What others had seen and experienced was mostly in different seasons, years, and places beyond my opportunities during one week in June 1998. Their luck was different from what mine would be. I didn't want to get my hopes too high. I had Bonnie Chartier's book about finding birds around Churchill. It has lots of non-bird information about the natural and human history of the area. I resolved to take only that book, three relevant bird identification books, and one other: *Diary of a Left-handed Birdwatcher,* by Leonard Nathan. I had promised myself to read again about Churchill when at last I was on the train. Even then, I planned mainly to watch the landscape change and see what I could see as the train rolled north toward the reality of Churchill.

Perhaps I was wasting a lot of money on a boy's quest. After nearly five decades of life, school, reading, television and movies, and nearly a quarter-century of extensive world travel, mainly for work but always seizing every opportunity to have a good look around, I suspected there might not be many surprises, much less momentous discoveries, left to uncover.

Nearly all this anticipatory anxiety melted away as I sat staring at Saskatchewan from my breakfast table. There was no going back. I was committed to this adventure, and it would unfold at its own pace, come what may, regardless of my hopes and fears. The train and I were operating on real time, the present.

A long train ride might be a good metaphor for helping my son understand life. In a car on the road, you appear to have far more choices than life really offers. In an airliner, you feel almost blessedly disconnected from reality. A transoceanic voyage by ship is too featureless. A train rolls through the real world, beautiful or ugly, familiar or not, and you have to give yourself to the train – its speed, its tracks, its route, its destination. You can choose what you pay attention to and how you react to what you see, but the train rolls on regardless.

The train is my Arrow of Time. I literally have a window on time. I can see only the present, as it rolls from past to future. I can face forward to strain for a glimpse of the future as soon as it becomes the present. I can face backward to savour the present just as it disappears for good into the past. I can look out on the people, animals, plants, land and buildings present along the tracks. I can look to the side as far as I can see into the distance to the present horizon. What I cannot do, no matter how hard I try, is look straight into the future or straight back into the past. I cannot see beyond the horizon of the present (unless the train ceases to be a metaphor by going round a curve in the track, or I'm in a domed observation car!). I have to give myself up to the present – its speed, its tracks, its route, its destination.

Memory of the past allows even a simple-minded animal to anticipate the future. Situations often repeat themselves and become predictable. If the shifting shape of a cat once meant a terrifying attack and a hair's-breadth escape, it probably will lead to the same right now – time to flee! The past cat helps the animal to anticipate the future cat. A healthy human can do a good deal more with memories, thanks to an ability to label memories and communicate them in abstract symbols – words – that stand for real things and events. We can pass these symbols back and forth and change their meanings as we talk to each other – and also to ourselves. We can think, and think about thinking – about the past, present and future. Language and the brain to use it give us the god-like ability to think about our memories, sometimes consciously, sometimes unconsciously, and blend them with the memories of others to experience what we've never personally seen, felt or done. Imagination allows us to reassemble these building blocks of thought into things, events and places that no one may have ever known.

We can build fantastic distortions of reality. Building distortion upon distortion, we can mentally travel way beyond the horizon of the present, sometimes even guided by wonderful logic. The results can be very useful as social and technological innovations with real survival value. That's what has allowed humans to go beyond the boundaries of nature as other animals know them and create a man-made overlay that often seems like a completely different reality.

There is a price to pay in having this god-like ability to travel mentally beyond the present. We can, and most of us do, go so far beyond the present that we find it difficult to impossible to return and dwell in the present tense for more than a moment or two at a time. The chatter going on in our minds, no matter how rational, incessantly pulls us forward and backward, anywhere but the here and now. Yet here and now is where we live, the only *reality* we have, the only reality we share with the rest of nature. The Vietnamese Buddhist Thich Nhat Hanh puts it succinctly in his book *Peace Is Every Step*: "Our appointment with life is in the present moment."

Instead of savouring the present and living the life we've got, we dwell on the past and worry about the future. Some of us soar on our mental chatter transformed into elegantly logical systems of thought. Some of us are literally driven mad by our own mental chatter turned into delusion. All of us are very often terribly distracted. We highly value the brief times when our minds are stilled by intense focus on what we are doing, seeing, feeling *right now* – when we are living like an alert animal.

That's how I was, at last, as I watched Saskatchewan roll by and waited for my breakfast.

The attendant was serving only the two tables closest to the kitchen. Soon the German-speakers were eating at the other table. Their language and camaraderie didn't invite my interaction, so I enjoyed a good breakfast in contemplation of the countryside, hoping for elk. Watching for wildlife from a train, especially toward the rear, is not the most productive tactic. By the time two locomotives and three cars have rolled by, you're looking at fleeing rear ends already some distance from the tracks. I saw lots of water and lots of ducks, especially Ring-necked Ducks – I came to recognize "departed duck" in the spreading circles on the water. They jump straight up into the air. I finally glimpsed a distant elk just before it vaulted into the forest. So I kept up an intense vigilance with binoculars on the table before me.

A middle-aged woman came back from coach – not the same one as the night before, proving that passengers could get on after Winnipeg. In fact, the whole crew had changed at Dauphin (rhymes with "coffin") except the dining-car waiter and cook, who doubled as sleeping-car attendants. They were the only ones going all the way with me. The woman looked hesitant, seeing that the only tables in service were occupied. Mine was set for four so I gestured with my hand that she'd be welcome to join me. I said, "Please!" And she sat down with a smile. I told her about the elk I'd seen, and she and the waiter proceeded to educate me about the differences in habitat where you should see elk and moose. The conductor (or *chef de train,* according to the French on his name badge) and his deputy joined us for breakfast. The conductor knew the woman, whose husband had worked for the railroad. Still watching the landscape – you never know when something exciting will be flushed – I was allowed into a gossipy central-Canadian conversation.

The crew would change again in The Pas (pronounced "Pa"), the first town after the crossing back into Manitoba. Almost at the provincial border, we passed into spruce-dominated boreal forest I recognized from central Québec. The woman lived in The Pas. She had boarded around midnight at Portage la Prairie, where she had visited her parents. Her husband and one of her sons worked for the new Hudson Bay Railroad (HBR). I learned that a Denver-based firm, Omni Tracks, had a year earlier purchased the rail line from The Pas up to Lynn Lake, and also the line up to Churchill. The same firm had purchased the Port of Churchill and had already turned what had been a financial burden on the federal and provincial governments into a profitable private enterprise. I also learned that Canadian National owned the tracks from Winnipeg to The Pas and supplied the crews to run the VIA Rail train. The woman's husband had worked for CN and was hired by HBR at substantially the same wage rate and benefits. HBR now supplied the crews to run the VIA train from The Pas up to Churchill. Anticipating the sale for years, CN had done little maintenance on the roadbed. The train would go progressively slower until it was down to about 20 miles an hour over the tundra. HBR was investing in maintenance and upgrading now, but there was a lot to be done yet.

Back to work for the two trainmen. The woman and I continued our conversation – and my education.

I was beginning to explore in my mind the distinctive features of Canadian English, more different from American than I expected, more than using "Eh?" instead of "Huh?" Central Canadians seem to have a light Scots melody, with harmonics from Ukrainian, Scandinavian and Aboriginal languages, I guessed. Canadians don't speak of "Indians," but of Aboriginal or First Nations people. In the more northern towns, Aboriginal people are a near-majority of the locals. The Métis (MAY-tee) are less-evident descendants of French–Aboriginal marriages generations ago, but no less numerous, I suspect. The woman from The Pas told me her husband's father was Métis. Her parents were from Belgium. It struck me that central Canadians were remarkably diverse.

We continued our travel through unrelieved spruce forest. Perhaps only an ecologist would notice, much less appreciate, the subtle variations of jack pine and white spruce on better-drained soil and the spiky, stunted black spruce of the sodden muskeg swamps. I also noticed that one strand of wire (a phone line, I suppose) followed the rail line, held aloft not by single vertical telephone poles but by tripods of wooden poles at regular intervals, one pole longer than the two, with the wire attached to the protruding, angled top. In some sections of the route, vertical concrete poles had been given the job of holding the wire aloft, but the obsolete tripods were still there, in all stages of collapse. No doubt the tripods were an accommodation to the difficulty of maintaining a single vertical pole upright in alternately sodden and frozen ground, frost-heaved annually. Why the concrete poles would be more successful, I cannot say.

An hour or more back into Manitoba, we pulled into The Pas. It had the feel of an unpretentious market town in Iowa, but in the midst of wilderness. I had 30 minutes to walk around. I remembered to photograph the train for a friend who has a passion for trains and had taken this route in the 1960s and again in the 1980s. It was pleasantly cold and cloudy. I got accustomed to the Canadian use of the Celsius temperature scale – it was perhaps 5°C, or in the low 40s Fahrenheit. The woman and the German-speakers got off, and a new crew of trainmen and the Weir Guys got on board.

They were heavy-equipment operators, big, hard-laughing guys from Thunder Bay, Ontario. They were on their way to spend the summer and fall in Churchill building a weir, or diversion dam, on the Churchill River, to contain the upriver intrusion of marine water into the Churchill water source, or something like that. They took over the lounge area of the dining car, then descended on my solitary vigil at lunchtime. With some unease, I invited them to share "my" table, but found them to be congenial, even good fun.

I wished my wife were with me, because she shows me again and again how interesting people are when you get them telling funny stories and teasing each other. I did my best in her absence and learned a great deal about heavy equipment, which they had loaded on freight cars in The Pas to come to Churchill a couple of days behind them. I learned even more about the workingman's Canadian bush. They are involved in very seasonal but highly remunerative construction work in remote places, scrambling to earn a living from multiple lines of work. The most articulate among them had trained and worked as a wildlife biologist, but now operated a fish farm and owned and drove his own dump truck, worth about $200,000. Only one of them had been to Churchill before. Try as they might, they couldn't hide their apprehension about what lay ahead.

The men were politely curious about the States, especially California. I've felt many times the subtle awe my California residence evokes in fellow Americans who have never been to the state. For them, California is Fantasyland, where the sun shines impossibly and the people radiate health, wealth, happiness and power – and never blow their lines. I suppose the United States in general has a similar effect on non-Americans who have never visited, but I was surprised to find this reaction among Canadians. My own ill-informed stereotype of Canadians was that they held us Americans in genial contempt, perhaps covering for the kind of benevolent resentment one might feel toward a more "successful" sibling, perhaps regarding the States as a self-important El Dorado where all that glitters is not gold. In return, the American nation is ambivalent about Canada. Some of us dismiss Canada as our 51st state, while others of my acquaintance think of Canada as a kind of City on the Hill – a frozen city! – where the government does right all the things we think our government does wrong.

The Weir Guys showed no such prejudice – only a genuine, innocent curiosity about a place they had heard good things about. They were also respectful of the purpose of my trip. They could relate to my attraction to wildlife, even birds. Nature was a very important part of their lives, too.

Seven hours from The Pas, through equally unrelieved boreal forest, we pulled into the Thompson station, in the midst of nowhere, it seemed. I had an hour to walk, and I did. It had warmed up to 15°C (60°F or so), and the sky had partly cleared. I discovered a road with a sidewalk in what appeared to be pure forest. The road went up and over a low rise, and I followed it. Topping the rise, I was amazed to find a major town before me, a model of modern North American suburbia. Of course! A company town serving the nearby nickel mine, reported to be one of the world's biggest.

I was surprised to hear a Least Flycatcher and an Ovenbird in the roadside woods. Surely they were at the northern extreme of their range, at least in Manitoba. I was reminded that even familiar birds are rare and exotic somewhere in the world. I take special interest in birds making a living on the frontier of their species' range, advancing in good years, getting knocked back in the bad. Species boundaries are fluid, suggesting key limiting factors in the lives of a species. I never have had time or commitment enough to delve and discover what these key factors might be, but I enjoy seeing a pioneer making a life on the frontier. I set to wondering what such a life is like, what risks are faced. It was my fascination with life in remote outposts at work again.

While evidence of the North was all around, the South was not yet letting go. The oh-so-familiar American Crow and Red-winged Blackbird were still present and conspicuous, but would soon be gone as I headed farther north. Starlings would become a prized find around Churchill. Even the Song Sparrow and White-throated Sparrow, which thrive around Thompson and farther south, would soon be hard to find. Yet American Robins would remain ubiquitous, perhaps more so, around Churchill, even on the tundra. And I would discover a vibrant colony of House Sparrows established within easy flight of the grain elevators at the Port of Churchill. My admiration for these hardy, adaptable species would grow.

There is memorable delight in clearly seeing a bird in its finest breeding colours and pattern, especially a breeding pair. I had two such lucky encounters during my walk from the train. A pair of small ducks, Blue-winged Teal, tried to make themselves invisible by gliding under the overhanging shrubs of a roadside pool. The white crescent on the drake's face is unique – "diagnostic," an ornithologist would say. My view with the binoculars revealed exquisite shades of blues, grays and browns with such speckles, fine striping and scalloping of these colours as to baffle any utilitarian explanation. Later, a singing pair of Philadelphia Vireos flitted in and out of view in the low foliage, like large, slow, deliberate warblers, pausing for long moments to calmly look about before making their next moves. Each of the pair displayed a similar warm wash of yellow on their sides, where they would be pale gray to white out of the short breeding season. This is one of the more curiously named species. It is the only bird named after a city. Even more strange, their breeding range is a narrow east-west strip across south-central Canada, far from Philadelphia.

It is one thing to see a bird well enough to identify it, to see its diagnostic traits and make the call: "Blue-winged Teal." That satisfies the birder, not the birdwatcher. The birdwatcher wants intimacy with the bird. Not always a contact as direct as I had with my first Ruby-crowned Kinglet, but an encounter close enough to see fine detail of eye, bill, feet and plumage, even relaxed behaviour – what its mate might see. Even when using binoculars or a scope, along with clever use of concealing cover, the element of chance is predominant. Some combination of events has to deliver the bird to the birdwatcher, and the birdwatcher to the bird, in a special moment of apparently good luck. But there are soul-stirring, magical moments when it feels like the encounter has been arranged. Perhaps the same distinction holds for our interactions with people. We seek intimacy, but mostly we just identify each other and move on.

Many new passengers climbed aboard in Thompson, mostly Aboriginal people in coach, but also a trio of elder birders from the north of England on their way to Churchill. The dining-car crew clung to their two-table limit, causing quite a backup at dinner, and even then they seemed overwhelmed. But the food was good.

My dinner companion was one of the Weir Guys, a heavy-equipment operator named Victor. He was fairly young, perhaps early 30s, and pleasantly soft-spoken with an archetypical Anglo-Canadian accent and manner. Victor was different from the rest of his crew. I couldn't doubt his skill with machines. The others seemed to defer to him as the specialist in operating some types of equipment. But he was not cut from the same cloth. He was relatively slight of stature and almost delicate in his handsome face. Gentler, more serious, more thoughtful, even introspective, he wanted to talk about himself, though not in a boastful way. Still, I sensed the others had grown tired of his story, and Victor saw me as a new audience.

Victor was so refreshingly open, I couldn't help being interested in his story. He was working through some maturing experiences of his life – a wife, a young son, a divorce, and the agony of trying to understand what went wrong and how to be a good yet absentee father. He wanted to share his questions and his insights. He struck me as a man on a spiritual journey, so it came as a shock to learn that Amway, the global marketing company, had become his vehicle. My first reaction was amused dismay, but being in an unusually open state of mind, I thought again and wondered how well his vehicle served his purpose.

I wasn't about to pump him for information about the spiritual qualities of Amway, knowing that could become an evening-long conversation and I was eager to turn my attention back to the scene outside the train. And people were waiting for our table. Still, I was reluctant to dismiss this earnest young man's peculiar path to becoming a better person. He also gave me the first intimation that I had chosen no less peculiar a vehicle – this train, this trip to Churchill – for a spiritual journey of my own.

I excused myself to resume the watch from my tiny compartment. The boreal forest continued to roll by relentlessly, broken by frequent swamps and ponds, sometimes rivers and lakes, on which I focused intensely in search of waterfowl and other wildlife. What was there was hard to see, much less identify. I was awed by the gorge of the great Nelson River. But I had lost the morning's sense of profound relaxation. I felt agitated. I had been trying to drink in the Canadian wilderness, to savour it. At the same time, I was trying too hard to see wildlife that mostly wasn't there to be seen. I was repeatedly distracted by my mental chatter, asking where all the animals were, wanting to see more than I was seeing, remembering similar feelings of disappointment in Québec. I tried to still my mind and return to the present, thinking to myself while breathing and smiling, as Thich Nhat Hanh teaches in *Peace Is Every Step*.

> Breathing in, I calm my body
> Breathing out, I smile
> Dwelling in the present moment
> I know this is a wonderful moment

Focusing the mind this way works well for me. I've attempted to teach my son the technique, but he won't really try it – yet. After all, he's not quite seven years old. When he wants to be a baseball pitcher and has to learn to still his mind to let his body perform the proper mechanics regardless of the number of runners on base and the count of balls and strikes, then he may listen to me. But I shouldn't bet on it. It is surprising how much our children mimic our habits, bad as well as good, yet shrug off our earnest attempts to teach them some particular, useful trick.

Purposeful breathing and smiling, even when I don't feel like it, do bring my awareness back to appreciation of the scene in front of me. Yet now I had to admit to boredom with the endless boreal forest. The fact that it seemed endless was an interesting observation in itself, but I was bored nonetheless. I could not will my mind to be still. I had to settle for a slightly agitated contentment as I kept up my vigil for wildlife.

※

My mental chatter kept drifting back to thoughts of Victor and Amway. I found myself regretting that I hadn't given him a more thorough hearing. Setting aside the immediate reasons, I knew that I hadn't wanted to listen more, because I could not allow that Amway had spiritual value beyond the comfort it seemed to give a man in emotional distress. Amway offers a world view that very effectively motivates people to sell lots of product, not just with carrots and sticks, but with a powerful vision and peer support. To motivate this way is to move the human spirit. Even so, I was thinking that Victor would not have taken so to the Amway world view if he had received as much education as I had. This thought brought me up short – a rather arrogant contention! Victor was an intelligent, reflective guy. He was clearly using his reason to seek truth in his life, explanations, purpose to guide his choices. But

The Wilderness Train: June 4–6

his reason must be flawed if he found profound truth and purpose in Amway. His search must be misguided to settle for such a commercial world view, I convinced myself. Yet, as I looked down my intellectual nose at Victor, I felt an upwelling sense of vertigo. I had to step back and collect my thoughts before losing my balance.

The boreal forest and muskeg wetlands and ponds kept rolling inexorably past the window, and I kept watching too intensely for animal form and movement. It became a loop of videotape repeating a series of landscape scenes over and over and over, until it dissolved to memories of Québec. I was the 17-year-old boy again, with about as many years of education as Victor, but much less life experience. From that moment in time, my memory played forward through my senior year of high school, four years at Cornell, another five at the University of Arizona, through the bumming-around-the-world years and two years working for the United Nations Environment Program in Kenya, then other jobs around Africa, back to Tucson as a researcher at the University of Arizona again, coming to rest on a ridge on the north side of the Santa Catalina Mountains, overlooking the San Pedro Valley of Arizona. Along this time sequence, I searched for evidence of the superiority of my world view.

I discovered this vista from the ridge when walking in the Catalinas with my fiancée's dog, Mac. He was a mix of black Labrador retriever with something rather larger and more aggressive. He needed occasional room to roam where kids and other dogs were scarce. Mac was very nasty to both, due to some bad experience in his unknown younger years before we first met him as a full-grown dog. But he was gentle with us, and a good walking companion, so I often took Mac to the desert or the mountains to give us both some outdoor time, even if his mistress couldn't join us.

One day, it was just Mac and me in the higher elevations of the Catalinas. Mac found and followed an old path obscured by a thicket of shrubs. It was marked for future visits by a rare and stately Arizona madrone, its peeling bark revealing smooth mahogany-red "skin." I followed Mac out onto the oak- and pine-covered ridge that projected from the main mass of the mountain. A dreamy odour of vanilla exuded from the bark of the ponderosa pines heated in the high-altitude afternoon sun. After a quarter of a mile, the path crossed an opening in the woodland that allowed a grand vista across the backcountry of southeastern Arizona, a succession of valleys and ranges, progressively paler and bluer as they stair-stepped toward New Mexico.

I sat down in some shade at the edge of the clearing, while Mac continued his exploration of "facts on the ground" beyond detection by the human nose. I must have fallen into a long meditation on the scene, because Mac eventually came back and lay down to wait me out. I was working through my experiences around the world and my education as a scientist, especially as a biologist schooled in evolutionary theory, the organizing concept for everything I knew to be true. Everything since the origin of the universe was surely the unfolding of a blind process driven by "chance and necessity," as the great molecular biologist Jacques Monod had summed up. This was Truth. It left room for mystery regarding what there was before and beyond the universe. My fiancée could use the term "God" to refer to the "before and beyond," and I respected that decision. But that sentiment was effectively irrelevant to me and the dog and the trees and the mountain ridge and the sweep of valley and mountains beyond. We were all there thanks to physical, chemical, geological and biological processes that I understood or had been assured that others smarter than myself could understand. God was not necessary to the explanation.

I thought more deeply about how I, my fiancée and Mac the dog fit into this world view centred on natural processes. The human species was of course a product of these natural processes.

And the evolutionary process within this species led to capacity for elaborate culture, beyond anything seen among animals. Culture evolved differently, overlaying genetic evolution. I had teamed up with another scientist, Ron Pulliam, to write about cultural evolution, so I thought I knew something that was true about this new process – that it was driven by a combination of chance, necessity and human cognition and intuition working with ideas rather than with genes. I also thought I had a fairly accurate mental map of how the human world works, based on my reading of history and the variety of economic and political systems I had witnessed and the various institutions I had worked within. Again I saw no evidence that God was necessary for this understanding.

The logical and reasonable conclusion was that the structures and processes of the universe, the earth and the human species have no purpose, divine or otherwise. In fact, the whole notion of purpose seemed most likely a side effect of the evolution of the human brain – a fantasy our brains insist on creating just to reckon with the real world. The lack of purpose did not bother me, because I still found rich meaning in the marvellous progression from Big Bang to Big Mac. It was all so fascinating. But the lack of purpose did pose a problem as I meditated on the mountain ridge with Mac the dog waiting patiently for the insights to come.

With no externally mandated purpose, I concluded, each of us is left to create a personal purpose, to choose our own reasons for living. I considered what purpose would make sense for me. I didn't notice that I was applying moral values to compare the alternative purposes that came to mind – that these values had to have come from *some*where I did not think to explore or even acknowledge. I settled with deep satisfaction on the purpose for my life. I declared that mountain ridge sacred ground, the site of my enlightenment. I named it in honour of Mac the dog, who had found the ridge and the vista for me. Mac relaxed his black, silky ears and wagged his scimitar tail in appreciation, then trotted on ahead, following his long, black nose back to the main trail.

I came back to myself with a slight, silent gasp. The boreal forest was still rolling by, but at 10:30 p.m. it was finally getting too dark to watch for wildlife.

What evidence had I found in my intellectual life history that could show my world view was superior to Victor's? I had come of age among people whose command of scientifically established facts was indisputable. But I could not remember a single well-reasoned argument to refute other world views or even show that they were inferior to the one these very well-educated people had passed on to me with assurances of its truth. They simply asserted that nothing could be true unless it was scientifically observable or predictable – true in their terms, by their rules. The very definition of Truth comes from their world view. I was beginning to find this assertion a bit too narrow-minded.

Victor's world view offered him meaning and purpose. Hadn't I just rediscovered that the world view I had developed, with a good deal of help, did not offer purpose beyond what I personally invented? I could say that Victor's works for him and mine works for me. "Roll your own purpose" could be our motto. That would make it a draw. Our world views would be equivalent, equally shallow, for all the scientific facts I could hang on mine. But I didn't want a world view that was simply useful. I wanted one that was true! As for meaning and purpose, my intellectual mentors, like Darwin and Einstein, had left me at naught, ground zero, the starting line. Even Thich Nhat Hanh, my spiritual guide, had given me only a meditative technique and a positive lens for looking at the world, not an explanation. I could offer nothing to Victor that Amway could not offer, perhaps even less.

What could I honestly offer my own son? Is it not a parent's most solemn responsibility to pass on to a child a world view that offers workaday meaning and purpose? My wife has no doubt on this matter. She believes her Christian world view has done well for her (I must agree), and so, she will pass it on to our son. I certainly do my son no favour if I challenge his mother's God-centred world view, redolent with meaning and purpose, with my Scientist world view that leaves humanity hanging there in an implacably cold universe.

More disturbing is that I don't have to openly challenge my wife's world view to cast doubts upon it in my son's mind. As I observed earlier, children readily mimic their parents, like it or not. Kids notice and absorb everything – including, perhaps especially, differences between their parents' world views. I wouldn't be able to hide my world view by remaining silent, and my son would certainly be exposed to it favourably and relentlessly by our predominantly post-Christian culture. In effect, without saying a word on the subject, I would be endorsing the antithesis of his mother's world view. As my very wise wife warns me, I will have to say something someday. I will have to explain myself.

I could already feel the heat of my son's questioning gaze.

Now I was purely agitated, no longer content. I had a headache from an extremely full day of watching and was glad to shut my eyes at last. In contrast to my first night, I slept comfortably as soon as I admitted it was too late to solve my problem of purpose. Like Scarlett O'Hara, I would think about it tomorrow.

∞

I completely missed the long stop and crew change at Gillam, where the track turns due north and heads straight for Hudson Bay. I woke to my alarm clock at 4:00 a.m., before the sun was due to rise, to see caribou and other wildlife most active at dawn. The train was moving slowly but steadily, at perhaps 20 miles per hour. It was a processional pace with a gently rolling gait. I lifted the window shade and looked out on a new world.

3

The Real Adventure
June 6

Horned Grebe

I was seeing the landscape in silhouette. At first, it reminded me of saguaro cactus desert in Arizona. Then I could see I was looking at dwarf, stick-figure spruces standing widely apart among rounded hummocks of – something – looking frosted in the early light. Many small pools of water gave dimension to the hummocks – the size of large, smooth boulders. As the sun rose, the mottled appearance of frost on the hummocks turned to lush white growth of lichen, as well as thick green/yellow/orange mosses and low-growing woody plants. At last, I was looking at Arctic tundra, utterly different from anything I'd seen before. Technically, since tundra is by definition treeless, I was not quite there, but the spruce were clearly struggling and had conceded dominance to the plant life of the Barren Grounds.

I was up and out to the dining car well before the 6:30 start of breakfast, just to drink in the scene from both sides of the train at once. Often the stately procession slowed to a crawl and then a stop and then back to a crawl as the train negotiated a particularly bad stretch of roadbed. Without a lot of special maintenance, a rail line across permafrost is subject to buckles and dips. Since the train made this run three times a week, I chose not to worry about derailment.

I was happy for the slow pace and stops, which allowed me to carefully scan the surroundings for birds and mammals. I saw my first Willow Ptarmigan, a legendary Arctic grouse that turns all white in winter and back to camouflage browns in summer. It is adapted for snow with heavily feathered feet that work like snowshoes. Then I saw another sitting on top of a dwarf spruce, looking like an oversize Christmas ornament, half pure white and half mottled with grousy brown. The ptarmigan (with a voiceless "p") is a signature bird of the tundra, emblematic, on stage in any explorer's dream of the North. To see a ptarmigan is surely confirmation of arrival.

Then again, the other birds I saw were not so confirming. Thanks to seasonal migration, there are many other species of the North that are familiar in winter in the South as well. I was seeing lots of Canada Geese and some familiar ducks – Greater Scaup, Oldsquaw, White-winged Scoter, Mallard. Also a group of Sandhill Cranes, a Common Raven, even a Bald Eagle. Just distant glimpses, sufficient only for identification. I thought I would see lots of shorebirds, that motley collection of birds that make their living with long legs in shallow water and on mudflats, probing with long bills or gleaning with shorter bills: sandpipers, plovers, and more exotic names. All I saw was a very out-of-place Upland Sandpiper, with its huge eyes in a round, plain head balanced on an upstretched neck, giving it the appearance of being as startled as I was to find ourselves on the tundra. This was my third life bird of the trip, even more unexpected than the Clay-colored Sparrow in downtown Winnipeg.

No caribou for me, but one of the Weir Guys reported seeing an unusual loner.

The Real Adventure: June 6

By seven o'clock, I could see the Churchill River to the west and the landmark grain elevators of the Port of Churchill up ahead. I felt a slight shock that I was about to arrive in Churchill after all these years. At our pace, however, it would be another hour before arrival. We were into treeless tundra now, but the lichen and moss hummocks were gone, too. The land was a more familiar marshy grassland in appearance. Time to do final packing and get ready to start the real adventure. I asked the dining-car cook what he thought the temperature might be. About 1°C, but pretty pleasant with the sun shining, he said.

When I stepped down from the train, the morning had the cool, crisp, dry feel of the High Plains. The light and shadows were sharp – not from high elevation but high latitude. I inhaled a refreshing memory of westward transcontinental travel, somewhere near the hundredth meridian, where corn and soybeans give way to wheat and open range. Where space and sunlight draw the eye to horizons beyond horizons. My first impression from the train station was that Churchill had the spacious, dusty, pale-gray utilitarian look of a small town in Nevada. There were wide spaces between buildings with exposed gravel and dirt between. No trees, no futile attempt at landscaping. I smiled at how the familiarity of the anything-but-beautiful scene made me feel comfortably at home.

My first Churchill contact, Lawreen of Tamarack Rentals, was at the station with the ocean-blue Ford half-ton pickup I would be renting for the next six days. The only regular cars I saw in Churchill were maybe three taxis plus a handful of others, including a nicely maintained "classic." The rest of the vehicles were pickups, vans, a couple of school buses, sport utility vehicles and lots of snowmobiles under wraps for the summer. Lawreen drove me to her office, pointing out the important landmarks – places to eat (four or five of them) and hotels (about five, all small). Also the Arctic Trading Company, the Northern (grocery and hardware store that used to be the Hudson's Bay Company), and Northern Images (for Aboriginal art) – all in the space of five blocks along Kelsey Boulevard (a.k.a. the Highway), the only paved road. The buildings were low prefab-looking boxes. The only real colour was the red provided by several Canadian and Manitoba flags. Looking up the dirt-surfaced side streets, I noticed the Royal Canadian Legion hall and the Métis Hall. Churchill was as likely a tourist destination as a military installation on the lunar surface. Yet here I was.

Lawreen was a big, friendly middle-aged woman, full of useful information. She and her husband were former government employees now working several businesses, it seemed. I asked my standard questions: "How long have you been up here?" and "What brought you up here?" Twenty-three years was the first answer. She had come to visit a girlfriend and never left. She was originally from the Winnipeg area. She had never ridden the train. The government gave its employees airfare "out" twice a year, and even now, when she wanted to go "out," she wanted to go quickly.

Her office was in the midst of what looked like a motor vehicle repair shop managed by a Métis or Aboriginal person. She recorded information from my California driver's licence, took an imprint of my credit card, had me sign a form, and that was it. Later I realized that I had no rental contract to prove that I had a right to drive this vehicle on the lunar surface or anywhere else. If I had asked for a copy of the contract, I suspect Lawreen would have laughed. I *had* asked about the arrangement for returning the truck and then getting to the airport. She said that I could drive the truck out to the airport, park it and leave it unlocked with the keys in it. No one would steal it, she assured me: "Where would they take it?" With only about 50 miles (82 km) of road, and none "out," I realized that stealing a truck was not a practical venture. She went on to say that sometimes teenagers would steal a vehicle in winter, for a joyride; people park their vehicles without turning

The Real Adventure: June 6

off the engine! Relax, don't worry, be happy. I liked Lawreen, and I was pretty sure I was going to like Churchill.

I drove the Highway, feeling the freedom of a man with choices and no accountability except to himself for the next six days. I passed the Weir Guys exploring on foot, waved and turned up a side street to an unfinished-looking building that called itself the Aurora Inn. I pulled off the dirt road into a dirt lot and parked at one of several standpipes, each with an electrical outlet. I had heard about this from a friend who once lived in Fairbanks, Alaska. I got out and checked the front of the truck. Sure enough, there was an electrical cord for plugging the engine block heater into the outlet provided by the hotel. Fortunately, I wouldn't have to use it in June (the frosts would be light), but it revealed what life is like much of the year.

In the modest lobby, I found a note on the desk asking me to call a certain number for service, which I did. Soon the owner, Gavin, a big, 50ish man with a broad, encouraging smile, was escorting me down a long hallway to my room at the end, near the back door. He offered to track down a back-door key for me so I could more easily come and go. By now, it was already around 10 a.m., so I decided to spend the rest of the morning getting settled in and resting before setting off to explore.

I found myself in a spacious apartment with a full kitchen and dining/living room, and upstairs a loft bedroom and bathroom. I wasn't expecting such living space. I decided to shop at the Northern down the street for breakfast foods and take advantage of my kitchen, taking one or two meals a day at the local restaurants. Looking out my living-room window, I had a view of two modern two-storey apartment complexes for locals (mostly Aboriginal people). Between these buildings was a dirt parking lot, beyond which I could see the grain elevators of the Port. In front of the building called Tundra Apartments was a fire hydrant surrounded on three sides by an open cage of thick pipes, to protect it from snowplows, I guessed. Looking up the street, I could see the tiny Anglican church at the crest of the low hill. This would be my opening and closing scene for each day.

∞

At noon, I bundled up and set out with some of the typical nervousness I feel when stepping out the first time from my hotel into a new town. I recognized the familiar feeling and smiled at myself. On the dirt street, I was greeted by an American Robin singing and a couple of Tree Swallows cruising near the ground for flying insects. They immediately made me feel more comfortable – old friends, all the way up here. But what flying insects were they finding? No sign of mosquitoes yet, thank goodness! I headed up the street toward the Anglican church and my first view of Hudson Bay. I didn't have to walk far.

It was a frozen ocean!

I stood transfixed with surprise, almost alarm. It was a strange and forbidding scene. I doubt that I have ever been so unprepared for what lay on the other side of a hill. I had anticipated sea ice, but I had not expected the visual, emotional impact of the scale. To the horizon and beyond, it was like any ocean. But this ocean was *frozen*! Not a smooth, flat frozen surface, like an ice pond, but huge blocks of opaque white ice up-thrust and jammed together as far as the eye could see.

I'm still stunned and fascinated by my memory of the scene. The ice on Hudson Bay would draw my eyes at every opportunity.

I picked and jumped my way across the glacier-smoothed rocks along the shore until I could get close enough to touch the ice. I didn't dare step out on to it. My closer view showed a fair amount of open water in between the blocks. The ones close to shore were grounded and sticking up high in the air. Some blocks were the size of houses or even small ships. Repelled by the danger, attracted by the strangeness, I tried to imagine polar bears out there on the ice pack, hunting seals. No, really, I couldn't imagine it. Too strange!

As I looked out on the ice, I was standing on a low, rocky ridge forming the shore of Hudson Bay. The ridge and shore run east from Churchill town past the airport and beyond to distant Cape Churchill. This ridge separates Hudson Bay to the north from the low tundra plain to the south. At Churchill, the ridge curves to the northwest to meet the Churchill River flowing from the south. The town is sandwiched between river and bay on a narrow peninsula terminating at Cape Merry. In five minutes you can walk across the town from the river to the bay.

This exposed rocky ridge is perfect habitat for the Horned Lark and American Pipit, a couple of winter visitors to plowed farmland around my town in central California. There they are usually elusive, flying silhouettes against the sky, notable only for their similar call notes. Here they allowed me to approach very close and study them in detail. And they sang.

Like a sand-coloured sparrow from most angles, the male Horned Lark looks impeccably dressed from the front and side. It has lemon yellow on the face and throat with a black robber's mask across the eyes, a black band across the breast and a double crest of tiny black horn-like feathers. It walks and runs with a distinctive shuffle. I have never seen one perch; they're always on the ground. Through binoculars, I watched a male on a massive boulder singing its thin, rising warble of tinkling notes, then zoomed the focus out to the sea ice behind him and back again, several times, enjoying the sensation of watching a film of wildlife in the Arctic. Yet this was no illusion!

High above the tinkling lark was the slightly smaller, more drab gray, darkly striped American Pipit doing its showy aerial display flight and song. It started by simultaneously bursting into a series of effusive *tsweet* notes and rising on the wing higher and higher for several seconds, then plummeting back to the ground very near the lark. The pipit is also a ground-walker, but longer of leg and more upright. Most distinctive is the bobbing of its tail up and down as it walks, as if the tail has a mind of its own and the bird would rather it stopped.

Moving away from the bay toward the Port of Churchill and the ever-visible grain elevator complex, I discovered little ponds nestled in the rocky ridge top, surrounded by willows about to leaf out. Male Yellow Warblers, bright as gold, moved from branch to branch, stopping only to throw their heads back with mouths agape to belt out insistent variations on the theme *Sweet, sweet, sweet, I'm so sweet*. This may be the most widespread and numerous warbler in North America, so I was neither surprised nor thrilled to see it. Yet this species is one of the best arguments for using binoculars for a good look at familiar birds. It is an often-overlooked treasure. "Gold" doesn't do justice to its intense all-over yellow colour. I'd have to add "molten," as in glowing hot yellow. Its black eyes stand in such contrast to the hot yellow head that they look like tiny orbs of polished onyx. In the breeding season, the male adds red-orange stripes from throat to belly to wow the females – and the birdwatchers. These males had obviously recently arrived to set up shop in the willows that would be theirs for the short summer.

In these little willow ponds also lurked pairs of American Wigeons. These are familiar, gentle-looking, medium-sized ducks. "Cute" is what we call an animal with a relatively large, very round head and short muzzle or bill. Wigeons are cute, with "absolutely darling" dainty, blue-gray bills, and a kind of dark area around the eye, making it look bigger than it is. The males used to be called

"Baldpates" because of the broad white stripe from forehead to crown, flanked by an iridescent green swath from around the eyes to the back of the head and down the back of the neck, giving the impression of male-pattern baldness.

White-crowned and Savannah Sparrows were everywhere, singing. Though small, they are probably the most conspicuous birds of the Churchill area, due to their distinctive and oft-repeated songs and their ubiquity. Like the Yellow Warbler, these species are exceedingly widespread in North America, and I was not particularly pleased to see them so common around Churchill. Something a little more exotic, please! Yet the birdwatcher comes to appreciate them for what they are and congratulate these North American natives for being at least as successful as any introduced species.

The White-crowned's song is a variable pattern of pure whistles. Its black-and-white striped head contrasts nicely with its steel-gray body and its back and wings striped with black and warm brown. A beautiful bird, and generally looking rather relaxed for such a small, edible creature.

The Savannah is a tougher sell. Its song is a thin, three-pitch, descending *tee-tee-tee tzeeeeeeeeeeeeeeeee tip*, unaccountably favoured as "natural" background sound for television commercials (mostly shot in locales where Savannah Sparrows do not exist). Except for a tiny lemon-yellow patch between the base of the bill and the eye, the bird is all stripes of various shades of brown over white. Nonetheless, I find them attractive through the binoculars. Savannahs are secretive and always seem to be in a state of mild surprise.

Below the rocky ridge were several much larger ponds, called the Granary Ponds, which snuggle right up to the Port complex on the Churchill River. Lots of ducks of seven species and three gull species and terns flying everywhere. Were these Arctic Terns? I'd been looking at Common Terns for decades in hope of identifying an Arctic Tern. The two species are very similar, like small, dainty gulls – white to pale silver-gray bodies, white deeply forked tails, darker gray wings with a hint of black at the wing tips, black caps pulled down to the eyes, and blood-red bills and feet. Here they seemed to be nothing *but* Arctic Terns, but my best assurance was that the Arctic Tern is supposed to breed around Churchill and throughout the Arctic, whereas the Common is farther south and would be highly unusual around Churchill. I'd soon discover that Arctic Terns are as conspicuous and ubiquitous around here as the sparrows, maybe more conspicuous with their buoyant, butterfly flight and keening, kipping cries. At last – something truly Arctic in the background noise of Churchill.

I sat for a while on the edge of a small bluff of the ridge overlooking the Granary Ponds and immediately above a willow swamp, scanning with my binoculars. I hadn't brought the spotting scope for this introductory walk – I prefer to birdwatch without a scope because of the extra awkward burden when walking. I sat on the ground, propping my elbows on my knees. This was my version of heaven, I suppose – a scene of diverse habitat and bird life laid out before me, close enough for 7x35 binoculars.

This was a totally man-handled landscape of port facilities, grain elevators, fuel storage tanks, railroad beds and tracks, gravel roadways and footpaths, and dredged ponds divided by straight earthen dikes. But nature long ago moved into the interstices of this hotbed of human industry, and now it teemed with life in early June. The area was framed by the coastal ridge. Great bare rocks dwarfed all man-made structures. The rocks were splashed with bright orange lichens. With the yellow-and-beige of winter-bleached grasses, the blue-greens of emerging weeds, the reds, browns and grays of willow branches and buds, they painted an undiscovered Renoir. The intersecting, overlying songs of the ridge birds, punctuated by the airborne cries of gulls and terns, the gabbling complaints and whistles of ducks on the ponds above and below, and the piercing alarms of shorebirds blended to perform an unnamed suite in a minor key.

I am ever struck by the irony of our relationship with nature. We seek it in its pure, untouched state, yet it reveals itself in abundance even where we touch too much. I cling to the ideal of wilderness. It is the purest manifestation of time before civilization. It is very important to me to know it is there, even way out there beyond my daily reach. I treasure its mere existence. I would defend its right to be there with all my heart. But access is, by definition, reserved for the truly hardy and determined, those schooled in the "woodcraft" of Aldo Leopold and John Muir. Experience of it is only for the elite of mind and body, and therefore wilderness is profoundly undemocratic, not for mass public enjoyment.

On the other hand, as Thoreau and others have written, there is something in wildness that nourishes humanity, even in absentia. We may never personally experience pure wilderness, but there are many facsimiles that give us intimations of the real thing. They lack some important features, but we who have not had the real experience don't notice the gaps as much as what is still there and functioning without frequent human interference. They have a similar effect on the human spirit. They are accessible by air, rail or road, and therefore more equitable in their offers of spiritual benefit, even to my wife and young son, who are unlikely to wander far from the road. This faux wilderness must be guarded, too, to be available for nourishment of future generations.

The irony is that, unguarded here in this Port of Churchill and its myriad relatives in the man-mauled world, the wildness of nature has moved in to set up shop, challenging us to recognize its gifts to the spirit right in our midst. This, too, must be treasured – if only because it can be so easily shared with a seven-year-old boy.

There is always the prospect of an avian surprise at any moment. At this moment, it came as a small group of redpolls (stripy finches the size of goldfinches, but with rose-red foreheads) settled twittering and buzzing into the willows below. I was excited to see redpolls again after a span of more than three decades. They were a wonderful, rare surprise at my boyhood home in Connecticut in the dead of winter. But were these Common Redpolls or Hoary Redpolls? Both are in the area and supposed to be "common." Yet they are hard to distinguish until you get the hang of it. I had never seen a Hoary Redpoll. The birder shouldered aside the birdwatcher – I had an *objective* to track down and identify both. It seemed I was seeing both species, but I couldn't yet trust my judgment. I would have to look carefully at a lot of redpolls first.

The birdwatcher reunited with the birder to jointly appreciate a gorgeous, full-dress Horned Grebe as it appeared in an open pool of the swamp below my perch. I exhaled an unvoiced "wow" as I took in the colours and pattern. I've seen many hundreds, no, thousands of Horned Grebes in winter plumage on both the Atlantic and Pacific coasts – basically a small gray-and-white diving "duck" with a black cap and narrow, sharp bill. Not a duck at all, really, but a diminutive loon by evolutionary relationship, more comfortable diving than flying and almost unable to walk on land, because its legs and feet are so far back on the body as to almost replace the tail – an adaptation for more effective underwater swimming. Toward spring, a few of them on the coast showed hints of the summer colours, but nothing like this bird that sailed right off the page of a bird book: jet-black head with a bright yellow headband and rubies for eyes, atop a rufous red neck and body with a mottled dark- and light-gray back. This bird calmly cruised the length and breadth of its private pond, not diving for fish, just displaying its beauty to claim its territory and proclaim its availability. So far it seemed mate-less, but I couldn't imagine that would last long. If I were a Horned Grebe…

∞

At last my mind returned, reluctantly, compulsively, to the thoughts of last evening, regarding Victor's world view and my own – the question of purpose and meaning. Pretty sure that this collage of wonderful sights and sounds was not placed here solely for my enjoyment, I ruminated on the purpose of all this life being lived around me.

If I were a Horned Grebe, my purpose in life would be written in my genes: to put on these breeding colours and fly thousands of miles from the easy life on the coast over inhospitable lands to this pond so I could cruise it in splendid attire, drive off same-sex rivals, attract a mate, build a nest, guard and warm the eggs, let the little ones ride around on my back for a few days, protect them during their learning to fend for themselves, and then put on my grubbies and head back to the coast and my great love – fishing – before the snow and ice set in. Thereby I would have fulfilled my duty, my purpose, which the evolutionary biologist sitting up there on the bluff would say is to pass my genes on to the next generation. What the guy up there doesn't account for is that I am a Horned Grebe. I am descended of an ancient lineage, stretching about as far back in millions of years as the lineage of any living bird species. The meaning of that lineage is me, here today in this pond in this feathery finery. My purpose is to extend that meaning into the future, but the meaning of that purpose is much larger. I am a Horned Grebe.

"Glory to God, Give glory to God, Glory to God in the highest …" drifted through my thoughts at this same moment, giving me a bit of a start. Where did that come from? Many times I have attended Mass and sung that beautiful refrain from the *Gloria* as a gesture of respect for my wife and son, so the more appropriate question was why here and now? Is the meaning of being a Horned Grebe to give glory to God? *That* certainly comes from a different world view, no less dismissed by my world view than Victor's Amway one, and much more aggressively dismissed, since its venerable history and massive current following mount a more virulent threat to my world view.

Without pause, my Scientist world view challenged the God-centred one. Let's define terms. What is God, what is glory, what does it mean "to give glory," and what is the meaning of "in the highest"? No operational definitions in observable terms? How can there be any test of its reality? It is not a testable hypothesis. Let's get real! Let's move on.

But I couldn't. I was unable to show the superiority of the purely scientific world view over Victor's Amway-inspired world view, either for offering purpose and meaning, or even for being more true. At best, these world views are equivalent in value. I faced the same problem with the God-centred world view. In fact, the problem was worse. I couldn't use the ad hominem dismissal of its adherents for being poorly educated or misinformed. I know very smart people who hold the God-centred world view, people like my wife. She tries occasionally to explain it to me, but she is working from underlying assumptions that puzzle me. C. S. Lewis gives intellectually brilliant, highly sophisticated, yet straightforward explanations, as in *Mere Christianity*. That helps me some, if only to make me pause long enough to consider the possibility that knowledge – how we know – might be approached differently.

So, as I sat there watching this magnificent grebe, looking very much as though it knew it was magnificent, I allowed myself to slip the leash of my world view long enough to feel that this Horned Grebe gave glory to God – without defining my terms, much less testing the truth of my feeling. It just *felt* like Truth. The same feeling I get when I read a trusted author or hear a trusted lecturer. But the trust was placed elsewhere this time. I knew the Truth as an intuition rather than an irrefutable hypothesis.

The Horned Grebe seemed to "know" it, too.

∞

I ambled a wide arc around the Granary Ponds toward the Port, noticing that the breeze off the ice was picking up and cutting through my layers even as the sun shone brightly. Wearing my baseball cap was better than being bareheaded, but I would have preferred my wool ski cap.

The Port side of the ponds was an "industrial estate." But that didn't bother the birds; at least there was no odour to contend with. I observed a large and actively feeding flock of Ruddy Turnstones working through what looked like a slag pile of old, rotted grain. This is an unusual-looking, pretty shorebird. The contrast of winter and summer plumage is almost as striking as that of the Horned Grebe. Again, I had never before seen the full breeding plumage, with boldly contrasting black and white in a complex bridle across head, neck and breast, with russet red and black on the back, white below and relatively short orange legs. The dark, short, slightly upturned bill looks like an awl, which the bird uses to probe under small rocks, seaweed and other vegetation, and to flip them over or bulldoze them out of the way to expose the bug life underneath. It is an amusing sight, a flock of turnstones flipping and bulldozing in the inter-tidal zone, but these birds had an easier time of it on the old grain pile.

I soon noticed they were feeding with Lapland Longspurs and Snow Buntings. All were resting on their journey to the high Arctic, far to the north of Churchill. Both species were still in transition between winter and summer plumage, so they looked a bit disheveled. Not realizing yet that the Lapland Longspur was a life bird for me, I focused on the Snow Buntings. I was rereading *Diary of a Left-handed Birdwatcher*, in which Leonard Nathan explores his obsession with seeing a Snow Bunting (which he almost did in Churchill) as emblematic of the larger question as to why birders get so excited about seeing species they've not seen before, or why they bird at all. I had seen Snow Buntings once before (at Plum Island), but not nearly so well or so near the mostly pure-white breeding plumage. I thought I was seeing something very special and wanted to share my find.

Just across the dirt road I spotted a couple of middle-aged men with scopes on tripods, looking out over one of the larger Granary Ponds. Birders. I approached them, and they recognized me as a birder and waited expectantly.

"Have you seen a Snow Bunting yet?" I asked.

They didn't seem too interested, but I went on to tell them where I had seen "my" Snow Buntings. Then I asked if they had seen a Snowy Owl. "No! Have *you*?" Now they were interested. "No, I was hoping to trade you a Snow Bunting for a Snowy Owl." One of them laughed and said, "Not a fair trade." Little glories to God were now commodities for trade.

We fell into a cautious but friendly conversation without exchanging names. They had been in the Churchill area for three days already. Clearly they were experienced birders and had been here before. They were from Winnipeg, with a school group that comes annually to spend a week at the Churchill Northern Studies Centre (the old missile test-launching facility way down the coast beyond the airport). One had an English accent. The other had been birding in southern California earlier in the year, where he had seen over 200 species.

When they discovered that I had arrived on the train that morning, they wanted to know what in particular I was looking for. I went down the list, as I could remember it, of the new species that I was hoping to see. They told me where to look for them and assured me that I had plenty of time to find them: except the famous Ross's Gull, a Siberian species that had shown up and bred annually at Churchill for the past decade or longer. They had been declining in the past couple of years; the little Churchill colony may have finally died out. And no Sabine's Gulls this year so far. Had I had seen anything special from the train? I told them of the pair of Philadelphia Vireos at Thompson. They nodded their heads and made noises that told me I needed to do better than that. I tried again, "Early this morning, I saw an Upland Sandpiper from the train. Not supposed to be anywhere near here, but it was unmistakable." Their faces became serious, but they said nothing. I could tell I had struck a nerve – they were thinking, "Good bird! Wonder if this guy really saw one. Too bad we can't get into the area where he saw it."

Terns wheeled in the air overhead, screeching. I asked, "So, how positive are you that these are Arctic Terns?" They looked at me to check that I was serious. "Well, we haven't looked at every one of them to be sure there isn't a Common Tern among them." They had misunderstood my awkwardly worded request for confirmation of my own identification, but I let it pass and just smiled. They said that the Arctic Terns had arrived the day before (they winter around the coast of Antarctica!). There, right in front of us on a tiny island in the pond, the terns were establishing a breeding colony – as they had done for several years running, according to one of the birders, who had been coming up to Churchill with the students every year for six years or so.

One of them helpfully pointed out a Common Snipe (a shorebird) doing its aerial display, in which the wind in the bird's outer tail feathers makes a low winnowing whistle as it dives from a height. I pointed out two sandpipers that they hadn't yet noticed. They confirmed them as a Least Sandpiper and a Stilt Sandpiper.

I commented on the muskrat swimming very close to us with grass in its mouth for its nest. This was my first mammal for the Churchill area, and rather surprising. I wondered to myself how such an animal could withstand the very long, very cold winters, even in its underground burrow.

They said it was time to move on. Knowing that I was on foot, they offered me a lift out to Cape Merry (they would have to come back through town and could drop me off). I declined, because I had been out in the cold and sun for three hours (I hadn't thought to put sunscreen on), and I needed a rest. "Rest?" they said. "We've been out since 5 a.m.!" I didn't bother to tell them I had awakened at 4 a.m. on the train, but I held my ground. I was tempted to go with them, because I enjoyed the conversation, but I did need the rest and still had to walk back to the hotel.

∞

I woke from an unusual afternoon nap at five o'clock. The outside scene had changed dramatically. Fog was blowing from off the ice and through town, nearly obscuring my view of the elevators. Hmm, this might be pretty grim if it kept up. I hadn't anticipated fog.

I set out anyway with a mission to buy groceries at the Northern and then have dinner at the restaurant attached to the Arctic Trading Company just down the block. I ran into a pair of late-middle-aged women in the hotel parking lot. They asked if I had come for the birds. Like the men I met earlier, they were immediately interested in knowing where I was from and what I was looking for. They echoed the Winnipeg birders' advice, which was reassuring. They were from the States and leaving that night at 10 o'clock on the same train I had arrived on. Bonnie Chartier had been their guide for the week, and they were standing in the parking lot waiting for her to return any minute. I was a bit excited by the prospect of meeting her, especially as I had her book in my hand and would be studying it over dinner. She didn't show before I left, but the lead woman assured me that with "Bonnie's book" I had all the guidance I would need.

I don't take well to being an obvious tourist. I like to blend in as much as possible, imagining myself as passing for a local – not too difficult in Canada. I like to have a sense of *living* in a place, even if only for a few days, not just passing through. So I got an odd kick out of going grocery shopping at the Northern, as though I was setting up a household in this frontier town, a taste of what it would be like to live here. The unfamiliar brands, the way the store was organized, local specialty foods, interacting with the checkout person (Aboriginal), and paying in Canadian currency: I was living like a Canadian! Silly really, especially as I had to admit that there were so few differences between this store in Churchill and a grocery store in California – just a lot less crowded, like pretty much everything in central Canada.

I didn't kid myself that I fit right in. Even in California, I don't feel like a good fit, especially with a pair of binoculars around my neck. I still find it a bit awkward to appear in public with binoculars, but not nearly as much as when I was younger. For one thing, birders are more common these days. In a place like Churchill, where birders are not only common but also welcomed as important contributors to the local economy, I felt positively comfortable in my role as visiting birder. Even so, birders tend to be "geeks" and older folks. Ignoring the hard facts that I've always been the former and am rapidly becoming the latter, I preferred to blend in as I could. I didn't carry my binoculars on this outing for groceries and dinner, only Bonnie's book, which I kept under my arm so as not to be too obvious. Over a meal of soup, steak, cooked vegetables and a Canadian beer, all of which were very good, I studied Bonnie's detailed descriptions of the various sectors of the Churchill area.

I was wary of rushing all over the place and wearing myself to a frazzle. I wanted to relax and enjoy these six days – to savour the subarctic experience. Yet I also had expectations and hopes. I had come a long way and wanted to maximize my chances to see at least the species of birds and mammals *regularly* seen around Churchill. The swift change that afternoon from pleasant, sunny weather to cold, wind-blown fog reminded me of Bonnie's warning over the phone that it could be shirt-sleeve weather one day and a blizzard the next at this time of year. I had allowed myself six full days in Churchill with the understanding that some days might be too miserable to be outdoors.

I would have to seize the first good days to see as much as I could, and not count on tomorrow. This was a strategic problem to be solved with good intelligence (the book) and planning. It took me a while to plot the sequence for exploring the sectors. I decided to cover almost all of them in the next two days, giving each a thorough look. Then I would go back to the ones I found most interesting during the following three days. Such was the luxury of having six full days for a relatively small area (small only in terms of truck access).

I couldn't help thinking about the potential "life" birds and mammals I might see. I knew I couldn't expect to see a Snowy Owl or Gyrfalcon or polar bear at this time of year, but I would be alert for them nonetheless. I now knew that Ross's and also Sabine's Gull hadn't been seen so far this year, which was not a good sign, but I would be looking. I had also heard from the Winnipeg birders that the Three-toed Woodpeckers that regularly nested in the Twin Lakes area had been burned out last year in a large-area forest fire to the southeast. So I couldn't expect to see them either.

My birder side had figured months ago that I had a very good chance of seeing 10 new bird species and perhaps a few new mammals, such as caribou, Arctic hare, Arctic fox and beluga whales. This arbitrary objective was lurking in the back of my mind, and I knew I was going to have to manage my expectations to avoid letting disappointment taint what good fortune I was bound to have. I would have to accommodate the number 10, nonetheless. I good-naturedly let myself indulge in keeping a running count of the species seen so far and how many lifers were among them. I was already up to four life species for the trip, but only the Willow Ptarmigan and Arctic Tern were expected as Churchill regulars yet completely new to me. I had many more lifers and near-lifers to track down and see to my satisfaction. How easy or difficult it would be to find them, I had no real idea. I was thrilled by the uncertain prospects of discovery, but apprehensive about becoming obsessed with the hunt.

After dinner I set off in my truck out of town, past the Port and the Granary Ponds, where I had spent the early afternoon, and out to Cape Merry at the end of the rocky peninsula where the broad Churchill River meets Hudson Bay. I don't say "flows into" Hudson Bay, because it depends on the tide, which ranges up and down 12 feet, driving Hudson Bay's seawater and ice miles upriver and back twice a day. This evening the flow was out to the bay. The river was not as full of ice as the bay. Toward the riverbanks, fast ice grounded by the dropping tide stood up high and stationary above the water. In the middle of the river was a procession of ice floes gliding low in the water and slowly past the honour guard of fast ice and out to join the glut of ice in the bay. Often I heard *crump,* like the report of a distant shotgun, as huge blocks of ice collided or collapsed.

Across the evening light on this remarkable scene, the fog was blowing in rolling billows of deep, soft-gray moisture, dimming and obscuring, lightening and revealing, letting ghostly sunbeams spotlight fantastic shapes of rock, only for a moment, then nothing. All cheer was drained away as the wind-chilled cloud swept the ground of orienting features and smelled of menacing ocean somewhere out there, too close and too cold. Sound was numbed and sucked away. My mind filled with haunting images of the early Hudson Bay explorers lingering too late in the season, their wooden ships caught and crushed by the ice. So many lives lost in search of the Northwest Passage to the Orient, lost in the despair of freezing fog.

Equally haunting images of Eskimos, the Inuit, venturing out to risk their lives for the hunt on the sea ice, adopting the life of the polar bear without all the bear's unusual adaptations for swimming and hunting in salt water colder than 32°F. More lives lost in the despair of freezing fog.

The huge rocks of Cape Merry revealed in the gloom the impact of ice – rocks ground down to smooth, flat and fluted surfaces by the millennia of glacial movement. Miles thick overhead, the glacier weighed so heavily and so recently on this land that it is still in isostatic rebound, rising steadily a few centimetres each year since being relieved of its icy burden.

In the gray half-light of this foggy subarctic evening, I was deeply chilled – by the steady light wind, despite my several layers covered by a ski jacket, my wool ski cap and lined gloves – but even more by the feeling of being at the edge of life on earth.

But I was not alone. A tour group of birders, about 10 in all, had already made their way across the rocks to near the very tip of the Cape. Every one of them had a hefty tripod topped by an enormous block of optical equipment. I'm invariably outgunned when I encounter true birders these days. My 35-year-old Bausch & Lomb Zephr Lite 7x35 binoculars and my dinky 30-power Bushnell spotting scope on its ancient, rickety but lightweight tripod do the job for me. But they don't earn me any points with the aficionados of modern birding hardware. At the same time, I can't help feeling pity; the real superiority of their equipment is more than counterbalanced by the word "lug" that invariably comes to mind when I see them walking around with this stuff over one shoulder. I guess I'm just a "lightweight" birder.

I wondered if this might be Bonnie Chartier's group of the moment. Thinking that I might overhear their identifications and even get into conversation to gain more intelligence on the local birding scene this year, I set out across the rocks directly toward them. Now I could see that they were more warmly dressed than I, with huge hooded parkas. One of the parkas had "Great Bear Tours" on the back, so I figured this was the guide, but not Bonnie, because her company is Churchill Wilderness Encounter. Then I noticed "Bonnie" in letters on the guide's sleeve. It *was* Bonnie; it had to be. Naturally, they were looking out on the river and bay rather than at me, so I felt I could sidle right up and fall in with the group. They were spread over a long, ragged line and shifted back and forth to talk with each other. I tried to get as close to Bonnie as I could without appearing strange. I looked out on the water and ice and listened to their identifications and confirmed them for myself.

The heavy-looking Common Eiders were indeed common out here, seeming at home in the water among the ice floes, males in their spectacular black-and-white breeding garb and the females the warm brown pattern of a hen pheasant. Two months earlier among the snowy Baltic islands near Stockholm, I had seen this same species in large numbers and was very pleased to see them again. Such cold-weather birds – they winter at sea as far north as the ice permits, I believe. Incredibly hardy, circumpolar creatures.

There were also good numbers of Red-breasted Mergansers, some Oldsquaw and Common Goldeneye, Arctic Terns, Bonaparte's

Gulls, and other gulls. My companions were concentrating on the harder gulls, trying to find something unusual. Bonnie was calling out to them, "They've all got flat heads!" Herring Gulls and Ring-billed Gulls, that's it. Bonnie seemed to have a lot of joy in her voice. She was a big, broad-faced smiling woman, though it was difficult to tell how big as she was wearing a huge parka. Listening to her I was drawn even closer.

"It's not *cold*!" She shouted over the wind to the group with a laugh. I figured she meant what she said. She knows what cold is. For me, and probably for most of her group, it *was* cold! I realized I would have to seek the shelter of my truck pretty soon; these people with their parkas could easily stay out here a lot longer than I could.

Given my proximity to her, I tried to think of some way to connect with Bonnie – like introduce myself. But somehow that seemed an odd thing to do out here, while she was trying to give this group their money's worth. What would I say? "I have your book and think it's great"? "We talked on the phone years ago. Now I'm here talking to you in person!"? "I've come all the way to Churchill because of your book"? "I'm not paying you to show me around, but I'm still trying to get some pointers from you"?

Just as I was pondering my options, Bonnie turned suddenly to me with a smile on her hooded face and asked in a boisterous voice, "Have you seen the Glaucous Gull at the dump?"

I was stunned. "No, I haven't." I was pleased to be that coherent. "Neither have we!" she laughed and turned back to her group. I had talked to the celebrity! She had given me a hot tip – unsolicited! I wanted to follow up with something intelligent, but I felt too cold and silly and outside the group. I remained a loner. So I withdrew.

The Real Adventure: June 6

Anyway, it was time to get out of the cold. It had been a long day, and a very productive one. I had five more whole days ahead of me. What a luxury!

4

The Big Day
June 7

Blackpoll Warbler

I had gone to bed deciding to sleep until I woke on my own. I had been chilled, slightly sunburned, and awake since 4 a.m. And it was hard to go to bed before the sunset at 10:30 p.m. I needed to sleep enough to catch up and avoid getting sick. So I woke gradually on June 7 and felt good. I was not outside until about 10:30 a.m. Birdwatchers have the reputation of getting up at the crack of dawn to catch the birds when they are most active. Not me. I am definitely not a morning person, not well adapted to being a dedicated birdwatcher, much less a true birder. But even *I* seldom set out as late as 10:30 a.m.!

It was a clear, relatively warm day. I was surprised but pleased. Better make the best of it, I thought. Heading in the opposite direction from the Port and Cape Merry, I set out on the paved two-lane highway into the tundra and toward the road junction called Akudlik, where there are marshes and lakes on which the famous Ross's Gulls had nested for the past several years. The tundra just outside the town looked like dry grassland dotted with large boulders and a few ragged clumps of dwarf spruce. Bonnie's book indicated that I should keep watch for Short-eared Owls sitting on the boulders. None. And I was to look for a left turn in about a kilometre or so, where I would go north across the tundra and then ascend the low rocky ridge facing out to Hudson Bay. Just before the ascent, I should stop and scan the tundra for nesting American Golden-Plovers (a lifer for me) and singing Smith's Longspurs (another lifer).

I parked the truck on the ridge, got out my spotting scope, and for the first time since leaving California, extended the legs of the tripod. This was like saying to myself, "Open for business." Time for serious birding. Looking out over the tundra from this slight, maybe 30-foot rise, I could distinguish little with the naked eye on the gray-brown flat plain stretching south for several kilometres to the Churchill River, visible only because of the ice floes. This country was flat and nearly monochrome. Hmm, was this what the tundra is all about? Then I scanned with the binoculars and rediscovered its texture. Hummocks. Not nearly as much white lichen and orange moss as I had seen from the train early yesterday morning. A lot more standing dry grass and very low-growing woody shrubs that were starting to turn buds into leaves. Spring had just begun. It was like March or early April in the northeastern US. Naturally everything looked gray-brown, except for the lichens and mosses, which were not as abundant here.

Into the view of my binoculars came a vision of shorebird beauty. I knew immediately this was an American Golden-Plover, standing robin-erect on medium-length, blue-gray legs at the top of a hummock, but soon disappearing down between the elfin hills and up again briefly, then down. "What a great bird!" I said out loud to myself. Jet black from face to under the tail, including all the chest and belly. And a truly golden and brown speckle from the top of the head down the back to the rump. My confidence in Bonnie's book soared; it had delivered me right to this bird.

While getting some good views of the plover through the scope, I heard a clear, sweet whistle song from the other side of the road. Smith's Longspur? The women birders in the parking lot of the hotel had said to look for them singing from the tiny clumps of white spruce on the drier tundra. So I swung the scope around to examine the three or four spruce clumps nearby. And there it was! A lovely finch, all mustard to ochre colour below, with a black bridle over a white face. I watched it sing several times and tried to memorize the pattern of seven notes. The song carries beautifully across the tundra – and it was right where Bonnie and the women said I would find it.

Starting off the morning with two life birds in as many minutes puts a birder in a very good mood, relaxed enough to settle down to some birdwatching. I spent many minutes gazing through the scope alternately at these two very different, characteristic species of the tundra: the plover moving and stopping like a motorized toy, occasionally bending stiffly and deliberately to pick something off the ground – its similarity to an American Robin working a lawn was striking – and the longspur content to sit atop its clump of spruce and serenade the tundra with its clear, sweet announcement of ownership and availability.

Back in the truck and feeling confident, I chose not to return to the Highway, but instead drove a rough track along the ridge toward Akudlik. The day was becoming warm. With no sign of a house nearby, I came upon a ragged array of widely spaced doghouses spread over a quarter-acre of tundra. Chained to each was, of course, a dog. All were large huskies, about 15 sled dogs. Some lay in the shade of their little structures, some on the rooftops. They were far apart and their chains were short enough to prevent direct contact between the dogs. As the truck came abreast of them, a few of the dogs sat up. All ears were perked, and all those pairs of wolf eyes stared with eager intensity at me. They looked friendly, so I had to remind myself that they would not be chained out here in the middle of nowhere if they were nice dogs. They looked capable of deadly defence of their territory, even when chained up.

I drove on slowly with the window down, watching carefully. A tiny bird flew across the track and lighted in an isolated spruce, far enough ahead to allow me to break to a gentle stop beside the tree. The bird popped in and out of view as it worked its way among the branch tips. I'd have to be lucky to get a good view. Binoculars ready. There! A male Blackpoll Warbler – black cap pulled down over a white face, with a black mustache radiating black stripes over white below and over a blue-gray back – in perpetual motion but sticking with this one tree long enough for me to see it well several times from the comfort of the driver's seat. It sang *tseet, tseet, tseet, tseet, tseet* on one pitch, beak wide open, labouring hard to push out this thin sound. Unmistakable once learned, and a good thing, too. I would hear this sound almost every time I drove past stands of spruces and would be grateful for not having to stop every time to identify the singer.

Like the Arctic Tern, the Blackpoll Warbler has a remarkable story. The tern wins the contest for the longest annual round trips, shuttling between the Arctic and the Antarctic. But this tiny warbler seems to win the prize for longest non-stop flight – from New England or Nova Scotia straight to South America in the fall, covering several thousand kilometres over some two to three days without a rest. How is it possible? Why does it bother? In the spring, it takes a different route, working its way up the east coast after making landfall in Florida. Why not take the same route south?

Think of the navigational achievement of any migrating bird, finding its way to a pre-ordained winter home and then back to the very place it was hatched. As an undergrad at Cornell University, I was lucky enough to know Steve Emlen, fresh from his dissertation work and continuing to refine his demonstration that birds (Indigo Buntings in this case) do orient themselves to the stars, taking their bearings in relation to the one star that doesn't move during the night: the North Star. But what if it is a cloudy night? Steve's colleague, the late Bill Keeton, one of the best university lecturers I ever had, later showed that homing pigeons could detect and orient themselves to the earth's magnetic field. Much more research since the late '60s, when I was at Cornell, has refined but not completed our understanding of birds' abilities to migrate huge distances, many species "knowing" the way even if they have never been before and cannot follow others who have.

Now I was thinking about this little Blackpoll Warbler, foraging for insects among the spruce needles and belting out its thin *tseet, tseet, tseet, tseet, tseet*. This little guy, who could barely cover the palm of my hand, had all this navigational equipment inside his tiny head, tuned to rhythms and sensations of the earth and the sky, which I'm only aware of through my ability to read. He can't do most of the special things I can do, like writing about birdwatching and picking up coins with my fingers and exchanging them for something to eat. So we're both pretty special – just very, very different.

But Blackpoll manages to be special *and tiny* (and rather snappy looking in his black-striped suit of feathers). What's more, he is not only a far better navigator than even Prince Henry the Navigator himself, Blackpoll is an astute weather forecaster. At least he had better be, if he is going to be back here in this spruce next June. I picture this little warbler in September, feeding steadily among the spruces of the rocky coast of Nova Scotia, trying to increase his body weight in fat just enough to fuel the journey over the ocean but not too much to carry all that distance. He is watching the weather, waiting for a cold front to pass over, giving him a tail wind and the signal to launch. He is a gambler – with his life – betting that he can follow the front much of the way, that it won't betray his trust and leave him to fight a head wind until he can sustain flight no longer and be forced to ditch in the sea and drown.

This one might not make it across the ocean this September, but many others of his kind would. I was looking at a miracle. Perhaps no more miraculous than any other little packet of life. But knowing the story of *this* miracle, and sitting beside it in privileged audience, I was more aware than ever of the miracle of all living beings.

Tseet, tseet, tseet, tseet, tseet.

∞

How fortunate Blackpoll is to be unaware of his destiny and the internal machinery designed by evolution to get him there – especially the risks he faces along the way. He is an alert animal, living in the present moment, unconscious of his past, oblivious of his future. How awful it would be for him if he really knew the risks. Would he be able to overcome the fear, if he did? Wouldn't his daily anxiety be heightened to the point of paralysis, rendering him unable to function as he was designed to do? His confused thoughts would compromise the natural order of his species. Aware of the nerve it takes to be a Blackpoll Warbler, he would surely lose it.

I am reminded of my son's present-tense innocence of what awaits him in adulthood.

I've noticed that all major religions (underlying their diversity of language and concepts) place high value on clearing the mind of thinking about one's self. Better to "see" God, they might say, to be alert to God's presence. We humans struggle with self-consciousness and self-absorption – our mental chatter. For the religious, this gets in the way of their relationship to God. Our mental chatter drives us back into the past and forward into the future as we dwell on regret and anxiety but spend little time in the here and now focusing on what God has put before us. Living in the present is essential for clearing the mind to be open to whatever meaning there may be in the universe. From the Christian perspective, C. S. Lewis wrote in the 15th of *The Screwtape Letters*:

> For the Present is the point at which time touches eternity. Of the present moment, and of it only, humans have an experience analogous to the experience [God] has of reality as a whole; in it alone freedom and actuality are offered them.

This leads to a surprising thought. Blackpoll doesn't have the problem of clearing his mind to focus on the here and now. Perhaps Blackpoll lives closer to God than I do.

That does not mean he sees God any better than I do. In fact, if God is unseeable (as I'm sure God is) and can only be imagined or intuited by a self-reflecting mind, Blackpoll's focus on the present doesn't enable him to know God at all. It allows the working of evolution on the Blackpoll species to take charge of his life and direct it toward a destiny. It is not thwarted by free will. Blackpoll is a pure manifestation of universal forces – God's will.

Some people, otherwise unreligious, agnostic or even atheist, speak and write with reverence for wildness and wilderness, contending that human control and even human influence devalues nature. Even if we don't destroy or impair the functioning of wild species or their ecosystems, our interference, even our mere presence, disrupts the natural order and thereby reduces its value. There is implicit religious significance here. On one hand, this contention invokes the "fallen" state of humanity, its corruption of free will, its sinfulness. On the other hand, it acknowledges a transcendent cause or order, universal forces of creation and sustenance that came before humanity, that shaped humanity, and with which humanity now interferes in an ultimately futile effort to control its own destiny. Many of us would not say, or believe we mean, that wildness and wilderness derive their high value from living more in line with God's will, but we might say and believe that being wild – nature – is a purer manifestation of the universal forces than being man-made, human controlled, or outright "civilized."

What will I say when my son is old enough to want to know what set these forces in motion, what created them, what continues to control them now? These are questions of origin. Charles Darwin lucidly described the rules of evolution, the way natural selection winnows the variation offered up by nature. Genetics and molecular biology have refined the theory of evolution, and there are still questions about "macro" evolution, but I firmly believe that Darwin got it mostly right. This is not sufficient to decide that Darwin supplants Jesus or others who personify or speak about God. Darwin's work amplifies the wonder about the origin of so much natural variation, just as the Big Bang theory, in trying to explain the origin of the universe, only invites deeper questions: What set off the Big Bang? What was there before? What lies beyond the expanding (or contracting or oscillating) boundaries of the universe? What is the dark matter and vacuum energy that makes up 98 per cent of the universe? And so on and on and on.

I see no conflict between science, as a body of knowledge or method of inquiry, and belief in God. Equally firmly, I believe that evolution – process and result – is a manifestation of God. What is increasingly difficult, however, is to conceive of God as "personal," operating like a super-human being directing the daily details of all Creation, like the individual destiny of Blackpoll or me.

Ockham's Razor, an old philosopher's rule of thumb, says the least complex of possible explanations is most likely the closest to being true. For this reason alone, I have to believe that *something* outside the universe, which I am willing to label "God," initiated certain events and set the rules by which these events would un-

The Big Day: June 7

fold, without determining exactly how they would unfold. Not just once, but in at least three events of creation – the creation of the universe about 15 billion years ago, the creation of life about 3.5 billion years ago, and the creation of human language perhaps less than 100,000 years ago. Our language is the capacity that makes us truly different from other animals, even the chimpanzees and other brainy animals that can be trained to use symbolic language in humanoid ways. Language makes possible the evolution of complex culture and, perhaps more important, the development of consciousness and thereby the ability to conceive of God.

In his manifestation of the universal forces shaping the evolution of his species, Blackpoll can do miraculous feats of navigation and weather forecasting, not to mention all the more mundane tricks of his insectivorous, predator-dodging, mate-finding and young-rearing trade. In my manifestation of these same universal forces, I have my miraculous hands and fingers freed from locomotion to make and manipulate tools, and I have my miraculous language and even more remarkable brain to use it, so that I can share experience with my wife and son and others in complex social ways. Perhaps as a mere artifact of this distinctively human survival kit, I have the ability to think about my thoughts, about others' thoughts, and to conceive of things beyond my own experience, even beyond human experience, to conceive of and perhaps even "know" God. But I, like the great majority of humans, waste this ability on counterproductive worry, regret and worse.

We have the opportunity for a special awareness of God, a closer relationship than Blackpoll can achieve. But this same special ability allows us to live mentally outside the present and to imagine "realities" that have no eternal reference point. We can allow ourselves to be distracted by our mental chatter and the distortions it creates, logical or otherwise, distracted from the actual moment in which we live and therefore from the eternal – distracted from God.

I have experienced so many years of distraction that it seems perfectly normal. It is very difficult to still the mental chatter and return to awareness of real life and an occasional glimpse of the Eternal. Compared with the vast majority of the human species, Blackpoll and his fellow non-human but alert animals dwell closer to God, more in tune with the universe than I, at least so far in my life.

∞

This meditation was broken by piercing cries. A much larger, louder miracle than Blackpoll alighted awkwardly on the spike-like leader atop another spruce and had to dance and flap to maintain its post at the very top – like the star on a Christmas tree. It was a Lesser Yellowlegs, looking outrageously out of place. Before this moment, I had only seen this fairly large, exceptionally long-legged, graceful sandpiper padding quickly across mudflats exposed at low tide. Insisting on being seen (and admired), *kew, kew* rang out from this teetering ornament. I did admire its long, impossibly thin yellow legs. Bonnie's book had prepared me for this spectacle, but it still made me smile – a comic miracle, this one.

My eye then picked up a darting mammal movement on the ground. I finally got the binoculars on it and discovered a red squirrel. I was truly surprised to see one this far north, especially in an isolated line of spruces surrounded by tundra and marsh. I always delight to the sight of these well-dressed, herky-jerky windup toys, but my admiration for their hardiness soared at this moment of discovery. I could hardly believe this little animal had survived the harsh winter. I knew it collects and stores food for the winter, and noisily guards its food caches, but without a burrow and without the ability to hibernate, these squirrels must often perish in the long, harsh cold. I wondered if the squirrel could spend much of the winter under the blanket of snow.

The common and familiar had suddenly become exotic and surprising. This was a developing theme of the trip. The red squirrel was only the second mammal for me, the muskrat being the first – both frequent companions in the South and unexpected around Churchill. I had expected the North to expand my perspective, but I did not anticipate seeing my home world in such different perspective, giving me new appreciation for it.

Two more tiny packets of Life came tumbling, buzzing and twittering from the sky into the spruces. Redpolls. My intensity ratcheted up. Which one? Common or Hoary? Like a setter on point, binoculars poised, eyes wide and sighting over the double barrels as a hunter along the top of a shotgun, I watched for movement. Nothing. "Come on you little twerps! Show yourselves!" Flit, flit, flit from one tree to another, and a *tweee* call formed into a question. Binoculars up, sighted on the landing area. "Sure enough – redpoll," I said to myself out loud, admiring the rosy forehead and rosy breast and brown, stripy back. The rump looked whitish, and there was a lot of white along the sides. "I do believe it's a Hoary," out loud again but whispered reverentially.

I settled back in my seat with satisfaction and reflected on the merit of sitting in one place, soaking up the scene, and letting the birds come to me. It is the difference between searching for particular species and seeing whatever is there, just posting myself in an attractive spot, getting comfortable and watching life on parade. I never know when and where a parade will come, but whenever and wherever it passes by, I hope for a good view.

I revel in being able to attach a label to each species of animal and plant and then to see associations. The label is not simply descriptive. Just as our family names represent distinct genetic lineages and cultural histories, a species name symbolizes a natural history, a story of evolutionary twists and turns in response to a challenging and changing world. A species name represents all the current members of a population of potentially interbreeding individuals. The name also labels an ideal type around which all the population varies in individual ways, the average result of a progression through time.

The quality of available field-guide books makes birds the easiest group for labelling with the names of species. The species' stories I've read or seen for myself are evoked by these labels. Being able to name birds lets me file my stories and associations under those names and call them up at will, to add, revise, relive. I suppose I list the names of species as a way to record the stories and organize them in my mind. It is not the list but the listing – the collecting of stories and weaving them together into a bigger story.

The appearance of something unnamed sounded the "all alert": finch sounds from the other side of the truck. The unknown challenged the recorded stories. The hunter emerged from his relaxation and went to work again. These turned out to be more redpolls, but they were difficult to see well enough to distinguish Common from Hoary.

One after another, I heard twittering and buzzing high in the sky, then I'd see the bird plummet to the top of a spruce. Every time I manoeuvered closer, the bird would disappear for good into the foliage. I suspected they were going to nests all along the line of trees and naturally being rather secretive as they got in close to the nests. Difficult as it was, I managed to see several individuals well and came to realize how variable they were in the amounts of red, brown and white, with marked differences between males and females but also between individuals. I began to doubt that I had seen a Hoary, as I saw so much variability in the Common Redpolls.

The uncertainty was unsettling. I felt agitated – and annoyed with myself for feeling that way – and distracted.

∽

My mind returned to concern for winter survival. Even on a relatively mild but wind-driven rainy day in the California winter, I wonder how the birds outside are surviving, how they keep from getting soaked and then dying from exposure. I am sure a number must die in each storm. In the same way, I worry about a homeless man huddled on a winter sidewalk. Yet he is up and around the next day, usually, and so are the birds – most of them. I am in awe of this simple ability to survive, to hunker down and wait it out, or even worse, to get out there to find something to eat despite the elements. For empathy, I can only reach back in my mind to that rainy, cold August in central Québec. How far removed my life is from that reality, and how much I want to protect my wife and son from it!

If I worry for the red squirrel, what about these Common Redpolls? Their story is the opposite of the Blackpoll Warbler story. The redpoll miracle is that they stay put in the far North through the winter, here in this place farther north than the *summer* range of birds like Evening Grosbeaks and Pine Siskins, which appear in Connecticut only to escape the harshest northern winters. I have read that even tiny birds can survive the cold if they have enough to eat. But with day length down to a few hours, how do they get enough to eat to make it through the night? Perhaps these redpolls dive into the snow for insulation of their body heat, like grouse or ptarmigan. I don't know. I am simply in awe of the miracle of their survival.

Still, their lives are often scary, and more often sooner than later, they die. If these animals are more in tune with the universe, closer to God, is that good? Is it good that the natural order for them is so dangerous, that they risk aggression from their own species, terrifying death from predators, agonizing death from freezing or hunger, lingering death from disability or illness? Suffering is embedded in the natural order for all species. This is reality. Is suffering therefore good? Perhaps what is Good in the *eternal* perspective can be either good or bad for individual packets of life. An individual redpoll may fall prey to a falcon, which is bad for the redpoll but good for the falcon, and good for the natural order, which is in tune with Eternity.

Maybe so, but this feels like a naturalist's equivalent of moral relativism – a most unhelpful perspective. But it might just be true. If so, we cannot characterize any act as good or bad. What is good for one species is bad for another. Nor can we say one species is better than another, given that all species are products of the universal forces, creatures of God. How can there be any universal Good in the whole of Nature – all this eating and being eaten, all this suffering and dying? Unsympathetic urbanites, like Woody Allen, might be forgiven for comparing nature to one great big "restaurant." I believe in God, that God created nature, but there is very contradictory evidence that nature, or even God, is good. What can it mean for any part of nature to be called good?

Setting aside the question of nature's goodness, the question might be whether it is *better* to be more in tune with nature. Better than what? Is Blackpoll, because he is closer to God, better than me?

Perhaps the comparison should be solely within a species. Is Blackpoll a better Blackpoll Warbler because he is more in tune with God? Think of a very different Blackpoll Warbler hesitating on the coast of Nova Scotia in September. If he were as distracted by the risks of the Atlantic crossing as I would be, he would suffer a failure of nerve. He would probably abandon the program and find some clever rationale for spending the winter in Nova Scotia (no risk of drowning, less distance to travel back to the breeding grounds next spring, weather here seems fine, definitely better than Churchill). And he would perish from lack of food in the long Nova Scotia winter. That would be bad for him. Also for his mate, if he had had one that summer and they had bred successfully, because she would return next spring to the same breeding site looking for him, and not finding him, her chances of successfully raising young might be fewer. More often than not, it would have been *better* for him and her if our Blackpoll Warbler had stuck to the program laid down by his evolutionary history, in tune with eternal forces.

What might this mean for guiding my son? Should he live his life totally in the present, with no thought to planning for the future or learning from the past? Should I extol to him the virtues of animal-like existence as having higher value than those of "civilization," as a true misanthrope would do? Such strange parenting would ignore the survival skills given him by our own evolutionary history. He was born to think and think about thinking, even to be rational. It is part of his special heritage, our program in tune with the eternal forces. It is *better* that he goes with that program. Of course, the human program has so many versions, due to the remarkable overlay of cultural evolution on biological evolution: one biological species with many cultural versions of its evolved program, each tuned to specific social and ecological circumstances. Still, it is *better* if he goes with a human program, any version, rather than a non-human program.

Is it *better* if we use our human abilities to live more in the present, to live closer to God, even as we give due importance to learning from the past and planning for the future? No matter that different cultures define what is good and bad differently. The answer seems deeper and more universal for our species. Think of the people who are *better* at living their own lives and living with others. They are fully aware of themselves and the place, the people and the other creatures around them. They accept all with gratitude when the present is pleasant and with patience when it is not. Their actions respond to what is happening more or less right now. They are not fixated on past hurts or heroism or on future fantasies or fears. While such people might not recognize they are living closer to the eternal Good, closer to God, are they not *better* – in *any* culture?

∞

Time to move. Akudlik Marsh was just ahead. In fact, I had been lingering all this time on the outskirts. I could have left the truck where I was stopped by the Blackpoll Warbler and walked. I didn't know, so I drove.

I parked at the start of an earthen dike between two ponds. With the intention of hiking some distance with scope and tripod over the shoulder, I locked up the truck. I felt a little self-conscious about being paranoid, but rationalized that I didn't want to get out of this "civilized" habit. I walked out onto the dike, which continued out across a large lake with a sheet of ice still floating in the middle. A few Semipalmated Plovers ran ahead of me with cries of protest after I nearly stepped on them. They blended well with the bare, rocky soil of the dike and remained immobile until the last moment. The Semipalmated Plover looks like a smaller, more compact version of a Killdeer, with only one black band across the chest instead of two, a bandit's mask across the forehead and eyes, and orange legs. Their protests reminded me to beware of stepping on any of their eggs. They lay them on practically bare ground hoping the speckled eggs will look like small stones to a predator, such as a gull.

The day was getting warm enough for a light jacket – sunny, low wind, very pleasant – a balmy, sunscreen-and-hat sort of day. The ever-present Arctic Terns were in the air. I scanned for an unusual gull (Ross's or Sabine's?) with more hope than expectation. Like the lottery, you have to play to win.

What I *did* see, cruising close to me in the water along the edge of the dike, was a pair of Oldsquaw. This is a rather odd duck with an even odder name. Before this moment, I had seen them only at a distance – from the train and offshore from the winter coast of New England. In fact, on the same day I did *not* see the Snowy Owl at Plum Island, I *did* see a large flock of Oldsquaw bobbing and diving in the wind-driven "chop" of the tidal mouth of the Merrimack River. I could never get a really good look at them. Later, I noted in the bird guide that I could see this species on its nesting ground around Churchill. As I planned this trip, I had looked forward to getting a closer look at an Oldsquaw.

And here they were: a male with its bicoloured brown-and-yellow bill and half-bald-looking head, dark-chocolate-brown body with golden streamers across its back, and a few long, stiff pinfeathers sticking up from its rear at an elevated angle from the water, and a female with far more subdued colours and contrasts and no long tail spike. Appropriately, the Europeans call them Long-tailed Ducks, but I prefer the more picturesque, if less politically correct, Oldsquaw. (My preference notwithstanding, the American Ornithologists' Union has recently changed the official common name to Long-tailed Duck.)

The Oldsquaw pair were cautious of my movements but allowed me to stay close. They dove regularly. Some diving ducks signal an imminent dive by flattening or sleeking the feathers on the crest of the head a moment before, and then they seem to arch up a little and dive straight down. The Oldsquaw's head seems to be sleeked all the time. It lowers the head, rolls forward and is gone below, reminding me a bit of a swimming muskrat going under. I've read that the Oldsquaw is one of the ducks that uses both wings and feet to propel itself underwater, so this difference may be related to the different appearance of the dive. The last of the male visible on the surface is that spike tail – not sticking up; he seems to lay it flat on the water surface before diving, perhaps his own signal.

A couple of times, my close attention spooked these ducks into short flight, just to get a bit farther away while staying close to the dike. *Ooo-wah*, he called in flight. It was a sound as distinctive as the look of the duck, almost a mewing call, both wild and gentle.

On the other side of the dike was a Pacific Loon, quite a bit larger than most ducks. It was in full breeding uniform with a deep-purple throat patch, almost luminous pearl gray on the head and back of the neck, and a ruby eye. Magnificent! Unlike the sexual dimorphism of ducks, which presumably protects the female when on the nest, the male and female loons are identically gorgeous. It was easy to see one of them on a nest at the edge of the pond, while the other cruised the open water like a patrol boat with flags flying. The erect *en garde* carriage of long neck, head and bill and the stately glide over the water as it watched me carefully with fearsome ruby eyes, all reminded me of the Horned Grebe at nearly twice the size.

Transfixed by the patrolling loon, I almost overlooked my third life bird of the morning – a trio of Hudsonian Godwits. These large shorebirds stalked long-legged in the marsh vegetation on the far shore of the loon pond. They were carefully and deeply probing the wet ground with their long sabre-like beaks – orange with black tips and curved slightly upward. Tagging along behind the godwits were a couple of Short-billed Dowitchers, which are much shorter in the leg and more chunky in the body than the godwits, but with dark, straight bills almost as long. They also were probing as deeply as their bills would allow, seeming to have to rear back a little to get the bill into the ground, then probing rapidly up and down – like a sewing machine, some bird books accurately note.

There are lots of incredible body designs in the bird world, but I have to vote for these long-legged, long-billed shorebirds as the most improbable (barely beating out the hummingbirds and the woodpeckers). Why? First, think of a man walking on stilts, then think of him running on stilts, then think of him balancing on the top of a spruce on stilts, like the Lesser Yellowlegs did a little earlier this morning. That's the easier part to explain. More remarkable, I think, is the very long bill probing deep in the mud and detecting by the sense of touch a succulent denizen of the ooze, and *then* opening the tip of the bill to grasp the little critter well enough to pull it up and out, and finally using a long, thin tongue to move the morsel up into the mouth (they don't throw their heads back to let gravity do the job, as some birds do). What looks to my uneducated eye like a stiff, horny beak is in fact loaded with sensory nerves all the way to the tip and enough muscle and tendon to pry open just the tip of the bill (I've seen the related Marbled Godwit practise this trick while resting), as if by remote control. Yet the very long bill is stiff enough to be thrust repeatedly, rapidly, almost violently into fairly compact mud. To me, this avian instrument is almost as remarkable as the very thin probes doctors use to explore and fix arteries and veins.

The dowitchers are only "short-billed" in comparison to the ever-so-slightly longer-billed Long-billed Dowitcher, which fortunately does not occur in the Churchill area. I say "fortunately" because this is a pair of species that are so similar in appearance (but not their call notes, if you can hear them) that the prudent birder – and especially the sensible birdwatcher – calls them "dowitchers." Usually it irks me a little to be unable to say exactly which one I'm looking at. Not a problem here, since the breeding ranges of the two dowitchers are not even close to each other. Why does that make me feel more comfortable? Probably because here I can make sure I've put the right label on the story.

Both the godwits and the dowitchers, here on their breeding ground, had a great deal of reddish brown in their plumage – deep chestnut on the godwit belly, a more burnt orange colour on the dowitchers. I really like reddish brown as a creature colour. Creatures seem to like it, too, because so many of them have it, in a multitude of subtly different hues evoking comparisons with oranges, bricks or chestnuts or, failing that, forcing us to dig up archaic adjectives like "rufous," "russet," "bay," "fulvous" and "buff." How about "ochraceous" or "hepatic" (as in liver-coloured)?

These adjectives have been built into the common names of many species. Bird guide books, especially the older ones, can get carried away in their descriptions. Having grown up with such books, I hadn't noticed the peculiarity of words like "rufous" until a non-birdwatching friend asked what colour that would be. Knowing that "the colour of the sides of a Rufous-sided Towhee" would not help, the best I could come up with was "reddish brown." Another non-birdwatcher biologist friend once pointed out a ludicrous bird-guide description of the behaviour of a certain African flycatcher as "shy and confiding." How helpful is that? For me, it captured the bird's demeanour perfectly. For him, the bird would be whispering secrets in your ear while averting its eyes!

Having looked and listened too much, I shouldered the scope and headed back the kilometre or so to the truck. The bright blue truck looked small and distant, isolated. I was reminded how much I depended on that vehicle, my lifeline, my enabler. Fatigue, hunger and thirst didn't stop me from admiring the loons and Oldsquaw again. Couldn't get enough – but it was time for a lunch break. What a great day! And it wasn't half over.

Back in the truck and on the Highway, I soon could see I had barely left the town. It took maybe five minutes to reach the Churchill Motel Restaurant, about a block from my hotel. I pulled off the dusty street into the parking area in front of the restaurant and parked with all the other trucks and sport utility vehicles, feeling like Joel Fleischmann pulling up to The Brick in *Northern Exposure* (my all-time favourite TV show). In the middle of this long subarctic day, everything looked overexposed, a too-bright grayish white – even the sky, which had "milked up" (my father's apt description of an expanding film of high, thin cloud). It seemed a little too warm, especially for my layers of clothing. I stripped down a bit and went inside, where it seemed a *lot* too warm. No air-conditioning, of course.

Even though it was approaching 2 p.m., most of the tables in three separate small rooms were occupied. But I found a good spot near a window where I could watch the action in the street and in the restaurant. Seemed like local folks entirely, out for Sunday lunch. They were a diverse group of people, though not as diverse as urban Canada with its loads of fresh immigrants and second-generation look-alikes. This was a more frontier sort of diversity, with pure and mixed races and ethnicities, challenging identification with traditional labels. My waitress was a tall young Anglo woman with an interesting smile. I asked her what was going on with all the kids and the filled garbage bags around the Chamber of Commerce kiosk across the street. A special clean-up-the-town day, she explained. "Good day for it," I said, remarking to myself on the civic pride in this remote outpost.

I decided this would be my big meal and that I would take my time to reflect on my progress and plan my next moves with the help of Bonnie's book. After all, this was the heat of the day, the slow time for wildlife. I enjoyed a good meal, Canadian beer, and a sense of accomplishment.

I decided that it was time to really experience the tundra by slogging around in it. For this purpose, I had packed big rubber wellington boots that, along with the scope and tripod, had rendered my duffle bag a serious threat to my middle-aged back as I lugged it in and out of airports and train stations. Bonnie indicates a prime spot for such slogging south of the airport. She warns her readers not to do this on a cold or rainy day, because when the slogger scares the shorebirds off their nests, the eggs or chicks are exposed and likely to succumb to the elements. Do it on a warm day, she wrote. What better day than this, and in the middle of the afternoon?

By 3:30 I was back on the Highway heading out of town again. A kilometre beyond Akudlik junction, and before ascending the coastal ridge to the airport, I turned south on a gravel road running parallel to, but well below, the main runway, which is raised high above the surrounding land. An expanse of marshy taiga lay on the west side of the road – a lot of standing water amid grassy vegetation dotted with anemic, isolated tamarack trees looking like dead sticks. It didn't match my mental image of tundra, nor what I had seen from the train yesterday morning, nor even the hummocky dry tundra I had surveyed this morning. Thinking I had not found the spot Bonnie was writing about, I pressed on, only to find the density of trees increasing. Clearly I was getting into the forest. I doubled back to take another look at the land below the runway. It seemed uninviting, even uninteresting – no displaying shorebirds, no singing longspurs. Figuring that it might be the wrong time of day, I turned around again and continued on south to Landing Lake.

Officially named Farnworth Lake, it is the former float-plane landing lake with the remains of a dock and service buildings on a spit of ground built out into the lake about 50 metres. This very large lake still had sheets of thin, porous ice covering much of the water surface except along the shores. Spruces and willow shrubs lined the shores, but patches of tundra were not far beyond. I parked the truck near the dilapidated buildings and ambled around with binoculars only, not sure how long I would be. White-crowned and Savannah Sparrows sang half-heartedly in the afternoon warmth. A pair of Pacific Loons was lurking along the shore and then took up diving at the edge of the floating ice, which seemed to be crumbling continuously at the edges and contracting noticeably as I watched. The loons surfaced right in the midst of the ice, as though it had no substance at all, like floating slush.

A lovely song floated out from the dense but leafless willow shrubs standing in the shallow water along the shore. Its tonal quality was finch; its pattern was wren. It was fairly loud, what a bird-guide writer might call "insistent" or "emphatic," meaning "Hey, here I am!" I had no idea what to expect. As often happens, the bird did not want to be seen, just heard. I searched the shrubs with the unaided eye in the direction of the song, alert for any movement. The singing stopped. After a couple of minutes, I scanned with binoculars as hope dimmed for this one. Binoculars are best for enlarging what you can see already, but if you're lucky, you can pick up a motionless bird with a quick scan in the general direction of a song. Nothing. I remained frozen on the alert for a while, and then relaxed back into my amble.

Soon I heard a sort-of-familiar, sort-of-different song from one of the taller trees in the middle distance. It immediately made me think of the Harris's Sparrow I was hoping to see. Somewhere between the songs of its close relatives, the White-crowned Sparrow and the White-throated Sparrow, this was a simple series of two clear, sweet, single-tone whistles dropping down to three or more whistles at a lower tone. I moved quickly, saw the bird high in the tree, and got it in the binoculars. And there it was, the black mask characteristic of Harris's Sparrow. Not a great view, but good enough to give me lifer number four for the day.

Having been thrilled to see my first Smith's Longspur through the scope, I decided to go back to the truck for the scope. It was a 30-metre walk each way, so I didn't have much confidence the sparrow would still be there when I returned, but it was, and I got it in the scope. Better, but still not a great view due to the backlighting. I started to circle around to get between the bird and the sun. Then it flew some distance across a patch of tundra, perhaps a hundred metres, to another treetop. Again I got the scope on it, but only verified the view I had already had. I wanted a better look – this was, after all, a life bird – but the only way to get closer was to go across the tundra, flanked on one side by Landing Lake and on the other side by a large tundra pond.

It looked dry enough, so I shouldered the scope and ventured cautiously out toward the closest hummock. My first step onto tundra was unforgettably alarming! The mat of vegetation gave way as though I was stepping onto a very thick, sodden sponge. Water appeared from nowhere to collect about an inch deep around my shoe. I stepped back to more solid ground in a moment of panic, thinking about being out here alone, beyond sight or sound of another human being, imagining my sinking into the muck. "It was only an inch of water," I reminded myself. Scanning the horizon with heightened awareness of the wilderness around me, I felt the edge of fear evoked by unfamiliar, potentially dangerous natural surroundings. It inflated my life preserver, Caution, but lured me with possibilities for Discovery.

I tried again, this time stepping lightly and quickly about four squishy steps until I mounted the target hummock, relieved that it held my weight without much of that sinking feeling and no water pooling around my feet. The hummock was broad enough to spread out the legs of the scope's tripod. I was still eager to see the Harris's Sparrow, but I knew I wasn't much closer than before. In fact, it was gone, never to be seen or heard again that day, like a spirit having completed its assignment to lure me out onto the tundra against my better judgment.

∞

Giving up on the bird, I looked carefully around me. Feeling stiffly secure but constrained on my hummock perch, I didn't dare move. I might as well have stepped out onto an ice floe on Hudson Bay. I was as fearful *for* my spongy surroundings as I was *of* them. Bonnie's book had warned me about treading on the tundra because of its fragility (footprints could last for years) and the likelihood of stepping on the nests of the birds who also prefer the drier heights of the hummocks.

With feet firmly planted on my hummock, I surveyed the local scene, becoming aware of its coarse pattern of shapes and fine pattern of colours. I remembered a comparison of tundra to coral reef, and could see the similarity. Like coral heads or blooms, this tundra's hummocks seemed to well up like bubbles to the surface of boiling water, frozen in place until they were crowding each other on the surface. The hummocks, which stood a foot or so above the surrounding lowlands, seemed composed mostly of lichens and mosses, with very low-growing woody plants in between and up the sides. This tundra didn't have the same gray cast I had noted in the morning. Here were the variegated red, pink, brown, green, yellow, white and orange of an eastern deciduous forest starting to leaf out in late April, early May – a lovely ordered chaos of colour and pattern.

I bent down to look closely at the plants underfoot. It was like looking into a terrarium – a diminutive world of stems, leaves, branches, buds and flowers, and even last year's fruits, which reminded me of my favourite, blueberries. But they weren't. Nothing here was familiar, except for what appeared to be sphagnum moss, very spongy and yellow-green. There were little white puffs of reindeer moss (lichen, really), sort of spongy, sort of brittle. Was that a miniature Labrador tea shrub with its leathery evergreen leaves? Another, leafless woody plant had feathery flowers like those of the fairy duster of the Sonoran Desert. I could distinguish up to 10 species of plants within a two-metre radius of my feet, but I could name only a couple. My biologist's memory recovered the word "ericaceous" (of the heather family) in association with tundra vegetation, but I had no idea what an "ericaceous" plant would look like. Anything smaller than trees and the larger shrubs, and I'm lost in the plant kingdom.

I've tried half-heartedly to learn to identify the smaller plants, but I've never taken a course in botany or found a field guide that is very helpful. The species are too numerous and too variable for me to remember. It's the same with insects and spiders. They are all around me when I'm out in the world, but I can't label them and remember the labels. I've tried to content myself with learning to recognize the Orders of plants and insects, but I still have trouble. And without labels, stories can't be filed away as easily for future enjoyment.

It is so much easier to label and remember birds, mammals and trees, even reptiles and amphibians, because the field guides for these groups are so much better than for other groups of animals and plants. Plus there are far fewer numbers of species. I need a field guide that I can page through in idle moments to see the species and memorize the names and read about their relationship to other species, their ranges and habitats and habits, so that I can weave my personal observations together with what is written. For me, a field guide is a mnemonic device, an almanac and a personal diary.

I started to recognize that black spruce, white spruce and various shrub willows were not the only trees around. There were quite a few tamarack (a.k.a. larch), which have the distinction of being the only deciduous conifer I've ever met. In early June, they were starting to leaf out, pushing out their tiny bundles of soft, bright-green needles.

Bonnie's book was very helpful for identifying the calls of the two frog species, which I was hearing everywhere all the time, it seemed. The boreal chorus frog sounds like a thumb along the teeth of a comb – *pr-r-r-r-eep*. The wood frog call is an abrupt, nasal quack or *ank*. Multiple individuals chorused together, and often I heard both species calling at once. These delightful frog sounds became part of Churchill's background noise, along with the songs of the White-crowned Sparrows and the Savannah Sparrows and the kipping cries of the Arctic Terns – and, near the river or bay, the occasional *crump* of ice floes.

∞

I was now getting comfortable with my surroundings. I wanted to explore and experience this patch of tundra. "Well, this is what I brought those boots for," I said out loud to the surrounding landscape. I left the scope on its hummock and squished my way back to solid ground and to the truck. I had bought these "wellies" especially for this trip, and this was their maiden voyage. They were very comfortable over the thick socks I bought with them. Clump, clump, squish, squish back to the scope, over the shoulder, and off I went to see if I could find that Harris's Sparrow in the far spruces. The water never went above ankle depth, but the boots gave me a nice sense of security and freedom to move. I just had to be cautious about stepping on lichen and bird nests.

As my appreciation of the colours of the tundra vegetation grew, I felt some regret that I had come too early to see the tundra in full leaf and bloom. It must be spectacular in early July when flowering would be at its peak. But that is also the season when biting insects are in full bloom, too. Maybe, I thought, I should enjoy what colours there were on this lovely warm afternoon on the tundra *without* insects.

Ooo-wah. I had company. An Oldsquaw pair on the very near tundra pond was watching me with edgy concern. The female hovered in the grasses along the far shore – near a nest, I'd bet. The male was bravely showing himself in open water. I could hardly believe how closely I was able to examine these beautiful birds with the binoculars and then the scope.

I reached the cluster of taller spruces on the far side of the patch of tundra – a screen of trees separating the tundra from a watercourse and more tundra beyond. Bearing left, I picked a way through the trees and willow shrubs to the willow swamp edging Landing Lake. I decided to hold still for a while, remaining concealed among the trees to increase my chances of glimpsing any shy creatures that might be going about their business in the swamp. Soon a female Common Redpoll was hopping from branch to branch almost within my arm's reach. She eyed me very nervously but refused to back off. Must be a nest nearby, I thought. Without moving my feet, I looked deeper into the spruce branches. There it was! About halfway into the tree and a metre plus above the ground, a little open nest with eggs.

My first impulse was to move away quickly. As a teenager participating in the newly started Nest Record Card program of the Cornell Laboratory of Ornithology, I had spent several weeks in the summer of 1964 tracking down active bird nests and returning daily to document their progress. I was distressed by the number of nests that were abandoned or raided by predators (probably

Blue Jays tracking *me*). From my reading and this personal experience, I had figured that it was not in the best interests of nesting birds to have a human visitor, no matter how well intentioned. I immediately but slowly withdrew without making any approach to the redpoll nest, trying not to further alarm the mother or to attract any third party's attention to the site.

I headed back in the direction of the truck, skirting the edge of the willow swamp and lake. Again I heard the finch-wren song from the willow swamp, this time quite close. There was the bird, lurking in the willows just above the water line, ready to dart back into the thicket. Hard as they are to identify, I was certain it was a Lincoln's Sparrow: a grayish face, buffy breast and sides finely streaked black, breaking sharply to a clear white belly. I always get a little thrill from sighting one, perhaps because they are hard to see in the first place due to their swampy habitats and reclusive nature. Lincoln's is also hard to distinguish from the much more common and conspicuous Song Sparrow. And I see them only occasionally each winter. It makes me feel competent to find and identify Lincoln's Sparrow. But I also find this species rather attractive. When you can get a good close look, in good light, sparrows are beautiful for their variations on the colour brown, broken into intricate patterns filled in with pearl gray or ivory white or even grassy yellow, and often accented boldly with dashes of rusty red, lemon yellow or jet black. Many of them are also good songsters. I had never heard Lincoln's Sparrow sing its lovely song.

Sudden, startling, loud. *Whoop!* What was that? For a moment, I was on the East African savanna, chilled by a hyena's siren cranking up the volume, climbing up the scale. A truly unnerving sound for anyone out in open country, far from vehicle or other cover. I could almost smell the sun-baked, vaguely barnyard odour of the savanna, filled with antelope and other hoofed mammals and their predators. I gratefully recollected my geographic position and

Life List: A Birder's Spiritual Awakening

realized the sound came from Landing Lake, where I had seen the pair of Pacific Loons. The call shared the tonal quality but not the pattern of a Common Loon's haunting cry-call-warble. Must be the loon – of course. Whew!

I reached dry land again and started toward the truck. Not so loud, but equally weird, a mechanical *oonk-KA-choonk, oonk-KA-choonk, oonk-KA-choonk* came from what seemed like just the other side of the old float-plane dock. I knew this comical sound immediately – American Bittern (of the heron family). More often heard than seen, this guy sounds like he is playing bass for a jug band. Eager to see the bittern for a change, I hurried to the dock and searched the waterside vegetation carefully. Nothing. *Oonk-KA-choonk* sounded again and still seemed close by – until I realized from the direction of the call that it was carrying a good half kilometre across the lake from the far shore.

∞

I retraced the road I had come on. I stopped as the truck came abreast of the tundra area Bonnie's book advises is good for tundra slogging. I had left my boots on to give this area a try, inspired by the pleasant experience of the tundra at Landing Lake. On the way in, the area didn't look particularly interesting, and looked even less so now. No calling or displaying shorebirds – a bit too early in the season yet? No hummocks and variegated colours – a different sort of tundra? Just a grayish-to-blonde grassland with lots of small pools of open water and scattered stunted spruces and larches. I hesitated a while, but then said to myself, "Okay, let's give it a try and see what gets scared up." Off I went.

At first, I stepped on the grassy areas, but then I decided to see what it was like to wade through the open-water pools. Clearly I wouldn't get far if I tried to avoid the pools. I also wanted to minimize the chance of stepping on some bird's nest. Just one problem;

the bottoms of these shallow pools looked like nasty ooze. I stepped in and immediately felt myself sinking into sucking mud. Alarmed, I threw my weight back on the other foot, still on the much firmer grass, and gently tugged until the mud released my foot. That was enough for me. I had gone only three or four metres out from the road. I regained the road with relief. No, thank you. Too scary to be out in that stuff, especially when all alone out here.

Back in the truck, boots off, I gazed with puzzlement over this very wet tundra, wondering if I was failing to understand something here. Bonnie's book had served me so well until now that I still wondered if I had found the right place. Oh well, I would move on.

∞

I was quickly back on the Highway and up onto the coastal ridge and driving past the turnoff to the airport buildings not far off the road. Now I could see Hudson Bay for the first time today. The coastal ridge lifted me quite a bit higher here than near the town, perhaps 50 to 100 metres above the level of the bay. I had a breathtaking 180-degree panorama of "frozen" Hudson Bay. This forbidding ocean of ice stunned me again. There was hardly a suspicion of open water. "Incredible!" I said out loud. I felt like an adolescent boy exclaiming "Cool!" as he encounters some dreadful scene of destruction that would make his mother recoil in horror.

I pulled off at the recommended overlook – a vehicle track that appeared to head straight into the tumbled blocks of ice stretching to the northern horizon (it actually disappeared down the steep slope to a shoreline road). I stopped before a bilingual sign framed by the too-bright reflection of white ocean: "Do Not Enter – Défense d'Entrer." I laughed, "I don't think anyone needs to be told. Who would want to enter *that*?" I got out with my camera to capture the visual joke on film.

Bonnie's book said I should look from this point for seals resting on the ice. I could see several black dots on the dirty gray-white ice, so I got out the scope and studied the scene. There were two types of seal bodies laid out on the ice, one about twice the size of the other and solid dark. The smaller seemed to be a dappled gray with a yellow cast. I decided from reading Bonnie's book that these must be the big bearded seals and the small ringed seals. The only other commonly seen seal in this area is the harbour seal. I thought I knew what harbour seals looked like, from all the ones I'd seen on the coasts of Maine and California – dappled gray on white, not yellow. Neither of these seals looked like that. They lay on the ice like big burlap bags full of grain. Through the scope I could see them lift their heads occasionally to look around, sometimes lifting the rear flippers, too. Where there are seals, why not polar bears? I spent a fair amount of time scanning the ice with the scope. Nothing but these scattered lumps of seal on the flattest sections of sea ice.

To my left, I could see Cape Merry and the tiny tops of the Port's grain elevators on the horizon to the west. To my right, I thought I could just see on the horizon to the east the wreck of the *Ithica*, a Greek nickel ore ship that ran aground in 1961 outside Bird Cove. At my back, south, were the very large once-and-future military hangars of the airport, Canadian flags fluttering in the weak southwesterly breeze. A Calm Air flight (SAAB commuter turboprop aircraft) took off and headed north. I watched in fascination until it disappeared toward the horizon of ice. I was thinking of its probable destinations: Arviat, Whale Cove, Rankin Inlet, Chesterfield Inlet, Baker Lake, Coral Harbour, Repulse Bay, Iqaluit. Names of the Eastern Canadian Arctic. Names of Romance, Discovery, Adventure. Names of tiny, isolated, desolate communities of mostly Inuit people with little prospect of any life beyond the traditional.

That small airliner was their lifeline to the world (or the world's point of entry to their world). I tried to imagine what it would feel like to be on that flight over the frozen ocean. It should be no more unnerving than any other flight, our lives depending on the smooth functioning of modern technology. I've been on a good number of flights, sometimes over very remote parts of the globe (and many times, on polar flights between California and Europe, high over Hudson Bay). Yet I felt certain that, flying relatively low over the ice of Hudson Bay as the plane descended toward a tundra airstrip at, say, Rankin Inlet, I would be both unnerved and thrilled.

∞

Back on the paved Highway, I was soon into a land of boulders, tumbled and smoothed round by the crush of glacier. Then down off the ridge toward a little outwash plain on the shore. As I descended, I could see off to the right, south, thick smoke rising from a small fire smouldering at the Churchill dump. The dump road ascended the ridge again to the top of the dump, which spilled down the slope. It was a fairly tidy and contained area of only a few acres, I estimated. Below was a rather attractive wetland, well patronized by ducks (mostly Northern Pintails, American Wigeons and Green-winged Teal). Lots of Herring and Ring-billed Gulls were standing around the dump and on the road, waiting for the inevitable something to happen. I circled the dumping zone and stopped the truck next to a pile of what looked like soil and straw. From here I could survey the scene.

My eye was soon drawn down the slope of discarded appliances and other rusted rubble to a pure-white gull amidst the silver-gray backs of the other gulls. I got out and set up the scope. It was the size and shape of its Herring Gull companions, but totally white as new snow (except for the eyes, the black-tipped pink bill, and pink legs and feet). No question that I was looking at my first Glaucous Gull – probably an immature starting its third summer. The larger gulls take four years to reach maturity and full adult plumage, and en route, they pass through several distinctive immature plumages. I had made a dubious identification of an immature Glaucous on the California coast, but this one was "for sure." Lifer number five of the day. I immediately wondered if Bonnie and her group had seen it already. "Ha!" thought the competitive birder. But this bird was too gorgeous in its own right for me to care much if it was rarely seen by others or not. I kept watching and enjoying its pure white glow among the silver backs of the other gulls and the decrepitude of rusting appliances and scrap metal. This gull had "presence," as Leonard Nathan (*Diary of a Left-handed Birdwatcher*) would call it.

I noticed that the dirt pile next to me was alive – with several Lapland Longspurs, males and females. They were scratching around in the loose soil, which looked on closer inspection to be loaded with grain, as though the slag from the Port operations was occasionally cleaned up and dumped here. With my binoculars only, I had wonderfully detailed views. The male's yellow bill was accentuated by his jet-black face and chest, hemmed with a pure white stole separating the black from a broad chestnut-red nape patch, or half-collar. Some of the males seemed still in progress toward the final breeding plumage. The females had a hint of the chestnut nape patch, but mostly they could have passed at a glance for slim, stripy female House Sparrows.

On this day, I was still working under the illusion that I had seen this species once before in winter Connecticut (a later check of notes in my oldest bird guide convinced me I hadn't). Perhaps the chestnut collar was throwing me off. I had seen Chestnut-collared Longspurs once, poorly, in winter plumage, in Arizona; I kept thinking of these birds in front of me here as Chestnut-collared Longspurs. In short, longspurs were to me an unfamiliar group until today, when I saw both Smith's and Lapland Longspurs in superb summer colours.

A small flock of medium-sized birds shot across the dump slope in tight formation straight at me on set wings, like cruise missiles locked on their target – which was the dirt pile. They were Ruddy Turnstones, I could see with the unaided eye, as they settled down to their meal only four or five metres from where I stood next to the truck. There is no more distinctive shorebird than this. Chestnut and black again on lots of white, but much bigger and bolder than the longspurs, who held their ground and continued feeding on the pile. The turnstones set about demonstrating how they earned their name, using their short, stout, sharp and slightly upturned beaks to flip over leaves, bark and even stones to get at whatever was underneath.

One among them was *not* a turnstone but another shorebird – a full-dress Dunlin complete with large black belly patch, long, slightly down-curved bill, lovely scallops of rufous and black edged with white on the back, and columns of black speckle on the white breast as though someone had painstakingly made tiny arrowhead marks with a fine-tip black pen. The Dunlin seemed more ill at ease than the others with my being so close. It stood stiffly erect in a pose I thought uncharacteristic, probably because I'm used to seeing this species in large flocks at a distance hungrily probing the tidal mud during migratory stopovers on the California coast. This Dunlin seemed to feel out of place among all these turnstones, and my close presence didn't make it feel any better. Soon it gave off a sharp *kreee* and took off down the slope to the wetland below.

I stood stock-still as long as I could to enjoy the intimate company of these beautiful birds, carefully raising my binoculars

Life List: A Birder's Spiritual Awakening

to get even closer views of their fine patterns of colour and then slowly sweeping down the slope to get another view of the Glaucous Gull. Finally, reluctantly, I broke the enchantment by gently moving around the truck with the scope and tripod to get in on the opposite side, hoping not to disturb their meal. But soon the turnstones took off as a flock and were gone, leaving the longspurs to their dirt pile.

I left them, too, and drove back down toward the Highway, passing another pickup on its way up to the dump. Looked like a local, probably not a birder. He flicked his hand briefly off the top of his steering wheel in the perfunctory wave of rural folks passing on rural roads, a kind of courtesy that seems to say, "Good to see someone else out here." I imitated the rural wave in return. It did feel good to connect with another of my species. I was just plain feeling good.

∞

The Highway remounted the coastal ridge and led through a long stretch of even more fantastic glacier-smoothed boulders of all sizes. Some were ball-shaped; others were planed off like tabletops. Then it was downhill again and across the flood plain of Eastern Creek. Seaward, to the north, it was clogged with willow thicket, where Bonnie's book assured that Hoary Redpolls would be found. But I couldn't see a way into the thicket, by vehicle or foot.

As it was getting on toward 7 p.m., I decided to pass up this area for the time being and push on to Bird Cove. Yesterday, the birders from Winnipeg had assured me a couple of times that Bird Cove was the place to go for the migrating shorebirds, advice that is seconded by Bonnie's book. I drove past a pair of giant white golf-ball shapes (probably part of an old strategic defence or missile tracking communication system) and a small lake appropriately named Gull Lake, because it is dotted with small boulders on which many Herring Gulls were nesting. I found the road in to the west shore of Bird Cove, which I had decided to take so that the setting sun would be at my back, giving me good lighting on any shorebirds in the cove. The turnoff was partially blocked by an unhitched, unloaded boat trailer, but I managed to squeeze by.

This Bird Cove Road, as it is labelled on the map in Bonnie's book, was a two-rut track through willows and beach grass going 1.8 kilometres to an overlook on the wreck of the *Ithica*. Bonnie warns that the road is bad and to "take special care in driving here; it is a (long) walk back to town." With those words and the boat trailer that could have been placed there to close off the road until someone moved it aside, I was getting mighty nervous about pushing on through pools of water across the road, in which the truck's back end slewed side to side. It turned out that I had already crossed all the wet spots before having second thoughts. Still, the road became narrower and sandier as I went on, and there was less and less opportunity to turn around without risk of getting stuck in the loose sand off to the sides. Some distance still from the *Ithica* (which now seemed very large indeed, aground but looking imprisoned in the ice), the road had come close to the high-tide mark of the west shore of Bird Cove. Far enough, I decided, assuring myself that I could back up to a solid-looking turnaround spot.

The tide was out – way out. That meant the shorebirds would be scattered all over the place and pretty hard to find. The task was complicated by the tidal mudflat not being flat at all. It was littered with seaweed in the near-shore, hefty rocks in the mid-tide zone, and great chucks of ice stranded on the low-tide zone. Sweeping the area with the scope probably would not be productive. I'd have to get out there on the mudflat and see what I could scare up.

I didn't relish the prospect after my experience on the wet tundra. I felt even more isolated out here, some distance from the

Highway. I worried about getting the truck turned around. And I was at the edge of an ocean I found deeply disturbing, if only because I could not even see the water due to the ice, though I knew the tide would be coming back in soon enough. A shipwreck loomed nearby, its thoroughly rusted hulk turning redder and redder in the dying light of the day. This scene was starkly beautiful, just the kind of place and lighting sought by landscape artists and photographers. But I didn't take photos. I felt a foreboding strong enough to make me edgy, on the alert for a vague something I might not want to see out here.

Just as a bird has a presence or spirit you can feel at a distance, a landscape has one, too, but massive and embracing. This spirit can buoy your own spirit as if you are floating in the calm water of a tropical lagoon. It can weigh on your spirit as if enveloping you in cold fog. It can challenge your spirit with a presentiment of fear, longing or ecstasy, even all three at once, as this landscape was challenging me. It was as though it waited for my next move before showing its intention. It would respond to my choice.

I had serious second thoughts. Maybe I should come back when the tide was higher, driving the shorebirds in closer to shore. No, I was there and I would see what I could see. I got out the scope and put on my boots. Just then I saw a small bird flit into the nearby willow thicket. It made some redpoll sounds. I headed toward it. It flew up to a prominent perch about 10 metres away. I got the binoculars on it and could see that it indeed was a redpoll. But what kind? Okay, maybe it'll stay put for the scope, I thought wishfully. It did – the lighting was a perfect gift. It was a male with lots of red, and also lots of white – puffs of pure white feathers coming out of his flanks and rump. Bingo! "Yes, sir. You're a Hoary Redpoll. No doubt about it!"

He flew and was gone for good. I searched the thicket for the chance of another look, knowing that I couldn't do much better than I had already – seeing him through the scope, no less. That's the way to see a life bird, so that you never doubt and never, ever forget the first identifying moment. I had had six such moments that day alone.

Had the spirit of the landscape rewarded my choice, to seize the moment by suiting up and getting out for a good look? Perhaps the spirit of the redpoll interceded with the spirit of the landscape, literally animating the landscape with its tiny spirit of survival and beauty, to which my own spirit responded with joy, and all three spirits had struck a fine bargain together. Perhaps each of our spirits, in its uniqueness, manifests one and the same spirit.

I was feeling good again and ready to brave the mudflat. I moved through the stinky seaweed zone, where I flushed some more Lapland Longspurs, and onto the mud itself. I found that it was firm underfoot. I stopped to scan with the binoculars and picked up a Semipalmated Plover, then two, not far away. I approached them quickly, then froze in my tracks as I discovered a flock of five sandpipers feeding nearby on wet sand. I headed in their direction, and they let me get close enough to see them very well through the binoculars only. But they were "peeps" – the smallest sandpipers and difficult to identify, because they are so variable in appearance and so similar to each other. There are five species commonly seen in North America: Semipalmated, Western, Least, Baird's and White-rumped Sandpipers. I had seen all but the White-rumped and was hoping against hope that these might be it. Making a good identification was likely to be tough, especially as I was unfamiliar with the breeding plumage of any peep species.

These five birds had the requisite long wings and fine streaking on breast and flanks, but I had to see the diagnostic white rump. The problem is, you usually can't see it unless they fly. I watched a while to see if they might open their wings to scratch or move. No luck. I decided to make them fly and walked quickly right at them.

They calmly withdrew as though moving up a beach to avoid an incoming wave. I stopped; they stopped. I waited, and they started to move around me to return to where they had been feeding. Must have been a good spot. I stood as still as I could while using the binoculars. They got so close I could no longer focus. Then one of them started to display at another by drooping its wings, raising its tail straight up, lowering its head and advancing at the other with a prominent display of its *white rump*! No doubt about this identification. Lifer number seven for the day.

I heard a strange throbbing buzz and looked around for some sort of odd insect. It sounded rather like a whirring mechanical toy. The buzz was coming from the displaying bird! "Good grief!" I wondered. "What next?" Two of them displayed while the others tried to ignore them. They resumed feeding as though I wasn't there. Then suddenly the show was over; they took flight and were gone.

I continued to move farther out from shore, but lack of birds and increasing uncertainty about my footing sent me back. Instead, I walked parallel to the high tide line, on the firmer mud similar to what the sandpipers had been feeding on, and toward a large group of feeding Canada Geese. As I got closer, they raised their heads in alarm and started to move away and honk at my approach. I decided to let them be. I had been very lucky. Time to call it a day. So I headed back to higher ground. In the distance I saw a large hawk or something coming my way along the beach with a bouncy flight pattern and a large head. A Short-eared Owl, the first species I had looked for as I set out in mid-morning, now passed overhead to put the cap on my excellent day.

Back on the Highway, I turned toward town and felt like a million bucks in my blue truck bouncing along the shore of Hudson Bay, gleaming white in the long evening light.

∽

I was back in town in 15 minutes. Amazing! I had been virtually out of sight and sound of other human beings the whole day, except for lunchtime, on the Highway and at the dump. I wasn't ready to call it a day, so I kept on going, past the turn to my hotel, and drove up onto the railroad embankment at the south end of the docks of the Port facility. From there I discovered a lovely view up and down the Churchill River, and right below the embankment was a small sand-and-rock spit of shore on which gulls, terns, eiders and turnstones were loafing. Out on the river, I picked out a male-and-female pair of Common Goldeneye ducks, each with truly golden eyes set in a distinctively pointy head. By now it was around 9 p.m. The evening light was weakening but still touching up the bland colours of river and town with highlights of rose and gold. And it was surprisingly warm, allowing me the luxury of relaxing there on the gravel bank with the view of ice floes sailing upriver with the returning tide.

Tomorrow, I thought, would be my day for exploring the boreal forest in the Twin Lakes area, the most distant area accessible by road from Churchill, and well inland. Though Bird Cove was about half the distance, I wasn't sure how good or bad the road into the interior would be, so I allowed a whole day. I would start as early as I could, hoping to catch the early morning activity in the forest and perhaps see a large mammal or two. Better get to bed.

Back in the hotel room at last, I ate a late snack over my bird books and species list. One of the great pleasures of an excellent birding day is to sit down at its end to make up a list of the species seen. I was adding to the list started the day before and also reviewing in my mind all the wonderful experiences of the day. I thought about the significance of what I had seen – and not seen, checking reality against expectation. I compared what I had seen with what Bonnie's book indicated was likely to be seen at this time of year and in the areas visited. Most of the expected species yet to be seen were denizens of the boreal forest and awaited me tomorrow, with any luck.

Late as it was, I further indulged myself by adding up the number of life birds listed so far around Churchill – seven today alone, two yesterday. I was not including the unexpected Upland Sandpiper somewhere south along the rail line. I was still thinking I'd already seen the Lapland Longspur, so I wasn't counting that one. Nor was I counting the Clay-colored Sparrow in Winnipeg. My arbitrary objective was to see 10 bird species typically found in the Churchill area but new to me. The number 10 had no significance whatsoever, other than being a nice round number, which is why I was rather embarrassed to take it at all seriously. But I did take it seriously. The birder couldn't help it.

Who was likely to be number 10?

Judging from Bonnie's book, the likely candidates were the Parasitic Jaeger and the Bohemian Waxwing. Both are commonly seen in the area, and both have some particular significance to me. Jaegers are a peculiar gull-like group of predatory seabirds, of which I had never seen even one species. Bohemian Waxwings are a northern forest species that occasionally shows up in the US with flocks of the similar Cedar Waxwings, themselves a rather fascinating bird in appearance and behaviour, always looking dressed for a masked ball in a beautifully tailored beige-and-buff suit with black robber's mask and head coiffed with a neatly trimmed crest. Where I reside in California, Cedar Waxwings are commonly seen in winter, and for more than a decade I've been looking at them carefully to see if one or more in a flock might be a Bohemian. No luck so far. Tomorrow I had a chance to see Bohemian Waxwings at last, in the Twin Lakes area. En route, the Highway passes by a known nesting site for Parasitic Jaegers, so I might even see *them*, if it was not too early in the year.

Good heavens! I was getting into bed at 11 p.m. Not much sleep tonight, as I planned to get up at 4:30 the next morning.

5

The Boreal Forest
June 8

Common Raven

I was in the truck and en route by 6 a.m., but the sun was well up over Hudson Bay, and the day had already lost its cold nip. I was irritated with myself for taking so long to get ready – as usual. I was irritated that I had stayed up so late last night. I was irritated that, at this rate, I would likely miss the cool of the morning by the time I got to Twin Lakes. I was off to a good start!

But just out of town, a comical scene gave me the needed attitude adjustment. A Whimbrel – a shorebird the size of a small, long-legged gull with a very long down-curved bill – was calling its ringing *tew, tew, tew* from an improbable perch on the roadside power line. I stopped for a good look at this old friend in an odd place. How could it keep its balance up there? Three local ladies trooped by on their early morning power walk. We waved and smiled. The morning was off to a good start after all.

I quickly reached the turnoff to Bird Cove and pushed on into new territory. The massive buildings of the missile launch facility and Churchill Northern Studies Centre loomed ahead. The Highway passed through a gate prominently displaying a rocket with a Canadian flag emblem on its tail, giving the area an aura of official importance. Serious stuff happens here. In fact, on the train up,

I heard the Weir Guys talking about the Canadian government planning a missile test this summer; equipment for the test was already being shipped up for installation at the launch facility, they said. As I passed through the still-sleeping compound, I saw no sign of such preparations, only a Rough-legged Hawk circling the long-unused launch building, which Bonnie's book says is its nest site. Wondering what effect a missile test would have on the nesting hawk, I turned to the south on a pretty good gravel road and out into the wilderness again.

Soon I found Willow Ptarmigan along the roadside – a very conspicuous white-and-brown male calling from a dwarf spruce top and a well-camouflaged mottled-brown female on the ground below. Then another male farther on. Meanwhile, I was having some trouble finding the landmarks described in Bonnie's book, though I didn't know it yet. I thought I was farther along than I was when I entered a large patch of boreal forest on a significant hill and figured I had reached the Twin Lakes area. I watched carefully for a right turn onto a vehicle track into the forest, rather optimistically labelled "Cook Street" on the map. I couldn't find it. Then I came upon what I thought would have to be West Lake, but where was East Lake? It was supposed to be just on the other side of the road. I stopped and got out to survey the scene and take another look at Bonnie's book.

I hadn't read it carefully, and even now I was having trouble comprehending the kilometre markings she gave. I was tempted to go back and see if I could reconstruct the route with kilometre measurements from the launch site, but I was also eager to get to wherever I was going and start a bird walk while it was still early. As my mind worried over all this, my body was enjoying the still-cool morning air and my ears were picking up songs of the White-crowned Sparrow (of course), Harris's Sparrow, Blackpoll Warbler, Ruby-crowned Kinglet and, to my surprise, the thrilling, haunting melody of a Hermit Thrush in the distance. I walked the roadside for a while, hoping for another look at Harris's Sparrow, without success. What to do next? "Perhaps I haven't gone far enough" was my thought and decision.

I got back in the truck and moved on. Soon I was heading downhill again, which didn't seem right at all. Emerging from the trees, I was confronted by a huge tundra plain stretching to the horizon before me. Convinced that I had overshot the Twin Lakes area, I stopped and studied my predicament. In my mind, the plain ahead stretched south into the vast interior wilderness of Manitoba. For a moment it seemed no less forbidding than the vast sea of ice to the north. I felt lost and a bit scared, for no good reason. It was not as though I was about to run out of gas; I had not run off the road and become stranded; I knew precisely how to get back to Churchill. Get a hold of yourself! I turned the truck around – carefully, so as not to get stuck and have *real* reason for concern. I went back several kilometres, up and down, in and out of the boreal forest, then up, down, in and out again until I was halfway back to the launch site. Still no sign of Cook Street or the East Twin Lake.

I stopped, got out Bonnie's book, with no small amount of frustration building up, and read the Twin Lakes section – again. There was the problem! I had missed the significance of a very short paragraph that takes you up and over two "rises" on which you should look for such birds as the Blackpoll Warbler and Harris's Sparrow. The paragraph does not make specific mention of the boreal forest on these two rises, but forest is implied by the forest birds mentioned. Beyond the second rise is "a large open marsh area" (my huge tundra plain?) and then another rise up into the Twin Lakes area. Good grief! Such self-inflicted confusion. I should have laughed, but I was in a hurry. I turned around again and retraced the route up and over, up and over and down toward the tundra plain. I stopped again, still wary of the vast expanse. The road across was a causeway. I could now make out the rise beyond, bearing a darker (forest) colour. Bonnie says there are six turnouts along this causeway. "I'll count them to make sure I'm on the right track," I reassured myself. And off I went. One, two, three …

Halfway across the tundra, I stopped because I could hear what I thought might be Smith's Longspur. I listened carefully. I scanned the hummocks – lots of them here, much like the tundra I walked on at Landing Lake. There were a few isolated clumps of stunted spruce and scattered, still-leafless tamarack. On one of the hummocks, I spotted the longspur, confirming my identification of the song.

I scanned some more, wanting to get a sense of the typical bird life on the typical tundra (if this could be called typical). Canada Geese once again, several on nests. Savannah Sparrows singing. The cries of Lesser Yellowlegs in the distance. Those three and the longspur were the most conspicuous species. I was again surprised by the lack of other shorebirds. Thinking back on the past day, as well as this location, I could recall roadside sightings of an occasional Hudsonian Godwit, American Golden-Plover, Short-billed Dowitcher, Whimbrel, Common Snipe, perhaps a Semipalmated Sandpiper, but never numerous or predictable and certainly not conspicuous. Also a few surreptitious ducks – Northern Pintail and Green-winged Teal, at least. White-crowned Sparrows, American Robins and even Common Redpolls were more conspicuous than shorebirds or ducks on the tundra, especially where there were a few scattered dwarf trees. A Common Raven or two were predictable, as were Arctic Terns cruising well overhead.

That was my first impression of the tundra bird community and no doubt coloured by the time of year – a bit early, perhaps. As much as I prefer solitude in nature, I longed for occasional interaction with a local expert who could answer some questions and give a broader perspective to my own observations. Birding is enhanced by knowing where to look and what to look for, and the local context, which helps the birder become a birdwatcher, appreciating each species for its distinctive adaptations and life history and role in the ecological community. Such good intelligence is gained from sharing with others, through books and now CDs and websites, but most effectively through real-time sharing with fellow birders in the field. Especially when the goal is to see lots of species in a short time, the birder must tap the knowledge and goodwill of other birders.

Still, I prefer solitude in nature. I am uncomfortable with the competitive aspect of social birding and the conventional language of birders talking about birds. In this parlance, birds are treated as trophies to be displayed, commodities to be bought and traded, puzzle pieces to be found and placed on the board. A "good bird" is a rare bird, or at least one that hasn't been seen yet by at least someone in the group. By implication, a common bird, or one that has been seen already, is no longer a "good bird." A super-abundant species might even be called a "trash bird." I know why a birder speaks of "good birds," and I'm enough of a competitive birder to appreciate the sentiment and use the lingo myself. I also know that birders don't become birders without being moved, at some emotional level, by the mere presence of a bird, no matter how common. Often the term "good bird" is applied to a moderately uncommon bird that is particularly distinctive or attractive, which is a more respectful use of language. I would feel more comfortable around birders if we would talk with more evident reverence for these little "glories to God."

The language problem goes beyond birders to our general culture and its conventions for masculine interaction. Clearly, birding is a masculine activity, no matter the number of ardent women birders. The great majority of truly fanatic birders are men. And the language of men notoriously excludes explicit recognition of matters of the heart and spirit. For me, birds are a matter of the heart and the spirit. A single birding companion is okay, because we can share at a deeper level one on one. More than two birders and it becomes a different story. The convention rules the conversation. In contrast, if I can get non-birders, like my wife and son, to use binoculars on a bird (I choose carefully which birds I insist they look at), they will often marvel at the colours and patterns of a bird seen up close. They are not even birdwatchers, really, but they are bird appreciators. It is great fun to show them an attractive bird, no matter how common. I admit it is even more fun to go on a hunt for species with a real birder, but I do wish we could talk more as though we truly appreciated the birds we see.

I drove on, getting closer to the higher, drier ground beyond, where the density of scattered spruce and tamarack increased. Singing American Tree Sparrows became conspicuous. This was another species I got to know well in winter Connecticut but hadn't seen since. They are notable for their rufous cap, pearl-gray face, neck and underparts marked with little more than a black "stick pin" in the middle of the breast. I had the opportunity to educate my ear by comparing their sweet whistled songs with the longspur's in the distance. Quite different, once you hear them together, but it was still surprisingly hard to remember the difference. Farther up the slope, the tundra was gone and a sparse spruce woodland took over. Driving along, windows down, I heard several Blackpoll Warblers singing their laborious *tseet, tseet, tseet, tseet, tseet*.

Going farther up, the white spruces dominated and grew taller and closer together, but it was an exaggeration to call this a forest. A lot of sunlight penetrated to the ground cover here, and I could see it was rich with small and varied plant life. I was eager to get out and walk in it.

Finally, I found Cook Street, just a forest track, delightfully narrow through the trees and covered by spruce needles, soft and quiet under the tires. I drove in as far as an old gravel quarry and parked. I locked the truck, despite the solitude, and walked. It was getting almost warm, about 8 a.m. now. I went only a few metres before a Gray Jay appeared to investigate my intentions. It was smaller, drabber, fluffier and cuter than any other jay I know. Fluffy plumage, large, rounded head, short bill – all the features of cuteness, like a stuffed animal designed to be adorable. All the better to ingratiate itself with campers of the North Woods. And nearly fearless, of people at least. Accepting my apology ("Sorry, no food"), the unflustered jay disappeared back into the forest.

A few more paces onward, I was stopped by rustling in the undergrowth. I crouched and peered through the spruce boughs. Only a metre away was an absolutely gorgeous male Pine Grosbeak, feeding on red berries from the ground cover. His red is hard to describe – somewhere between brick and rose – and he is *big*, for a finch. Like a stocky robin. He allowed me to watch for a minute before moving off. I couldn't follow, partly because of the trees blocking my view of his flight path and partly because the ground farther off the road was covered by very large patches of reindeer moss (lichen), looking very much like remnants of the winter snow. Bonnie admonishes birders to stay on the trails here, to avoid damaging the fragile ground cover, especially the reindeer moss. I noticed that the reindeer moss in the shade, still moist from the night air, was spongy under my hand, but in the sun it was dry and stiff, brittle under pressure. Walking on it would destroy this thick mat of delicately branching, puffy plants.

Reindeer moss was not the only fascinating ground-cover plant. There were perennials of two or three kinds, one still offering currant-sized red berries. Everywhere, it seemed, the forest floor was a thick, springy mat of beautiful plants. Again my botanical

Life List: A Birder's Spiritual Awakening

knowledge failed me, but I could appreciate nonetheless their variety and beauty and the total effect of the pattern these plants created on the forest floor.

The trail continued on to the shore of the West Lake, where there was a closed-tight A-frame cabin with an open deck facing the lake. I walked down to the water's edge and startled a pair of Oldsquaw (*ooh-wah*). Greater Scaup – good-sized, stocky diving ducks with distinctive head shape and large blue-gray bills – and a pair of Pacific Loons were out on the open water. Arctic Terns were making a ruckus over a long, thin, grassy island in the lake, probably thinking about breeding there. Bonaparte's Gulls, black-billed, black-hooded and almost as dainty as terns, sat in treetops along the lakeside. It was very strange to see even small gulls sitting in spruce trees. Bonnie says they nest there. It seemed that all sorts of improbable behaviour were the norm around here.

I took a seat on the edge of the deck and relaxed with the view of the lake. Except for the terns *kip*-ping and the gulls *kee-ahr*-ing, it was absolutely still. No other sounds, only the lightest of cool breezes. The sky was blue but beginning to milk up with high thin cloud.

∞

My mind drifted back 33 years to a similar lakeside peace in Québec. It was a good campsite on a lakeshore that was softened by a skirt of half-sunken sedges and grasses. The evening light cast each blade in paired silhouette and reflection on the glassy surface. Even as a 17-year-old boy I felt moved to watch with dreamy attention the reflected light from the lake fading imperceptibly to black, until only the campfire lit the tired faces of my companions.

My two tent mates and I woke to the call of the trip leader in the dark dawn. There was frost, the coldest morning so far. Our miserable trio broke down the tent, tossing aside the straight trunks of young spruce hewn and spliced and roped the evening before, as we had been taught (what seemed like months ago), to hold up the tent through the night, come rain or wind. There had been neither, only a still night that gave up the heat of the land to the brilliant stars and created ice crystals on every quiet surface. Billions of crystals seemed to glow as the eastern light began to promise its return to earth. Grubby boys in grubby clothes worn relentlessly for days, we huddled around the near-useless fire and remembered we must be waterborne before sunrise. It would be a very long paddle that day. Lake and river travel. At least we would not have to portage the equipment and canoes more than once. We almost looked forward to the paddling, because it would warm us as the fire refused to do.

With the canoe half in the water, I went with awkward speed to my place at the bow, straddling the tightly packed and rope-secured equipment, with a foot on each gunwale. I felt the bow settle into the water as I sat down and positioned my paddle. My stern man, Carl, pushed off, and the canoe seemed weightless in its glide from the shore into the sedges and grasses. We let the canoe glide, treasuring its freedom from land, the momentary sense of frictionless flow. The sun was still below the horizon but close enough to send pink, glowing hope through the mist rising from the lake ahead. A mink's head broke the still surface and fled before us, veering off toward shore before submerging again to underwater safety, leaving a widening V of evidence on the water, but not before I silently pointed out the mink to Carl, who smiled back in appreciation. Together, as one, we dipped paddle blades into water and accelerated the canoe toward the open lake and the rising sun.

These long-ago experiences welled up inside, and I floated on them for unmeasured time. At 17, I thought far more of the future than of the past. Now, at nearly 50, the past already dominates my relaxed mind, which is no doubt typical of aging. At 17, there is so much more "future" than there is "past" to think about, and the other way around at 50 and beyond. I like 50 better than 17, because I have a lot of neat stuff to remember, and I can manage to keep the regrets more or less under wraps. And remembering the past is so much more satisfying than daydreaming of the future. The past was real and memories of it can be vivid, even when not fully true to the original. The future, on the other hand, is fantasy, blurry and likely to never come true.

There was more to my lakeside reverie than memories. The real scene before me matched one imprinted in the depths of my brain. It wasn't just the spruces-and-water of Québec 33 years ago. The imprint seemed to be an amalgam of many similar forest scenes: in New England and upstate New York, in the mountains and plateaus of the American Southwest, even in the highlands of East Africa or the coastal mountains of Australia. I felt an instinctive, primal attraction to this place, a sense of comfort, of being at home in open forest or woodland surrounding a lake, the way a migrating bird would instinctively recognize the right habitat to settle in.

∞

Then I came back to the terns, gulls and this lakeside morning. And my assignment – to find the expected boreal forest birds. The Gray Jay and Pine Grosbeak had already reported in. Several more to find, still, and they were not hanging around this cabin, unfortunately. Time to walk on.

The forest track continued on past the cabin and away from the lake. I soon found lots of birds, first being alerted by singing or twittering, then patiently picking them out in the white spruce branches, darting in and out of view. Got to be fast with the binoculars. Not much time to aim and focus. White-crowned Sparrows,

The Boreal Forest: June 8

Common Redpolls and Yellow-rumped Warblers (yes, warblers with yellow rumps) were my main companions, to the point I had to filter them out of my consciousness to detect anything new, such as a couple of Dark-eyed Juncos trilling from high in the trees. This is the unmistakable pink-billed, black-and-white sparrow of the coniferous forest, displaying prominent white sides of the dark tail when it flies up from the ground where it likes to forage.

An unexpected Chipping Sparrow appeared. "What the hell are *you* doing here?" I asked out loud. This mundane bird of the suburbs is a real find here. Once again a new perspective on an old friend; the familiar becomes exotic. I took time to study it and remind myself that this little bird is very beautiful. Rather similar to the American Tree Sparrow, it has a pearl-gray head and body with a bright rufous-red cap over a white line above the black eye, and a black line through the eye, from both sides converging at the nape. The back and wings are red-brown overlaid with parallel black stripes from nape to tail, and cutting across these black stripes are two white "wing bars." All this happens on a bird only five and a half inches from bill tip to tail tip.

"Glory to God, Give glory to God, Glory to God in the highest" floated through my brain once again.

Several times, the quiet was shattered by the staccato chattering trill of a red squirrel. When I hear them, it is my habit to find and watch these squirrels. I like to see the fox-red, sleek coat, feathery red tail, the jet-black line that separates red back from white-to-buff belly, and especially the conspicuous white ring of fur around the big, dark eyes staring right back at me. Their beauty and intensity energize me. We seem drawn to the same kinds of forest. One sat frozen silent on a tree branch just off the track, at my eye level, and watched me coming. I pretended not to see it as I got closer and then very close indeed. It held its perch as I passed. I was pleased

Life List: A Birder's Spiritual Awakening

by the intimate moment and wondered how many animals that I had *not* seen were watching me walk through their forest.

I was startled by a sudden siren *whoop*. Since I was in the forest, it took me a few moments to realize that it was one of the Pacific Loons on the lake. This and the cries of the terns and gulls reminded me that the lake was a little way off through the trees, though I could not see it. I could also tell that the track was moving me away from the lake. Lesser Yellowlegs in aerial song pointed out that the tundra was not far, either. In the sun, I was now beginning to get uncomfortably warm in my dressed-for-a-cool-morning clothes. I decided to turn back to the cabin to sit and look out on the lake again.

After that long moment of still enjoyment, I started back to the truck. *Chick-a-zeeee* came faintly through the trees. I stopped to listen, then spotted some movement low in a distant tree. The bird wasn't getting any closer, so I figured it would be worth trying to approach. But how? I would have to walk across the forest floor mat of vegetation. Careful to avoid stepping on any reindeer moss, I tiptoed my way toward the bird. Soon I could see it was a pair of Boreal Chickadees, shuttling between the lower tree branches and the ground cover. These are like the familiar Black-capped and Carolina Chickadees, but with brownish caps rather than black, coloured tawny rather than gray below, and having a distinctly nasal voice. Berries were the attraction, it seemed. They were too busy eating to take much notice of me. I watched them a while, enjoying their nasal comments to each other. They drifted away, and I found my way back, satisfied that the woody-stemmed ground cover plants did not seem in worse shape for my stepping on them.

I was intercepted again by a Gray Jay, perhaps the same one. It gave an odd call or two as it approached and was soon joined by another and then another, sailing toward me through the trees on set wings. They hopped branch to branch, as close to me as the branches would let them come, and eyed me fearlessly. They flew to other nearby trees and repeated the inspection from various angles. I was surrounded. After this close scrutiny for maybe three minutes, each jay seemed to remember something more interesting and slipped away among the trees.

∞

I drove back to the main gravel road and a few kilometres onward past a view of both West and East Lakes to another side road. Here I parked the truck at the turnoff and walked the narrow vehicle track into the burned area where the Winnipeg birders had told me the Three-toed Woodpeckers had nested. Now it was a land of black sticks and ashen ground. There were several bulldozer cuts for firebreaks or firefighter access through the area. It was thoroughly uninviting and seemed to stretch as far as I could see. So I retreated and tried another, unburned, side road going the other direction from the main road.

Caribou tracks! Very distinctive, like cow tracks in size and overall rounded shape, but the two sides of the hoof were like crescent moons facing each other. The caribou had gone down the side road, so I followed the tracks to a small lake. I lost the tracks when the road turned right and paralleled the shore. It was getting warmer, probably well into the 70s Fahrenheit (I later heard that the high for the day was 25°C, or just shy of 80°F in the shade). How could it be this warm so far north in early June? I hadn't left hot California to be hot here. I wanted it to be cool, even cold! I was annoyed with myself for being annoyed by the heat, but even more for how it was probably slowing down the bird activity.

Where were those darned Bohemian Waxwings? That's what was really annoying me. "Oh, brother! You're not going to do this

Life List: A Birder's Spiritual Awakening

number on yourself, are you? You've seen most of the boreal forest birds, lovely birds, and great looks at them, too. Not enough?" "No," I thought to myself. "I want to see Bohemian Waxwings."

Grump!

I recovered my perspective as I walked along this beautiful lakeside track. The spruce needles matted on the ground gave a nice spring to my step. I started to relax again, and then *seeee seeeeee*. Sounded enough like a Cedar Waxwing to be a Bohemian call. Hyper-alert, I heard it again. It was high in a clump of tall spruce. I heard it again but couldn't see it and couldn't tell which tree the sound came from. I moved sideways a few paces to hear it from a different angle, hoping to triangulate. Nothing more. I waited. I waited some more. Nothing.

Getting a tinge desperate, I advanced across the forest floor mat (not stepping on any reindeer moss, mind you). Then I did what I never let anyone ever, ever hear or see me do. I made the sound *pshhh, pshhh, pshhh* with my lips and breath, like an unvoiced whistle, then a kind of sucking noise with my lips against the back of my hand. These are birder's tricks to get LBJs (little brown jobs) to come closer or pop up out of a thicket to take a look around for the source of the sound. It's presumed to simulate a young bird in distress. If so, the trick should be particularly effective in the breeding season and shortly after. It works well with some species, especially sparrows. But more often than not, it doesn't work at all, and you end up feeling rather foolish. It might work with a waxwing, but I'd never had occasion to try the trick on them. Who knows? Like I said, I was somewhat desperate by now.

Nobody but a White-crowned Sparrow showed up.

I had nothing better to do, so I waited for a long while. The sound came again. I could see nothing. I began to think that this might not be a waxwing at all. Maybe it was a fledgling bird calling out to its parents from a hiding place. Just then a couple of finches came flying in from far off in the forest. One landed on top of the clump of spruces I was staking out. It was a male White-winged Crossbill! A beautiful rosy-pink finch with a bill designed specially for opening up conifer cones (the tips of upper and lower mandibles don't meet but cross over and past each other, hence the bird's common name) with black wings and white wing bars. This species is much less common around here ("lucky to find" in June, according to Bonnie's book) than the Bohemian Waxwing ("should see"). The crossbill flew off over the small lake.

Shortly afterward, I disturbed something that flew low to the trunk of a tree next to the track. I had to twist around to get it in the binoculars. Almost immediately, it flew on down the road out of sight, but I got the focus just in time to clearly see that it was a black woodpecker with a ladder of white and black on its back and a yellow cap on the crown of its head. A male Three-toed Woodpecker! "Lucky to find" before last year's fire and even luckier now, I thought, given my impression that the Winnipeg birders feared it might not be found at all this year.

I needed to tell someone about this. I thought of the Churchill Wilderness Encounter Rare Bird Alert bulletin board at Akudlik. A "rare bird alert" by bulletin board, phone, e-mail or website is a node of the birding world's intelligence network, sharing real-time news of unexpected finds at the local, state or provincial and national levels. Contributors of news items are generally the more serious, socially networked, and therefore credible, birders. I've never gotten into the habit of using the system, even for planning birding trips. But people like me are welcome to contribute sightings of rarities, if they can be verified by birders with known credentials. Before putting my credibility on the line, I wanted a better look. I gave up for the moment on the waxwing, or whatever it was, and headed on down the road after the woodpecker. But it seemed to have vanished. I plunked down on the side of the road in the shade and waited for sounds of either the woodpecker or the waxwing. Thirty minutes or so and nothing.

Still, it was a very peaceful wait, punctuated by a red squirrel foraging in the ground cover, making a wide circle around me. I reflected on the irony of seeing two bird species, in as many minutes, that I hadn't sought or expected and that were reported to be less commonly seen than Bohemian Waxwings. It's always a treat to see something unusual, but I had to admit I would have preferred to see the waxwings. Why? Because I had seen the others at least once before.

I retraced my steps to the spot where I had sighted the woodpecker and made careful note of the location and the landmarks between it and the main road. I crossed the main road and wandered up a bulldozer cut toward the burn area again. I noted an American Robin, then another, and said out loud, "You guys are *every*where!" I decided to return to the truck through a bit of unburned forest before emerging on the main road.

As I entered the unburned patch, there was an explosion underfoot – heavy but fast wing-beats from the roadside shrubs, to my right. Suddenly, my memory flashed to the time when my son and I were startled by a covey of 50 quail bursting into the air from a thicket of coyotebush in the dunes of Bodega Bay – a wildlife experience we'll always remember together. An explosion of grouse or quail never fails to jolt me, but I immediately knew the perpetrator. This bird flew two or three metres to land on the open ground under a thick spruce. Even before I raised the binoculars, I could see this was a steel-gray and black Spruce Grouse, standing stiffly at attention with his tail fanned like a turkey; with him was a mottled-brown female. She was slinking off and away from me into the shrubby ground cover beyond, while he stood his ground in full display, showing me how big he could be.

Most remarkably, he let his fantail gradually close to half-width for a few moments and then audibly snapped it to full width again. He repeated this tail snapping several times over the three or four minutes I watched, close by. If I hadn't been a lot bigger than he was, I think I would have been intimidated by his snapping and stiff pivoting to present the full effect of his puffed-up display. But I could see he was very nervous and would have fled if only his instincts were not holding him in this formal-portrait pose.

I decided to let the Spruce Grouse stand down and withdrew slowly toward the truck, which was within sight at the end of the vehicle track. He remained at attention until I was a good distance and then allowed himself to move with slow dignity toward his female. I imagined him feeling relieved that his display had driven me away. Is it possible he was thinking, "I showed him!" and congratulating himself? Or had he even been conscious of what he was doing, much less drawing conclusions about cause and effect?

∽

I've often tried to imagine myself in the mental state of an animal like this grouse. Literally inconceivable. The mental tools of this animal are no doubt well suited to his reality. I can observe his behaviour and admire its adaptive value and even speculate how his nervous system works, but this does not describe what it feels like to *be* him, what he is thinking and feeling as he stiffly displays in the face of real danger. There is no question in my mind that he is thinking and feeling *something*. But I cannot hope to know how similar or different his thinking and feeling are from mine.

I like to think I've had better luck with our recently departed black Labrador, Shabo, successor to Mac the dog who discovered my "sacred" ridge in the Santa Catalina Mountains of Arizona. Mac was our loyal protector and problem child. Shabo was our pal, our shameless kid, then our son's big, furry brother. Shabo was the most beautiful dog my wife and I have ever known – perfect conformation for a Labrador retriever, with a shiny black coat that always looked freshly oiled but felt like dry silk to the hand. He had a wonderful attitude toward life – forgiving, easy-going, enthusiastic – and he was smart. Even for him, intelligent and "conscious" as he appeared, life seemed to be totally present tense, unreflecting on the past, and without any concept that the future might not be the same as here and now. I often envied and occasionally tried to emulate Shabo's mindset, to park my brain in neutral, to dwell solely in the present for a while. If Shabo had been me encountering the grouse just now, I think he would have frozen for a moment, then chased wildly after the grouse, to no purpose, and then trotted on without another thought.

Is that true? Perhaps Shabo would have mulled over the incident as he trotted on, even as he remained alert for the next one. Perhaps he would compare what had just happened with previous encounters with wild creatures and would file it among his memories. He might even be lost for a while in a canine reverie of sights, sounds and especially smells that create mental images beyond anything I could ever imagine. Images that would come back to him in sleep, causing his paws to flip and flop and eyelids and ears to flutter, accompanied by muffled woofs.

Our mental tools are different. How different after all? Would Shabo's brain constantly conspire against itself? Even out here, so far removed from my normal reality, my mind was almost constantly moving out from the present into the past, into the future and outward into the larger world, reflecting on cause and effect, on the meaning of it all. Whose mental tools are better? Better for what? It depends on the purpose.

Oh, yes, the question of purpose – beyond that which we make up for ourselves.

The Boreal Forest: June 8

We humans think of ourselves as special, "created in the image of God," which implies that God is like us and unlike the other animals. Yet we have a far better prospect of understanding other animals than we ever have of understanding God. However vast our differences, our kinship with other animals is much closer than with God. We are all carbon-based life forms, and God is surely not. We are all of this planet and share evolutionary roots in some period of life's history on earth. God is likely in us all somehow, but vastly beyond life and earth. God is, no doubt, unlike anything we animals on earth can even conceive of. Our frame of reference is too narrow.

I can feel just how narrow when I remember a night on a lonely roadside in the high country of Arizona, and a night on the Bolivian shore of Lake Titicaca at 12,500 feet above sea level, and a night with my wife and son at an amateur astronomers' outing below Lassen Peak in California. The dusty atmosphere bouncing back the man-made light of our normally low-elevation, over-populated lives is a metaphor for what diminishes our vision of the Divine. Occasionally, it is our privilege to stand at high elevation at night and dare to look deeply into the dark sky, clouded only by masses of uncountable stars. Through binoculars, one can get a sense of depth into outer space and of earth's suspension in the impossibly cold abyss of an inconceivably vast universe. It is almost too terrible for a sensible person to bear. It is only bearable when we also sense the grand paradox – beyond the boundaries of the universe, yet within each of us – that many of us label "God."

For us to conceive of God is like trying to describe a great building in which we are confined to a single room with one window looking out in only one direction. We cannot conceive what the building looks like, but we do feel the building around us. It offers us daily evidence of its existence, because we are in it. However, just as a fish cannot conceive of being wet until it is forced out of the water, we cannot conceive of this mystical medium we live in, except by intuition of its absence.

How unimaginative and constrained by our own mental tools we are to think that God is like a human being in any way! Nonetheless, we do have a closer kinship to God than the other animals do, perhaps, because we *try* to conceive of God. Our ability to think about things removed from routine reality gives us that "advantage," among the many other advantages and disadvantages of our mental chatter. We can become more aware than any animal of the presence or grace of God in our lives, even if we can never know what lies behind that grace. We can be aware of God's presence in other lives as well, even (perhaps especially) in a displaying grouse or a trotting dog. God's presence in all creatures, not just people, does not demean us; rather, it elevates them. But *we* can reach higher to embrace God's presence in ourselves and others. We can also fall lower by rejecting that true presence and believing, or at least acting as though we believe, that *we* are the only gods around. That's a tragic mistake neither Shabo nor the grouse would likely ever make.

∞

Driving onward, I pondered again the irony of seeing several great species I hadn't expected, yet still missing that which I was expecting and most wanting to see. It was expectation, not the real experience, that was bugging my brain.

The main road immediately narrowed to a vehicle track not much different from the side roads I'd been walking. It curved left to head east and then north along the top of a low escarpment, perhaps only 25 metres above the wet taiga below, which seemed to stretch to the horizon in the south. It was like driving the rim of the world with a vast squishy unknown below. The Twin Lakes lay on a plateau, raised a bit above the surrounding, much wetter plain.

The Boreal Forest: June 8

It was now hot in the truck, so I was travelling with the cab windows fully down. I heard a thrush's voice spiral briefly up the scale and then briefly down again. It certainly was not a Hermit Thrush; in fact, it was no thrush I'd ever heard before, which meant it was a Gray-cheeked Thrush! It was just off the road and below the escarpment. I braked to a gentle, quiet stop and jumped out to walk back to the spot. I patiently surveyed the trees below me. Nothing but a White-crowned Sparrow or two. I waited. No more singing. I walked slowly back to the truck, alert for movement. Nothing.

Would I count a species I had only heard? Sure, as long as the song or call was distinctive. In fact, I even count as "life birds" some species I have never seen, *only* heard, like the Eastern and Western Screech-Owls and the Whip-poor-will.

Is this cheating? I don't think so. If I had only seen and not heard these species, I would have more reason to doubt my identification. All have distinctive songs or calls, which I have learned and verified from published recordings. For that matter, who cares except me? Life and trip lists are for my own entertainment and edification. I would only be cheating myself. It is a matter of private integrity. For my purposes, the vocal is as important as the visual, sometimes more so, as in the case of the small, brown thrushes. In appearance, they are very similar, but they are very distinctive in song. Still, I was looking forward to seeing that plain gray face of the Gray-cheeked Thrush, just to complete the experience. Not this time.

The road came to an end in a large clearing between the shore of the East Lake and the drop-off to the plain to the east. Just to the left as I drove in was another small closed-up cabin on the shore, and at the far side of the clearing, a footpath continued along the edge of the rocky rim of the escarpment. I was tempted to hike the path, but it was in full sun, and I was feeling too warm and tired. I was at the end of the road, literally and in my desire to explore the area further. I was ready to turn around and drive back to my hotel for a break. I was feeling somewhat peevish about failing to see a Bohemian Waxwing, and irritated with myself for feeling that way.

I heard a locally unusual White-throated Sparrow below the escarpment – *Poor Sam Peabody, Peabody, Peabody*. This clear, sharp song of the North cheered me, so I walked over to the rim to listen for another. Just White-crowned Sparrows again – and American Robins! Rather than tune them out as "trash birds," I paid my grudging respects to these species that seem to thrive in a wide variety of habitats. Especially the robins. They seemed out of place, if only because they are so common in my home area, and just about every home area I've known in North America. I had to smile with a bit of admiration every time I saw a robin.

It was getting on toward two o'clock. I retreated to some shade at the water's edge with a bottle of water and a cinnamon-raisin bagel that tasted of home and comfort. I sat on the lakeshore sand, chewing and breathing deeply to enjoy the moment, the cool air out of the sun, the blue of the lake and sky. Flat, white clouds shared the sky. Toward the far shore, I could see a large sheet of ice floating on the water. Ducks at the ice edge but too far away to bother with – were probably Greater Scaup. To my right the shore curved in a long arc to a point a half-kilometre away. Unusually tall spruce trees cut a classic northern skyline – jagged, spiky – out to the point.

In one of the tallest spruces, toward the top, I noticed a large globular mass of something. Inspection with binoculars showed it to be a nest with rather large black, indistinguishable bodies in it, occasionally shifting about. I stirred myself to go back to the truck to get the scope. In doing so, I noticed on the distant rim trail a party of three hikers coming my way. Where could they be coming from, I wondered. Figuring that we would surely interact in a few minutes, I went back to my spot on the lake and set up the scope on the nest.

The scope didn't help identify the black bodies – until a Common Raven appeared over the treetops, soared in a circle and down to the nest. Sensing the parent's arrival, the black bodies leapt up and took shape. There were four of them, nearly as big as mom or dad, begging shamelessly with vibrating wings and open beaks. From that distance, I could only imagine the racket. It looked as though a slight sibling jostle would suffice to knock one or two from the nest. With the addition of the adult, the family of ravens bulked larger than its very large nest. Quickly the adult took off again and disappeared toward the north and the tundra I had driven across in the morning. No wonder the grown-up seemed eager to get clear of that rowdy crew. They quickly settled down but remained identifiably ravens.

Just then I noticed the three hikers emerging into the clearing and heading toward my truck. I expected they would see me sitting by the lakeshore and come over for a chat. I would share the ravens' nest with them. But they didn't – either they didn't see me, or respected my privacy, or wanted to maintain their own. They moved past the truck and on up the road. They looked weary and warm. They wore coats tied around their waists. One was a shirtless young white man; to my surprise and slight alarm, he carried a high-powered rifle. The other two were unarmed and appeared to be tourists from Asia, a man and a woman, older than the rifleman. They quickly passed out of sight, and I returned to the beautiful lake and the ravens.

∞

You don't have to be a birder or even a birdwatcher to have played the game "If you were a bird, what kind would you be?"

I used to give a variety of answers without much conviction. In recent years, however, I've responded without hesitation, "I'd be a raven." Why? Just a mischievous response to a fanciful question, I sometimes thought. No, it's more than that. I mean it: a raven. Because that's my favourite bird? No, I honestly don't have a favourite bird.

A raven is certainly not much to look at, just a rather impressive crow, really. It's big and it's black – that's it. Until you watch and listen to them.

I saw my first-ever Common Raven in the Great Smoky Mountains of Tennessee in April 1956. I wasn't even eight years old. It was a memorable trip, because my father, mother, brother and I had to fly – my first trip in an airplane. And the Smokies were the most exotic destination my family had ever visited together. The raven was to me a bird you would see only in such a place – mist-shrouded mountains far higher than I'd ever seen. Life as a raven meant living in the wilderness, beyond the boundaries of ordinary life.

After living for many years in Arizona, my view of ravens came down a little closer to earth. I encountered them as a matter of course in the mountains and canyon lands. On the desert grasslands southeast of Tucson, Chihuahuan Ravens were a commonplace. In fact, there were no crows at all, just ravens of one species or the other. I never failed to appreciate both, but the Common Raven still was for me a symbol of wilderness, of special places of beauty and escape from the ordinary.

My regard deepened when my wife and I bought a small cabin at an 8,000-foot elevation in the Santa Catalina Mountains above Tucson. Within less than a year, we were transferred to California, but we doggedly hung on to the cabin for another 13 years. My father used it regularly in the warmer months. Our son experienced his first snow there. We all developed a tradition of Thanksgiving at the cabin for over a decade. And we got to know Common Ravens better than ever. My father and I particularly enjoyed raven talk, the guttural croaks and cries as they sail over the ponderosa pines in ones and twos.

I always try to draw my wife's attention to these remarkably inventive vocalizations. Being an incorrigible tease, she never fails to intone in her deepest voice, "Nevermore," knowing full well that ravens have a lot to say, but never *that*. My father was a poetry major in college, but he takes ravens at their word and never alludes to Edgar Allan Poe (except to humour my wife). His and my love for raven talk is a bond.

I try to imagine what life as a raven is like. Mostly it's *not* a pretty picture. Sure, you'd get to live in remote, often spectacular places. But to make a living, you'd be picking at road-killed rabbits, plundering baby birds from their nests, killing and gobbling pretty much any living or dead thing you could get your huge beak into. Not having the good sense to migrate even from the high Arctic, you could wind up being the only living creature found abroad at Prudhoe Bay in the long, dark Alaskan North Slope winter (at the dump, of course). These are not nice birds leading an enviable life of peace in the pristine wilds. They are as tough and resourceful and ruthless as street-smart homeless kids – just as free and potentially just as miserable.

Ravens may not be enviable, but I find them admirable. Why is that? What do I admire? Maybe it's the combination of their ruthless toughness with their evident curiosity, their loyalty to each other as mates, their talkativeness, and their apparent *joie de vivre*, almost a sense of fun in their relaxed moments. In short, ravens seem intelligent, like they're thinking about and even enjoying what they're doing – for good or ill. Such potential for both mayhem and greatness. An almost mythic combination of the worst and the best that nature has to offer – like people.

Life List: A Birder's Spiritual Awakening

So maybe I don't quite "get" the question. Maybe I'm thinking it's "If you *had* to be a bird, what kind would you like to be?" And when I answer, "I'd be a raven," I suppose I am saying, "I want to be the bird most like a human being, since I can't be a human being but still want to be." What an amazing thought from a person who has spent most off his life profoundly skeptical of the merits of being human. I've heard it said that by the time you reach 50, chances are pretty good that you will have come to know and accept who you are, even really *like* who you are. That sounds about right to me. I suppose I could be saying, "I'd rather be me, a human being."

Okay ... but I'd sure like to soar out over the tundra, the forest, the high peaks, or the canyons, with my wife soaring nearby – I making rude croaking comments about the people we see below, she teasing with an occasional "Nevermore!"

∞

I checked the lowlands below the mini-escarpment for signs and sounds of Gray-cheeked Thrush, and paid silent homage again to the ubiquity of American Robins and White-crowned Sparrows. I settled onto the bench seat of the blue truck, rolled down the windows to let the heat escape, and took a good long gaze at the lake, taking stock of a very full day. Still only 3 p.m. I gave thanks as the engine started right up. Resolved to head straight back to Churchill, I nonetheless cruised slowly along the escarpment on the narrow track, alert for anything new, and enjoying the now familiar. I felt a tired satisfaction, calm but not quite content.

The Bohemian Waxwings still haunted me. I reflected on the contrast between yesterday, with so many life birds, and today with none. Not one, though I'd encountered several I hadn't seen for decades, and some I had hardly seen even then. There was a lot to smile about. "Don't let the waxwings ruin it for you," I counselled myself. "You got spoiled by yesterday."

The road widened at the burn-area turnoff, where I accelerated to a steady, fast pace for "home" – within the limit set by the uneven gravel surface. Soon I could see the three hikers ahead, the rifleman well ahead of the other two. There was plenty of time to consider the possibilities – in this heat they might prefer a lift. I carefully studied the Asian couple as I came abreast of them and passed by. They seemed pretty tired. I slowed to a stop just ahead of their leader and let him catch up to me. Before he could stop or react, I asked, "Are you all right?"

He seemed a friendly, confident 20-something with a mustache. He stopped and looked at me with a "Why do you ask?" expression. He uttered something like, "Yeah … sure," with a puzzled smile.

"Okay. Good. Just wanted to make sure," I replied and quickly drove on to hide my mild embarrassment. Still, I felt good for having done the right thing. Out here in the bush, a little consideration can make a big difference – people are friendlier and more concerned for each other, because you never know when you'll need the other's help. "Reciprocal altruism" is what we called it in graduate studies of evolutionary theory. I was surprised that he was surprised, that he didn't seem to share my romanticized notion of bush courtesy.

Soon I discovered at least part of the reason. A kilometre or two beyond, after the hikers were gone from my rearview mirror, I came upon an empty van parked on the roadside, facing my rising dust cloud. On the side was painted "Adventure Walking Tours."

I rolled on, reviewing my day in reverse. It always seems much shorter between landmarks on the way back from a new place, even across my huge tundra plain. I stopped briefly a couple of times, but generally kept on rolling and pitching along the gravel road and soon reached the launch site – only a bit over 17 kilometres from the East Lake cabin. From there the paved road felt fast but still bouncy in the springy truck – like we were dancing across the dry tundra of the coastal ridge. Coming over a rise and down, I was awed again by the frozen ocean spread across the horizon. Simply amazing. Immense. Forbidding. Fascinating. White! Sunglasses mandatory.

Just past the turnoff to Bird Cove, a falcon shot across my bow. Breaking to a crawl – thank goodness there were no other vehicles to worry about – my eyes followed the bird to a grove of tall spruce. It landed. I could see a track off the road to a man-made clearing in the tundra, not too far from the spruce trees. I drove in cautiously to where it was obvious that the ground was too soggy for wheels. I backed up a bit to be safe. I was still far enough away to have to use the scope.

I got out slowly with the scope, hoping my bird would stay put. It did. Through the binoculars, I was almost certain it was a Merlin – it was too small to be a Gyrfalcon or a Peregrine Falcon, too plain to be a Kestrel (and too far north, I thought). My hunch was confirmed by Bonnie's book, which says to look for Merlin nesting in clumps of spruce near the coast. And the Winnipeg birders had told me they had just seen a Merlin over the Granary Ponds. But I wanted more than a confirmed hunch. With the great views I'd been getting of birds on this trip, I wanted to see a Merlin at least well enough to pick out all the diagnostic traits: the vertical line from the cap through the eye, the short, vertical stripes on the breast and belly, the solid brown on the female's back, blue-gray on the male.

Even with the scope, I could barely see, perhaps only imagined these markings. It had to be a female. The sun angle was not good; the background gave poor contrast. I plunked down on the ground to wait for her to change position, move, fly. The intervening land was too wet to cross without putting on my boots. I preferred to wait and see what might happen – despite my growing eagerness to get back to the hotel room for a shower and a rest. After a few minutes, another falcon flew with Kestrel-like cries to the top of a much closer spruce, but the sun was almost directly behind. Luckily, it soon flew across to join the female, landing in the next tree over, with a much better background. Still small through the scope, but all traits were clearly there, including the blue-gray back of a male. Not great, but a very good view compared with the two or three times I'd seen Merlins before. Okay! Super! Let's go.

I packed up the scope, then checked the falcons again with my binoculars. Probably a nest in that grove of spruces. I thought of the proximity of Bird Cove, from which direction the falcons had come. That reminded me of seeing a Merlin on a cold January day flying across the mudflats at Bodega Bay. It flew low, fast, and directly toward a large feeding flock of sandpipers. As they rose into the air en masse, the Merlin accelerated right into the middle of the flock. The falcon veered off to light on a metal post sticking up from the mud, with a large bird dangling from its talons. The kill looked easy – a surgical strike – then dinner. Back in the present, it occurred to me that a Merlin's life might be easy where it could find tidal mud and lots of sandpipers. Almost a leisurely stroll down to the "restaurant," as I was planning to do soon.

∞

The Gypsy Café was the most stylishly colourful building in town, right on the main road with extensive unpaved parking in front. The lot was empty. It was barely 5 p.m. Three teenage girls came out of the café and across the lot. One was old enough to look sexy in her halter top and shorts, so naturally I looked. She looked back momentarily as if to say, "Thanks for the appreciation, but aren't you, like, way too old for me?" Which I was, of course, but it flustered me to have it pointed out, even so subtly.

My mind quickly transformed me from "dirty old man" to "evolutionary theorist," pondering the reasons older men are so often attracted to younger women. What a great defensive mental trick! But it's a good question, one that occurs to me rather too often. My wife claims she read somewhere that men think about sex every 15 minutes on average. I respond, with feigned thoughtfulness, "No, I don't think so. I think it's more like every 15 *seconds*." She laughs and hopes I'm not serious. Someday my son will be old enough to read this and be embarrassed for his old man. He'll have to learn to deal with his own sexuality, so for his sake, I'll be direct. The fact is that my "search image" for young, good-looking women is almost as well-honed as it is for birds. Use of binoculars is strictly limited to the latter creatures, however.

Since my days as a formal student of evolutionary biology, an offshoot field of interest called "evolutionary psychology" has emerged. It uses evolutionary theory to explore the origins, the "adaptive significance," of our own psychological tendencies. It's easy to get carried away with untestable speculation, but regarding men being attracted to younger women, I find the ideas pretty compelling.

The starting premise is that natural selection favours choices that lead to more healthy offspring than the alternative choices. The contention is that men who choose to mate with younger women father more healthy kids who grow up to have kids of their own than do men who choose to mate with not-so-young women. The underlying reason is that women are most likely to have healthy kids (and less likely to have started having them already) when they are in their late teens and early 20s. And certain features seem to go with healthy fertility-in-waiting, such as ... well, you know them when you see them. Just take a look at the women in magazines and movies. The idea developed by evolutionary psychologists is that male human brains evolved over millions of years to key on these features, to find them "attractive." These "secondary sex characteristics" are exaggerated in the women chosen as models and actresses, making them all the more attractive to the average man (up to a point, beyond which they become grotesque). Human cultures enhance "attractiveness" with overlays of clothes, makeup, hairstyles and mannerisms we learn to associate with young women.

It's highly doubtful that a man consciously thinks about healthy fertility-in-waiting when he sees and pines for an attractive woman. The immediate reason for what we feel is seldom related directly to the ultimate reason natural selection favoured these feelings. Our inclinations take on a life of their own, disconnected from their origins. Natural selection doesn't care about our daydreams. It's when we *act* that consequences unfold. "Whatever works!" is the motto of evolutionary change. If daydreams lead a man to pair up with a fertile lady-in-waiting, then whatever genes may predispose him to those daydreams get passed on to the next generation of daydreamers.

If men are, consciously or not, on the lookout for candidate mothers of their children, the logical corollary is that most women are searching for men likely to be good providers for them and their children. The best providers would be somewhat older men with the physical and mental prowess to achieve social status and control "resources." But not too old. Men in their "prime," their late 20s to early 40s. So says the plausible hypothesis.

I look younger than my age, because I've kept a full head of hair that has barely started to gray. Yet I dress like a respectable person of means – a gentleman on vacation rather than a bum on the run. Maybe that's why the girl in the halter top bothered to take notice of me taking notice of her. Was that an appreciative smile or a dismissive glance?

What if all this, or any of this, is true? I've been thinking that it is good to be in tune with universal forces manifest in a species' evolutionary history. But this kind of naturalistic thinking can be used to justify behaviour that is clearly bad, such as older guys going after underage girls. The defence that "It's in our nature" can be and has been used to delude ourselves that all sorts of evil behaviour are okay. Capacity for self-delusion may be the most powerfully dangerous consequence of our mental chatter. We can talk ourselves into just about anything.

What is it that holds me back from acting on a natural attraction favoured by natural selection? Fear of embarrassment when this girl spurns my attention? What if she doesn't? Fear of the law crashing down on my head? Loyalty to my wife? Respect for this girl's feelings? Realization that she and I most likely couldn't sustain a conversation? That sex is most satisfying for a couple that has lots of practice, especially together? That this girl doesn't look enough like the woman I love? Fear of losing the relationships on which my life depends? All of these, no doubt. All of these reasons seem linked to my learning over a lifetime, from my upbringing, my culture and my personal experience, not some primordial genetic constraint. It is a natural tendency held in check by human culture and learning. The criminals among us prove this check is neither universal nor foolproof. Yet it is very, very powerful.

It's helpful to think that our capacity for culture – the accumulation of learned behaviour and the transmission of this repertoire to future generations – is also a product of our biological history, part of our human nature, a manifestation of universal forces. Culture is the consequence of lots of learning animals engaged in mental chatter with themselves and each other.

But the specifics of our culture are not shaped directly by natural selection. The details are determined not by genes but by our individual learning and choices and actions – all of us together, in aggregate interaction. Natural selection works through births and deaths to increase or decrease the frequency of genetic traits in a population. In contrast, cultural traits – specific ideas and learned behaviours – are not genetically transmitted. We often pass them on to others without a single birth or death occurring, and for reasons that often have no connection to natural selection. Fashions of speech and dress and politics can sweep in and out in a single generation. Technical and social innovation can transform society in a single decade. It's cultural selection rather than natural selection that drives the process of cultural change. However, it's not clear what drives cultural selection.

Historically, and especially before recorded history, societies were more isolated from each other than they are now. They developed distinctly different cultures as their cultural selection worked in isolation. As a collective group of decision-makers, each society more or less stumbled into its own cultural destiny through the exercise of "free will." They adopted new ideas, practices and tools that fit, according to their brand of logic, what was already there. Eventually natural selection must have weeded out the societies whose cultural selection and evolution had increased their vulnerability to environmental change or to competition and destruction by other societies.

It is my native culture that offers me reasons to resist my natural impulses. If we, a society of humans, really do steer our own cultural evolution – *create* our own culture – then the reasons for my restraint are set not directly by the universal forces but by the collective free will of my cultural ancestors. I have been mostly cut loose from the forces manifest in natural selection. So how do I know these reasons for my restraint are good or right in some universal or eternal sense and not just the end product of a process driven by the distinctively human mental chatter of my culture? If we can talk ourselves into anything, what guarantees that we have talked ourselves into doing what is good? Is it good simply because it fits with our man-made culture-of-the-moment? I doubt it.

Wouldn't she have a good laugh, if this attractive young woman knew what mental chatter she triggered in my mind?

∞

The inside of the Gypsy Café was like a large meeting hall, with linoleum tables and simple chairs in keeping with that motif. At one end was a typical delicatessen-style glass case and counter, with glass-doored refrigeration units behind, featuring a variety of beers and soft drinks. Behind the counter was a short, rotund, dark-haired man with his back to me. I walked over and looked in the glass case. The man turned his attention to me. He had a broad Hispanic sort of face and a wonderfully friendly smile. "What would you like?"

Giving up any pretense that I knew what I was doing, I returned with my best smile, "Are you serving dinner?"

"Sure."

"Okay, how does the system work?"

He turned and pointed up to the display boards, the kind with the push-in white plastic letters, high on the wall over the refrigeration units.

"Oh, I see."

Various temptations were named up there, but one board featured the day's special: Arctic char. I asked about it. He explained proudly that he had just received a very large fish, "caught today and flown in from Chesterfield Inlet." Oh, the magic of that name! I had to have a piece of that fish. Then I examined the beer selection – some familiar, some not, but all Canadian, I was assured. I picked the most exotic sounding. I was up for a good meal and feeling adventurous.

I paid and went across the room to a window table with my beer and the books I'd brought with me: Bonnie's book, of course, and Leonard Nathan's *Diary of a Left-handed Birdwatcher*. This was my second reading of the latter, and I was about halfway through. I was really enjoying it, because it captured and characterized so many of the feelings I often have about birdwatching and birders. He knows the scene intimately, yet stands on the margins of it enough to look on with some objective ambivalence but also deeply personal attraction.

My first order of business was to taste the beer and to take stock of my survey of the Churchill area and its natural history. What was still left to see? The only major zone missed so far was the area to the south along the east bank of the Churchill River. From Akudlik Junction, Goose Creek Road goes through boreal forest and taiga to the Cottage Area. From there, the road crosses the broad multi-channel Goose Creek just upstream from its confluence with the much, much larger Churchill River. Then the road becomes a straight causeway, called the Hydro Road, making a beeline across open spruce bogs (muskeg) and ponds and willow thickets until it reaches a pump station and boat landing on the bank of the Churchill River itself.

Dinner arrived in the hands of a small, thin, 50ish man, bald, wearing wire-rimmed spectacles and dressed in a white T-shirt, an undershirt, really. His smile was impish and ingratiating. He looked like he belonged in a New York City deli, except for his smile. He invited me to enjoy my dinner. And I did. The Arctic char filet was perfection, firm like swordfish, but more moist and delicate.

While eating I continued to study Bonnie's book and to consider next steps. I knew I needed a break from intensive birding. I still had three full days ahead of me. So I decided that tomorrow would be a day off – just some relaxed birding around the Port and Granary Ponds and out to Cape Merry. And with renewed energy from a sumptuous dinner, I would use the remaining long evening to explore the Goose Creek and Hydro roads and complete my overview of the Churchill area. What tipped the scale toward that decision was Bonnie's promise that the boreal forest along Goose Creek Road was a reliable place to find what I was looking for – Bohemian Waxwings. Even Northern Shrike and Northern Hawk-Owl could be seen on the power lines or treetops. I had to make the effort today. Who knew if the weather would permit a visit in the three days ahead?

That decided, I relaxed over my beer and Leonard's book for another half-hour before rousing myself to action. Soon I was in the truck and on the Highway, heading out of town again. At Akudlik Junction, I turned south on Goose Creek Road. I checked the metal shed-like buildings for evidence of an office of Churchill Wilderness Encounter, where I believed I would find the Rare Bird Alert bulletin board. No sign of anything but a road maintenance facility – a few storage buildings with no office of any sort.

The road was paved at first but soon gave way to well-groomed gravel. After crossing a set of railroad tracks, there was a long straightaway with spruce forest edge on both sides. The forest was cleared back from the road by a good 10 or more metres on each side, so I didn't have the same feeling of being *in* the forest as at Twin Lakes. It reminded me of being on the train, passing through a wide corridor almost off-limits to the local inhabitants, except that in the truck, I could control the speed. I cruised along slowly at 20 to 40 kilometres an hour, trying to scan both sides at once, alert for any movement or sound. There was surprisingly little: Blackpoll Warblers and an Orange-crowned Warbler, the usual White-crowned Sparrows, a Green-winged Teal in the water alongside the road. The building of the road seemed to create narrow linear ponds on both sides, almost like wide gutters with standing water.

A couple of kilometres brought me to the second set of railroad tracks, the ones I'd come in on by train. Just before these was the turnoff onto the Nodwell Trail, which I took, following Bonnie's recommendation. I soon was tailgated by a very large dump truck on its way to what seemed to be a gravel pit. Letting him pass, I stopped, looked and listened, then followed him all the way to the excavation site. I quickly turned around and headed back to the place I had stopped, which is where the Nodwell Trail intersects with the Manitoba Hydro line. This is a series of high-tension power lines held up by very tall metal and concrete towers marching across the land along a broad, straight, cleared corridor through the forest. "Hydro" means electric power in this part of the world. The cleared corridor looked walkable, so I decided to try it.

The ground and vegetation were spongy and uneven underfoot, but I managed to make my way north to the third tower from the road. I had seen nothing to speak of up to that point, but there I discovered a large pond tucked into the forest to my left. Sharp whistled notes rang out from the pond, so I approached. I saw a shorebird at the water's edge, which I figured was a Lesser Yellowlegs. In retrospect, I can't be sure it wasn't a Solitary Sandpiper – it was certainly the right setting, and I wasn't alert to how similar they are. Then I saw what looked at first like a flycatcher alight on a dead snag, as though returning to its chosen perch after sallying forth to snap up an insect. But the more I examined this bird through the binoculars, the less it looked like a flycatcher. It was faded blue on the head and back and showed a peach colour on the breast.

"A bluebird? Couldn't be."

But the more I looked, the more it was! Had to be a female, then, with its pale colours. Okay, which one – Western or Eastern? I took a close look at the throat – same colour as the breast. Probably an Eastern Bluebird, but I'd have to check the book.

Just then I felt a sharp pinprick of pain on the back of my hand. There it was, the first mosquito. Big one, too. Slap – I got it. There were others in the air around me. Time to move. For a panicky half-moment, I thought of how far it was back to the truck. I loathe mosquitoes, even more than most people do, I think, which was a major reason for the early timing of my visit to Churchill. I'd rather risk blizzards and missing some of the later-arriving bird species than deal with the biting bugs of the subarctic summer. I was also hoping to catch some of the earlier passage migrants (like Snow Buntings) and winter visitors (like Snowy Owl) before their departure, but avoiding the hordes of insects emerging in the second half of June was a major incentive. It occurred to me, as I took a confirming look at the bluebird, that the early emergence of mosquitoes and the surprise visit of the bluebird far to the north of its range were both related to the unseasonably warm weather carried by the southwesterly wind of the past two days.

I made my way to the truck and had no trouble leaving the mosquitoes behind as long as I kept moving. Back in the truck, windows up, I studied the bird guide and agreed with my identification: Eastern Bluebird. I also scanned the checklist of species in Bonnie's book and was surprised to find she didn't even have the Eastern Bluebird on her list of "Seldom Seen." This was an unusual find! I'd definitely have to post this sighting on the Rare Bird Alert bulletin board. Still, I couldn't get very excited about seeing a bluebird. Much as I love to see bluebirds, seeing one here was like running into a fellow tourist from the States.

Continuing on Goose Creek Road, I checked out the various recommended spots with little result. The Cottage Area is an incongruity, a residential street in the middle of wilderness. I was reminded that Canadians seem to use "cottage" to identify any modest home in the country. These are not summer or winter cabins or vacation homes. They appear to be year-round residences.

Goose Creek was impressive, a broad, high-volume river flowing past and through thickets of willows. No sign of humanity upstream or down. Just this road and a bridge, which was substantial, like a long, narrow steel cage you drive through – one vehicle in one direction only. You must wait your turn, and there were just enough other trucks on the road that I had to wait my turn, but no one was behind me. Once on the bridge, the tires of the truck had to be guided on two thick wooden plank tracks the whole long length of the bridge. In the middle, where I stopped to take a good look upriver, I had a feeling of precarious suspension above the flood. The evening light and the darkening clouds above, and the strong, fast flow of steel-gray water underneath, added to my uneasy sense of solitude and vulnerability. Seeing nothing of wildlife on the river except a few scaup ducks, and not wanting to prolong my uneasiness, I moved on across.

The road beyond was soon a long, straight shot to the pump station on the Churchill River, raised well above the surrounding wetland of pools, marsh, dense willow thickets, and islands of ragged spruce. It made an attractive landscape in the slanted sunlight. It was now getting on past eight o'clock. I stopped and lingered several times, walked the road in a couple of places, hearing a locally uncommon Song Sparrow and the trilling song of a Swamp Sparrow in the willows – as well as a melody that probably belonged to a Fox Sparrow, but I couldn't confirm that hunch. I came upon a tight group of five Sandhill Cranes close to the road, cautiously feeding as I rolled slowly by. Shorebirds – Hudsonian Godwit, Lesser Yellowlegs and Common Snipe – stalked the shallow water. Ducks – Northern Pintails and Northern Shovelers – paddled the deeper water.

There were a few trucks parked at the pump station as I drove up. It was a clearing in the willows along the Churchill River, with a rough stony beach on the water. A small concrete pump house sat a few metres back from the shore. All there were locals – Aboriginal or Métis or both. They took little notice of me. The grown-ups were fishing; the kids were playing on an unhitched trailer, making it rock like a cumbersome seesaw. Their example gave me the idea to climb onto the bed of my truck to get a better view of the river. It looked a couple of kilometres wide at this point, maybe more. There were a few ice floes. Nothing much in the duck department, which was a bit of a surprise. I walked to the water's edge to get a better view upriver, a vast expanse of water flowing out of the interior of Canada.

I drove back at a pretty brisk pace, glimpsing another Merlin across the bow, two American Bitterns flying overhead. I lingered a little here and there, and stayed alert through the forest for shrikes, owls and – of course – waxwings. Soon I was back to Akudlik. Not fully convinced of its existence, I drove into the road maintenance compound and circled the sheds in search of the Rare Bird Alert bulletin board. I found it: just a whiteboard tacked to a shed wall under a roof overhang. On top in permanent letters was the title "CWE Rare Bird Alert." And there was a dry-erase marker pen. Column headings at the top said something like "species," "date," "location" and "name." There already were several entries: a Gyrfalcon, a Bald Eagle, an Upland Sandpiper seen from the train on the sixth (I smiled at this confirmation of both my identification and its significance – one of the British birders must have seen it, too) and a Red Phalarope in one of the pools I had examined south of the Goose Creek bridge. I think I would have seen it if it were still there.

Determined to do my civic duty, I was still nervous about this whole idea of exposing my identifications to public scrutiny and daring to say that I had seen a bird rare enough to go on this board. In the late '80s, I saw a very rare Rufous-necked Stint, an Asian sandpiper, at Bodega Bay. I reported it to the local rare bird alert co-ordinator, leaving a message on his machine. He called me back to interrogate me, which I found awkward, because he asked lots of questions using anatomical terms I'd heard before but didn't know anymore. He was impatient with my sloppy details. In the end, he put my sighting on their recorded message as a "maybe" for a day or two. I felt foolish, especially when no further sightings were reported. Clearly I had exposed myself as a rank amateur. Nevertheless, this rank amateur had definitely seen a Rufous-necked Stint, in full breeding plumage, and I had reported it so others might have a chance to see it. A remarkable sighting, a lifer for me, and duty done.

Here I was again. I got out my notes on exact locations and directions thereto, and I picked up the marker. Luckily no one was around to observe me and make me nervous. I put down my two birds: "Three-toed Woodpecker male" and "Eastern Bluebird female" followed by the day's date. Unlike the brief, even telegraphic, location descriptions given for the other sightings, I proceeded to specify how to get to the precise location of each of my sightings. It made for a lot of words and a couple of lines for each bird.

I got back in the truck and admired through the windshield my two entries on the board, an amateur's contributions neatly printed as they were below the others. "Oh well," I thought out loud. "I've shared my discoveries, for what they're worth." Then I drove off down the Highway into Churchill.

6

The Day Off
June 9

Parasitic Jaeger

The morning sun through the curtains downstairs bounced off the rust-brown carpet and suffused the loft bedroom with a warm half-light suited to lying half-awake and wandering through my thoughts. One of them was a desire for a leisurely breakfast at the Churchill Motel Restaurant. It was almost nine o'clock.

Downstairs I looked out through the curtains and discovered another sunny, probably warm day. I switched on the TV for only the second time, looking for news of the world. I also was curious to see how Canadians would present the news. There was a French talk show from Montréal, which I tried to follow but couldn't. The only other channel I could get interested in showed still photos of subarctic winter scenes, credited to a Churchill photographer, while the audio was a call-in radio show featuring gossipy news of First Nations communities I'd passed through on the train, such as Cormorant, Manitoba.

At exactly nine o'clock, the Canadian Broadcasting Corporation, CBC, took over the channel. Suddenly it was only seven o'clock – in Vancouver. A news program came on the air with great national style. As the music of the Canadian national anthem played, the video showed beautiful Canadian landscapes melding one into the next, progressing from the Maritime provinces, across the forests and prairies, to the Rockies and the British Columbia coast. A very stirring, even moving way to start a Canadian day. This reminded me that Canada's national symbols are nature-oriented – the maple leaf on the flag, the loon and other wildlife on its coins.

The Vancouver morning news show was indistinguishable in format from its US counterparts – except for the weather report featuring a map of British Columbia and then Canada, with forecast high temperatures for Whitehorse and Yellowknife, but not Churchill. The local radio-on-TV show had predicted a high of 25°C for Churchill, which seemed about right, given yesterday's heat. I was hoping for a map with fronts and such, to get some idea of what I might look forward to. The most I could discover was that Winnipeg would turn colder again in the next couple of days.

∞

I walked down the block and across Kelsey Boulevard, which becomes the Highway out of town, and through the restaurant door just before ten o'clock. I passed the untended cash register, poked my head into the small dining rooms to the right and left, and saw no one. I admired the walls crowded with large, framed, very professional photos of local wildlife – polar bears the most numerous, but also Arctic fox, snowshoe hare, caribou – most, if not all, in winter scenes. I wondered if folks in Churchill prefer the winter. I also wondered if I was too late for breakfast – a more unsettling thought. No sign of life except from the third eating area in the even smaller back room en route to the kitchen. I entered cautiously and immediately felt the eyes of four local men who had been enjoying coffee, cigarettes and talk until I stepped awkwardly into their midst. I stood for a moment, noticing there was

The Day Off: June 9

no way to sit down in there without breaking into their circle. I retreated to the cash register in confusion. Just about then, a short, round woman emerged from the kitchen with their food orders. I stepped back in to catch her attention. I stammered, "Still serving breakfast? All right if I sit out front?" "Yes" to both. Soon I was settled in for my anticipated pleasure – a big breakfast and more of Leonard Nathan's book.

The waitress was friendly, even chatty, but mostly I had the room to myself for relaxed reflection at the halfway point of my visit to Churchill. The hard work of orienting, exploring and discovering was mostly accomplished. Now I could burrow into this place and try to understand it. No more rushing around to make sure I wasn't missing a big piece of the puzzle. I'd focus on my favourite pieces, the most interesting pieces, and try to savour the experience of them.

Nathan's book was a perfect companion for reflection on the meaning of birding, the meaning of coming all the way here. It was at that moment that I first thought of writing about these days in a similar style of self-questioning exploration. This might help my wife and my son to understand the experience and thus to understand better an important part of me that was otherwise nearly inaccessible. Both of them enjoy seeing birds, and they take pride in knowing the names and correctly applying them to common species. Neither, however, shares my obsession to see in the living wild what is pictured in a book, preferably through a pair of well-focused binoculars or a spotting scope and preferably as it behaves naturally in its home environment – to see birds as part of the story of life. This obsession to identify generates discovery and then reflection on the meaning.

My wife is to me an indescribably lovely person, and we are each other's very best friend. All the more remarkable that she does not share my passion for birds and, more broadly, natural history.

I suppose it is not so unusual, and in fact is rather common, that spouses have some unshared passions, demanding understanding and forbearance from each other. At first, it takes a common passion, more than just for each other, to keep two people together long enough to get to know and trust one another. For us, dancing provided the initial glue as we developed our friendship. Then we enjoyed trips together, first to the Arizona mountains and canyons and later overseas. On these trips, I always managed to do some birding, often by going out on my own in the early morning, but also with her, using what I had already learned to accommodate non-birders. I confined our birding to beautiful natural areas with good walking trails. I was quick and quiet about making identifications and drew her attention only to unusually interesting birds that she could see well unaided. Soon she was sharing my binoculars and getting good looks at good-looking birds. She marvelled at the details of colour, pattern and behaviour. She enjoyed hearing some of their natural histories. But she has never picked up the binoculars and bird book and gone off birding by herself, much less fallen prey to the voracious appetite of the life list. Birding is my passion, not hers.

My wife does not simply tolerate my birding. She admires and encourages it. She likes to join me on occasion, and she encourages our son to take an interest, but she knows I get the most out of birding when I do it alone or with an equally passionate birder. She also keeps it from overrunning my life by making clear there are higher priorities. Time and place must be made for my birding, but birding has its time and place.

Sometimes the time and place can be rather unexpected. One day my wife and I were talking near a window, and my eye caught a movement in the tree outside. I froze, and fixed my eyes on the movement's source. Recognizing it as a thrush, "needing" it for my monthly bird list for the area around my town, knowing that I'd

The Day Off: June 9

have to see it well to identify it to species, and believing that she would forgive me, as most people would not, for interrupting our conversation to look at a bird – all this calculation in a heart beat – I moved quickly but carefully to the window.

"You're just like a cat!" she exclaimed. She knew I would take the comparison as a compliment.

I like cats – especially my first one, Gleep. She arrived as a very young kitten when I was 10 years old. Gleep was born of a half-wild farm cat in a Vermont hayloft. She grew up to be a very small, nondescript gray cat. But she was a most interesting animal. She brought the good and the bad of the natural world into my family life, for she always had the run of the land around our succession of rural homes in Connecticut. Gleep got herself pregnant after loudly declaring her availability to all within a mile radius (my mother wanted her to have the experience of being a mother before getting her spayed). I watched as her three kittens were born in the hay of a horse stall. Her maternal instincts seemed to extend to the dogs and us as well as to the kittens. That included providing for us through her considerable skill and determination as a hunter. She would spend the night outside, if she so chose (no point in trying to stop her), and in the morning would often leave us a freshly killed rodent laid neatly on the back-door step. She continued this charming practice for years.

When we moved into a newly built house on the edge of a great expanse of protected forest, she set to hunting the forest like the fearsome predator she was. I suspect the local mammal fauna had thrived until then in isolation from house cats and other subsidized killers. Gleep's first few months were the most productive she had ever known. Morning after morning, I found a present at the door. I was becoming very interested in identifying any living thing around, not just birds, so I identified Gleep's catches as she brought them to me. We were a team conducting a systematic survey of the small nocturnal mammals of the forest preserve. I was the young curator of mammals. Gleep was the professional collector delivering specimens to me for identification. I still have the list of specimens she delivered, starting August 28 (when we moved in) and ending January 27 (when Gleep's hunting was finally closed down by the winter weather and she went into her annual half-torpor on one of our beds): 20 deer mice, 13 boreal redback voles, 13 meadow voles, 4 southern flying squirrels, 3 woodland jumping mice, and 1 eastern chipmunk. I would identify the little body, almost always in good condition, as though asleep, and then hand it over to the proud little killer, who would then proceed to eat it head first.

Not all the rodents on the catch list were caught by Gleep, and not all were dead on arrival. We had kept one of Gleep's offspring, who became a rather large tiger-striped cat, named Tigger. He was as sluggishly domestic as Gleep was driven by wild instincts. But Tigger would hunt, too, and he accounted for a small minority of the list. He was not maternal, of course, but he did bring his catch to us once in a while – especially if it was not dead! My father had installed a "cat port" on a back door, through which the cats could come and go. If we left it open at night, Tigger would occasionally bring his prey inside the house, dead or alive. One night I woke to movement inside my pillow. I bolted out of bed and hit the lights. Cautiously I peeked into the pillowcase and saw an alarmingly large pair of eyes peeking back. It was a flying squirrel! I had never seen one alive. I quickly sealed the pillowcase, found a flashlight and carried pillow and all outside into the dark night. I held the pillow against a tree trunk on the forest edge, opening of the pillow case upward, and squeezed the squirrel out like toothpaste from a tube. It shot up the tree trunk, seeming to be in good condition, and was gone into the dark treetops.

The Day Off: June 9

For some reason, Gleep's collecting and my identifying did not continue when spring came. I think it was because Gleep's hunting success never again came close to that fabulous fall and early winter. Most likely, the rodent community around our new house was reeling in shock from the feline onslaught and never recovered as long as Gleep stalked the forest edge and beyond. My mother described keeping cats as a "conflict of interest" for nature lovers. She excused Gleep and Tigger as not being all that interested in birds, which was probably true. I do remember they caught a few birds, but the cats never seemed to take advantage of the bird feeding we did in the winter months. They were too interested in staying warm and dry inside at the time the birds needed the feeders the most.

Today I am more ambivalent about keeping a cat, because of their killing ways, but mostly because of the risks they run and the nuisance they create when on the loose. My suburban world is so much more confining for a cat or dog than the ex-urban rural world of my growing-up years (we lived in or near very small towns, but my father commuted to work in New York City). In my world view, a cat must be on the loose to be a real cat. Gleep was the paragon of felinity as I see it. I always had the feeling that she was a wild animal that had deigned to let us associate with her in exchange for a little food, warmth and affection when she needed it. She could have dismissed us any time, and often did for days at a time. She could not have lived as long on her own, which she grudgingly acknowledged by taking advantage of our offer of a fallback strategy. Not that she found us irksome. She just preferred her freedom to bear arms onto the hunting grounds and live like the self-reliant predator she always was. For me, it was like having a tiny tiger living with us. I could study her life and understand her at a level I could never hope to achieve by visiting a real tiger in the zoo or catching an unlikely glimpse of one in the wilds of Asia. Gleep was a privilege to have as a "pet."

What I learned from Gleep about predatory lifestyles included an admiration for profound repose. Cats in general, big and small, sleep a great deal. What really impressed me, however, was Gleep's ability to fully relax while watching the goings-on around her. How I envied that! But she could just as easily and suddenly transform into a coiled spring of riveted attention. My wife's remark on my cat-like stalking of a bird was the first time I understood the parallel. I seek to enjoy the natural world, to absorb it through my senses. My intellectual predilection is to be an observer of life, a student of its meaning. But there is a predatory instinct at a deeper, more fundamental level that has the power to transform me into Gleep stalking her prey. A birder's impulse is to identify and list. I think this impulse reflects a need to stalk and catch that underlies my civilized upbringing. Like all primordial tendencies, it is a fact of life to be controlled but never fully denied.

∞

Every predator alternates between intense seeking and profound repose. It eventually becomes satiated by a good meal, enters a state of relieved relaxation, and simply watches the world. I knew I had achieved that state in more ways than one when I went up to the cash register to pay for my breakfast. As I waited, I spotted a typed message on the counter that said, "I know where to find a Boreal Owl. For $50 I'll take you to see it. Call [a Churchill telephone number]." Talk about a town catering to birders! "Psst, hey buddy, wanna see a Boreal Owl?" Yes, of course, I wanted to see a Boreal Owl. This might be literally the chance of a lifetime. I thought about this pay-per-view offer for a long moment as I waited for the waitress to appear and take my money. The notion almost made me laugh out loud. I guess I'm not really a birder after all.

At least not that morning after three days of being a birder. I had stalked and caught, and now I was ready to watch.

After dropping off my book and collecting my binoculars, I set out for a reprise of the first walk I had in Churchill – up the street past the Anglican church for a view of the ice on Hudson Bay from the rocky ridge line and then onward around and between the Granary Ponds to the Port facility and the Churchill River. I had visited some part of this small area every evening for the past three days and had come to appreciate the variety and accessibility of the birds there. Some birds had become "friends" to be greeted as I walked the neighbourhood: the Horned Grebe and the American Wigeons cruising their private willow-rimmed ponds, the White-crowned Sparrows, Savannah Sparrows and Yellow Warblers affirming their territorial rights to shrubs and grass, American Pipits in aerial display and Horned Larks in tinkling song from the tops of boulders with frozen ocean backdrops, and an assortment of gulls, Arctic Terns, shorebirds and ducks on the larger ponds and along the river shore. Today I had time and warm enough weather (I walked in only a long-sleeved shirt) to allow more leisurely communing with each of my friends – and the prospect of new acquaintances.

Prominent and alone on the ridge top is a tall flagpole topped by a large Canadian flag showing the wind direction. It overlooked the bay to one side and the town, Port and Granary Ponds to the other. This was my first destination. En route, I stopped to admire the Horned Lark and American Pipit and to scan the open bay water between ice floes for Common Eiders and Oldsquaw and other marine life. Two young men in T-shirts below me at the water's edge were poking around among the fast-ice blocks. A spaniel-sized black-and-brown furry dog came charging up the slope from the two men, whizzed past me over the ridge top, and carried on another 10 to 15 metres. Soon it was busy working back and forth in the willow shrubs. A few minutes later one of the men came up from the water's edge toward me. He was an Aboriginal man of medium to hefty build with a broad, Asian sort of face framed by black hair above and along the cheeks and jaw line, and punctuated by a scraggly moustache. He seemed amiable as he called to me, "Did you see my dog?" Grateful that I could be helpful to a local (rather than the other way around), I pointed behind me and called back, "Just over there." He didn't answer, but kept coming toward me.

He stopped beside me, and I turned and pointed again to his dog. He called out in stern voice, "Button, get over here, you stupid dog." Button immediately looked up, got a fix on his master and came running straight toward us. What a good dog, I thought. I couldn't imagine my late Shabo responding so well to a single command. He always had excuses for not doing what he was asked or told to do. Not that he was untrained; he knew exactly what was wanted. He just lacked motivation to obey unless offered major incentives or a threatening tone of voice. So I was very impressed by this little dynamo named Button.

Button was not greeted with a "Good dog." Still amiable, the man reached down with one hand to grab Button's collar and made a fist with the other hand. "I ought to beat you, you f---ing bad dog," he growled. Alarmed that he was going to harm the dog, I jumped in with a polite advisory plea, trying to sound light and friendly. "You don't need to do that. He came right to you when you called him." He threatened the dog again, but without seeming to mean it – like he felt compelled to put on the appearance of a tough guy. I interceded again on Button's behalf by leaning down and petting him and marvelling again that he had come right away. I even talked about how my dog would never come like that. The man let go of Button, and, without altering his even-tempered mood, asked what kind of dog I had. I answered in the present tense, as though

Shabo was still alive, then added, "Well, he *was* a black Labrador. He died last year." I felt confused by my unconscious denial that my dog was gone. I was sad for a moment, as I looked down at Button's enthusiastic face. Again the man verbally threatened Button with physical abuse, using the f-word, but still half-heartedly. With some exasperation, I petted the dog to protect him. Finally the man gave up his posturing (for whose benefit, mine or the dog's?) and asked what I had been looking at out on the bay.

"Ducks and anything else that might be out there," I replied, not sure how he would react to such an objective. He fell right in with me, however, talking about the birds in the area and the people who come up to Churchill to see them. He asked how I had come. I told him I had arrived by train on Saturday but would leave by plane on Friday. He told me he used to work out at the airport. I remarked on the huge size of the airport facility, and he related how the Concorde had landed at Churchill, that's how long the runways were. He repeated, with a little swagger in his voice for emphasis, "The f---ing Concorde landed right f---ing here in f---ing Churchill."

"That must have been really exciting!" I enthused, imagining the commotion such an event could create anywhere in the world.

"Damn f---ing right, it was."

"Are you still working at the airport?"

"Naw, I work at the elevators loading grain on the ships." He seemed proud as he pointed to the Port facility. "Big f---ing ships come in to be loaded here."

"Yeah, I've heard. How much of the year do you load ships?"

"Oh, from next month to October or whenever the ice gets too much."

"What do you do in the off-season, when there aren't any ships to load?"

"We do repairs on the elevators sometimes – and I get government assistance," he said in a flat tone, looking down for a moment, sounding not quite matter-of-fact. Fortunately for both of us, his friend came up the slope from the water and joined us just at that moment. "He's a carver," the first man said, pointing at the other man by way of introduction and with renewed pride in his voice.

The newcomer was a bit shorter and thin, almost scrawny. He, too, was Aboriginal, but looked very different: prominent cheekbones, sunken and smooth cheeks, a thin moustache. Acknowledging his friend's introduction, the newcomer smiled a broad, ill-at-ease but friendly smile with large, uneven teeth, but said nothing. The first man went on to explain that "carver" meant carving soapstone figures, and that his friend's work was being sold in a lot of places around town. I had heard about the rather sophisticated Inuit artwork in soapstone and was a bit surprised, expecting an accomplished artist to look, well, different from this rather scruffy youth. I asked him directly if his work was sold at Northern Images, the recommended place to look for fine soapstone carvings. He said yes, confirming his artistic credentials.

"I'm planning to go there this afternoon," I said. "I'll look for your work. What's your name?"

"George Noah," the first one answered, and George Noah agreed with a toothy smile and nodding head.

I asked where they came from and got some exotic answers. The first man said he was from Rankin Inlet, about 150 miles due north along the west shore of Hudson Bay; the second said Coral Harbour, on Southampton Island at the top of Hudson Bay. I asked what the landscape was like up there, whether the vegetation was like it is around Churchill. The first one looked around and then stooped and held his hand about knee high from the ground and said, "Nothin' grows taller than this." He explained that these communities are supplied once a year by barges towed up there during the ice-free season. The first man pointed to truck trailers still on flatbed rail cars sitting between the Port and the train station (the ones that "my" train had picked up in Thompson and dropped off here). A company name was freshly painted on each one, something like "Northern Transfer." He seemed proud of the company as he indicated that it was the one that barges supplies up to the remote communities far to the north. Everything else goes in and comes out by air through Churchill.

I said I had heard that the administrative centre for Keewatin District had relocated to Rankin from Churchill a few years ago, and I asked if that meant there was a lot more activity up there now. The man from Rankin didn't think so; nothing was happening up there, he said. Of course, he may not have been back to Rankin for some time. George Noah didn't have anything to add.

I thanked them for all the information. They wished me well and walked on with Button toward the Anglican church, and I wandered on to the flagpole. I settled myself on a lone park bench nearby, enjoyed the warmth of the sun in the gentle breeze and studied the view of the Granary Ponds below. As I scanned the ponds with my binoculars, I thought about this interesting encounter with two young Inuit men. Modern-day Eskimos. Not what I expected, I thought, but then what *did* I expect?

∞

My mind drifted back again to Québec, to my first experiences with native North Americans. I especially remember one of our canoe portages that took us directly through a Cree village.

We were wet and chilled as we trudged uphill through the dark forest in the misting rain. I stooped and leaned into the tumpline across my forehead, holding the 65-pound box full of kitchen utensils to my back. It was much easier to study the ground at my feet than to look up for a view ahead. But I looked up when the dark of the forest opened to the light of a clearing. I was one of the first in the line of portageurs and could see the Cree men, women and children coming out of their wood and canvas huts to examine the unexpected transients. They stood by their doorways and stared dully without surprise or curiosity, as though watching a boring television program. I felt too awkward to use my high-school French to greet their stares. I noticed with surprise and a bit of disgust that trash was piled outside the huts in disorderly heaps. I thought how cold they must get in the winter in these crude structures.

The Cree people watched the line of white boys trudging past with their burdens. No words were exchanged other than a couple of *bonjours* between the trip leader and one of their adult men – not friendly, but not unfriendly either, just very, very distant. The portage required two more passes through the village with the remaining gear and canoes, but the residents had seen enough. The second and third passes went unobserved, except by a few young children. Once the portage was completed, neither we nor our trip leader made further mention of the event. It was just another portage.

That was not my first view of the "squalor" characteristic of many poor communities, but the event was so awkward that it left a deep but confused impression. With this early negative exposure to poverty, it may be ironic that my career has been spent mostly working with and for the poor. I often wonder what will be the circumstances of my son's first strongly felt encounter with absolute poverty. How will he accommodate it? Born rich or poor, each of us must find a way to come to terms with our place and role in this awful inequity. The way we finally choose profoundly affects and reflects our relationship with all humanity – and therefore, I must suppose, with the Divine in every creature.

The Day Off: June 9

It is a long, circuitous path from my graduate education to what I do now for a living. There is a thin thread of consistency along the way. My academic interest focused on the ecology and sociology of both animals and humans. To make a living in the real world, outside of academia, I was fortunate to become an ecological consultant in Africa. Concern for the environment led me to concern for the people who live there. The complex of poverty and population drives people to overuse and abuse the limited natural resources available to them. Logic, chance and necessity landed me in a career helping poor women reduce the many burdens of poverty on themselves and their families through an international non-profit organization that provides financial and educational services to groups of women in very poor rural communities around the world.

Surely this is a noble cause, responding to a grand vision of what life could and should be like, at minimum, for all people. Yet life cannot be lived in the abstract. Even a noble cause must translate to daily life, dealing with the present, moment after moment. I found my niche in this real world as an organizer of ideas and a manager of people, recognized for "people skills" I would never have expected in the shy boy I was – and still am, more or less.

In the right setting, I enjoy being with people, and mostly they seem to enjoy being with me. But my natural inclination is to stand to the side and observe the workings of human society with interest and reflection. I feel hope and despair for the future, sincere sympathy for the people I deal with personally and professionally, deep love and gratitude for those few who are close to me, especially my wife and my son. Still, there is no denying that my inner being is nurtured by solitude in the natural world. The fuel that sustains my life as a social being is delivered by these quiet reconnections to the power source manifest in nature. Unfortunately, this need for asocial "down time" puts me at odds with expectations of my society, or any society. I'm a member of an oppressed minority, incapable of organizing to demand our rights, because we, each of us, would rather be alone.

I often feel guilty for preferring observer status in the whirl of social interaction. Some would call me cold and uncaring, too aloof, reluctant to engage in what most of us feel is the most precious and meaningful experience of our social species. Many lovers of nature evince a distaste for humanity, but I suspect their distaste is often born not so much of philosophical objections to humanity as of discomfort in their interactions with people. I try to avoid falling into this self-justifying version of misanthropy, but I get tarred with the same brush nonetheless. I acknowledge that my shy ways can make others uncomfortable. They can sense that for me, socializing is often more work than fun, however cheerfully I work at it. Certainly this is a handicap. Frequent exhaustion with human contact cuts me off from many wonderful chances to learn from others and share in what truly is precious in the human experience.

This is who I am. I tell myself I can make this weakness into a strength by working with it rather than fighting it or giving in to it. Avoiding people is not an option and definitely not my goal. Being more aware of my limits helps me conserve my social energy and use it more consciously, I'd like to think. Ironically, when I do engage with others, they're usually not trying as hard as I am to create an enjoyable encounter. I grow weary from the feeling of not being met halfway, sapping my enthusiasm for more. And yet, I usually feel better for the effort, knowing that I've done my part. I reach out to others who are struggling even more than I do. Working harder means, I think, being more sensitive and caring about the feelings of others. This is probably what my colleagues at work admire as "social skill." But small talk can still be excruciating.

If being social is difficult in the best of conditions, think how much more so it is with people coming from very different worlds. The vast majority of my co-workers in the fight against poverty are not very poor or even from very poor backgrounds. What I was thinking about on the bench below the flagpole was my personal struggle to relate to people from other worlds, people who are struggling to come to terms with a modern world run by people more like me than like them. As in my early days as a field student of animals, I seek to understand what the world looks and feels like inside their lives. But it is hard work.

The two men from the far North were not unlike so many other "working-class" men I've met. The bravado is tiresome, but despite the liberal use of the f-word, this was a thin layer easily pierced. I enjoyed my talk with them. I was pleased that I had been able to understand them in a small way. It was a minor victory for me personally, because I had been a bit apprehensive as the first man came up the slope. Not that I was fearful for my safety, just uneasy about how the interaction might go, partly because young men of all types usually find birdwatching ludicrous or even incomprehensible, and they are unafraid to let me know it.

I'm also aware that some people feel like victims of an oppressive mainstream of society and are, therefore, hypersensitive and quick to go on the offensive or withdraw into sullen resentment. I sympathize with their sensitivity. I, too, resent being considered guilty until proven innocent of association with the "bad guys" who happen to look and speak like me. Combined with my natural awkwardness in making small talk, I feel doubly uncomfortable. There is a psychological chasm to be bridged. I am not good at taking the necessary personal initiative and risk to overcome what has taken centuries to create. So, my first impulse may be to withdraw or avoid, thereby adding to the problem rather than making it better.

Life List: A Birder's Spiritual Awakening

This time I did not withdraw or avoid, because I was at ease in myself, relaxed and unhurried, and open to learning as much as I could about this very different part of the world, alert to the presence of God in these men.

∞

I could hear people approaching from behind the bench. I turned to see two Anglo men: one in his 30s, the other, in his 40s, with a cowboy hat two or three sizes too small held atop his head by a string under his chin. Definitely tourists, like me. The older one was the leader. He asked if I'd mind if they joined me on the bench. "Sure, have a seat!" I said. Trading information on how long here and where from, I learned that they had arrived on the train that morning and would be departing with the train that night. They were on a transcontinental train trip. Just for the heck of it, they decided to get off in Winnipeg and do a little side trip up to Churchill and back. They were eccentric, friendly and talkative. They were definitely not birders. The older one lived in Connecticut and had embarked on the transcontinental train in Montréal. The younger one lived in Calgary and had flown to Halifax to start his train trip. They had met on the train and become travelling companions, both bound for Vancouver. They asked about things to do on foot, and I shared the little I knew.

They were looking for ways to occupy themselves until the 6 p.m. boat trip they had signed up for. They told me they had called Mike at Sea North Tours to book the daily trip on the river and into the bay. The idea intrigued me. I had not thought about a boat trip, because I had heard there was far too much ice for taking a boat across the river to the Prince of Wales' Fort (one glance at the river seemed to confirm it). I pumped them for more information, which they happily provided. I thought to myself that it might be a good thing to do, especially on a warm day like this.

I also thought that it might be fun to join the two of them. They seemed like good companions. I resolved to call Mike to sign up for the trip myself.

They decided it was time to walk on and left me to myself again. Soon after, I wandered down to the same rocky perch above the willow swamp where I had sat on my first afternoon. There was the Horned Grebe again. There were Common Redpolls and Yellow Warblers in the thicket. A swimming bird, much smaller than the grebe or a duck, was startled into the open water by my arrival. It made toward the willow swamp and its thicket of branches over the water as quickly as it could swim, which was still a poky pace. I keyed in on it with the binoculars well before it disappeared into the thicket. It was a Sora, a fairly common member of the rail family. It looks like a half-size brown-and-gray American Coot, but has a black face mask contrasting with a yellow bill. Like all rails, the Sora is so secretive in thick marsh vegetation that you seldom see them even when looking hard for one.

Savouring my good luck, I sat a long while and drank in the scene with all senses. An odd place to revel in nature, overlooking an industrial landscape of man-made ponds, railroad tracks, grain elevators and petroleum tanks. Yet the scene teemed with life.

I worked my way along the ridge to the north side of the Granary Ponds and then splashed through some wet ground to mount the railroad grading and walk south back toward town and along the edge of the largest pond. An inviting grassy path atop a dike separating three ponds headed west toward the Port elevators. I had developed a real preference for this path, because it felt more natural than the railroad tracks or the gravel roads in the area. It allowed more intimate contact with the water birds, which often hovered along the water's edge under the overhanging grass and willows of the dike. They would move out into view as I approached, but still were calm enough to stay nearby. I had lots of close-up views of the many ducks – Northern Pintails, Green-winged Teal, Greater Scaup, and Northern Shoveler – as well as Herring, Ring-billed and Bonaparte's Gulls, and of course the constant air traffic of Arctic Terns *kip*-ping and screeching and carrying minnows to mates. This morning I also identified Lesser Scaup among the Greaters and some Gadwalls and, most unexpected, a pair of Blue-winged Teal. Thinking of the close encounter near the Thompson train station, I admired again the teal's lovely colour scheme.

Among the shorebirds, I could count on seeing a couple of Stilt Sandpipers and one or more pairs of Red-necked Phalarope. As its name suggests, the Stilt Sandpiper has long legs, even for a sandpiper. They are a distinctive yellow-green. The bird also carries a moderately long black bill, drooping slightly downward toward the tip. It uses this equipment to work the deeper water near shore.

Farther out from the pond shore are the phalaropes – another type of sandpiper, but quite unusual. The breeding female is the more brightly coloured sex, rufous-red and white on the neck with black face mask, and the duller male is the one who sits on the eggs and tends to the young. Females may mate with more than one male, making these shorebirds rare examples of polyandry, the opposite of the far more common polygyny, where the male has more than one female mate. (The generic term "polygamy" applies to either sex having more than one breeding mate.) Phalaropes are also unusual for their feeding behaviour. Unlike other shorebirds, which walk around on the ground or in shallow water as they probe with their long bills, phalaropes float and paddle around on the water's surface, from which they pick at their invertebrate meal. They even spin or pirouette on the water as they feed. I've read that this is supposed to stir up the water, maybe even create some upwelling, to bring mosquito larvae to the surface. That's what these phalaropes were doing – putt-putting here and there over the shallower parts of the pond, stopping to spin and pick. It was worth a long look every day. Not only are phalaropes an unusual treat for a California-based birdwatcher, they are also the stuff of college biology texts, giving the sighting of phalaropes an exalted significance.

Continuing along the grassy dike, I drove a Savannah Sparrow before me. It would fly ahead about 10 metres and disappear into the vegetation. I would approach within two or three metres and the bird would flush and fly ahead again. After two or three times, the bird would fly out over the water in a tight arc and rush past me in the opposite direction to get back into the middle of its territory on the dike. Then I would flush the owner of the next territory and repeat the process.

I often stopped to get a good look when the bird alighted to get a good look at me before disappearing into the grass. Most sparrows are difficult to identify, and because they appear so drab, many casual birdwatchers don't bother. I've taken a perverse pride in identifying sparrows. Not that I'm particularly good at it, but lots of binocular time on sparrows has given me a great appreciation for their fine patterns of brown, gray, white, black and often rufous. The Savannah Sparrow is about as drab as a sparrow comes, but a good close-up usually rewards the viewer with a characteristic splash of lemon yellow between the base of the bill and the eye. Sparrows are almost as elaborate as the Blue-winged Teal. Granted, their colours and patterns give sparrows very effective camouflage, but the fine detail seems far more elaborate than necessary. It sets the mind to wondering how and why the process of evolution creates such exquisite excess. It seems the evolutionary process is far less economical than it is effective. It doesn't choose the easiest path to the adaptive result.

Farther along the dike, where there were more low-lying willow shrubs, I scared up a warbler of some sort. This was an odd location for a warbler, I thought. It might be something off-course and even rare for Churchill. (Something more for the Rare Bird Alert bulletin board?) It was staying in the thicket as it fed and moved along rather slowly, so I stalked it for many minutes, getting a good glimpse once in a while. But there was nothing much to see in the way of identifying marks. It seemed to be a female or some sort of immature male waiting to take on the distinctive breeding plumage of its species. I inventoried the bird's colours and patterns, reciting them to myself in an effort to remember until I could refer to the books in my hotel room. Knowing that identification of this bird would be a real challenge, I shadowed it for many more minutes than I needed to get fully acquainted. I kept hoping to see something more, a characteristic behaviour, a flash of colour, perhaps to hear it say something that would give away its name.

Finally, I was satisfied that I had learned all I could. I reached the end of the dike, headed to the riverbank at the south end of the Port facility, checked the usual spots, and saw more old friends. Then I retraced my path across the dike, moving more quickly this time, paying less attention to the ducks, phalaropes and sparrows, keeping an eye out for the warbler. I passed over the railroad tracks and onto the narrow gravel road through the willow swamp toward town. I stopped alongside the swamp to listen to the loud, emphatic song of the Northern Waterthrush. This is a warbler that looks and acts more like the American Pipit, walking (not hopping) along the water's edge as it forages, all the while keeping cadence with a bobbing tail.

From there I could see between the two apartment buildings to my hotel and the window of my own room. Just as I was exiting the swamp, I heard the buzzy twittering of redpolls descending from the sky. Two landed on the tops of nearby willows as tall as small trees. I could see lots of white and then more white and decided with great satisfaction and amusement that I was looking at Hoary Redpolls just 30 metres from my hotel room. Immediately after, I heard a sort of familiar whistled song. Up on the power line was a Harris's Sparrow! It flew down to the parking lot between the apartment buildings and foraged under a pickup truck among some House Sparrows. Not the first time that I have searched and searched for a species of bird only to later find the object of my desire right outside my window.

I checked my field guides as soon as I got back into the room. There was no way to identify my warbler. Frustrating as this can be, I took solace in the warning I've read several times that a good birder knows when to say "I don't know about that one." Too often birders will make a call when they shouldn't. Credibility is enhanced by admitting to doubt and even declining to try identifying some birds down to the species level. Feeling rewarded by so many other birds this morning, I was content to let my warbler remain unidentified.

∞

During lunch, I called Mike at Sea North Tours and discovered that his boat was full for the 6 p.m. trip; it could carry only 12 people. I asked about the next day. There would be one trip at 11 a.m. Timing depended on the tide, which ranges 12 feet in the river mouth, he said. He had seen the first beluga whales of the season in the past two days. Excited by the thought of seeing these famous white whales, I asked him to sign me up for the next day's trip. It would be $49 Canadian for two hours. I regretted not going that day, since it was rather warm. Whatever the temperature, it would feel a lot colder on the water. Who knew what the next day would be like?

I resolved to spend the afternoon exploring the town itself, starting with the Town Centre and then on to the Eskimo Museum and then the Northern Images shop to seek the soapstone carvings and other artwork I'd heard about. All was within an easy walk of the hotel. After dinner, I would spend the evening at Cape Merry and see what I could find: maybe a jaeger flying among the gulls and terns on the river.

The Town Centre is a municipal complex – huge for a town of fewer than 2,000 residents. A long, low building stretching along the rocky ridge for the equivalent of two or three blocks and facing out to the beach and Hudson Bay, it housed the high school, a hockey rink, a restaurant, the public library and other municipal services all under one roof, connecting by closed-in walkways to neighbouring buildings such as the health clinic. It is designed to let people spend hours and hours in various activities without having to emerge into the normal deep freeze outdoors. I was curious to explore inside. At first, I had difficulty finding my way into the building, not seeing an obvious main entrance from the road. Once inside, I found a clean, utilitarian atmosphere, much like a large, modern high school. There was a maze of corridors, stairs and levels. I wandered and finally found the library and then the restaurant-cafeteria, which is part of a much larger central atrium. You could eat at one of the tables of the restaurant and watch your young children playing on an indoor playground with a long slide housed inside the figure of a wood-panelled polar bear. The kids climb up the bear's back, disappear inside the huge head and emerge sliding out of the bear's chest. I thought of the fun my son would have on that bear.

In fact, that was the first thing, other than the train ride, that I thought my son would have enjoyed on this trip. I felt a little sad that he and my wife could not share all this with me, but I knew there was little here of interest to any but a birder or a starry-eyed adventurer. Nonetheless, there were some minor pangs of guilt for leaving them behind, despite their sincere, loving wishes that

I enjoy this special time to myself. I also felt some regret that I had not explored more thoroughly how I might arrange for my father to join me. The logistics of accommodating his emphysema (oxygen bottles, etc.) would have been problematic, and given the uncertainty of the weather, I had chosen not to even dangle the idea in front of him. Always one for an adventure, especially if birding is involved, he would have leapt at the chance. But I could not have guaranteed him a safe trip, much less a good time.

Deep down, too, I knew this trip had to be solo. The whole idea of visiting Churchill was so lunatic that I could not bring myself to encourage anyone else to go. And perhaps I had an intimation that this would become an inner journey to a very personal destination only I could hope to reach. Still, my wife, my son, my father, my mother had been with me at every step, along with beloved pets and cherished memories of other places and other wild animals I have met over the years. I was grateful for their companionship and guidance along the way.

The Town Centre had almost no windows, but I had heard that there was a great view of the bay, so I kept wandering to find it. It turned out to be not too far from the atrium, a sort of alcove with picture windows on three sides, looking up the shore to the northwest, down the shore to the southeast and straight out onto the bay. It provided a magnificent view of huge blocks of ice floating on the water. There was much more open water today than on the day I arrived. My first assumption was that the unusually warm weather of the past three days had melted all that ice. I was stunned by the thought of such dramatic change. Once again I was mesmerized by the sea ice and stood there watching for many minutes.

For a weekday afternoon, a good number of people were using the Town Centre. But often I was alone as I explored the various public areas. In solitude, I admired a whole wall of black-and-

Life List: A Birder's Spiritual Awakening

white photography of local faces, mostly older folks of all races, showing the weathering you'd expect in the far North. I noted the artistic talent of the local photographer and thought of how some small communities in interesting places can attract more than the typical share of talent.

I found my way out of the complex through a long, narrow corridor past multiple classrooms, probably part of the high school. Pleasant as it was in the Town Centre, I was glad to be outside in the open air and on the gravel again.

Across the way was the Catholic church: very small, with a roofline that sloped dramatically toward the rear from its high point under a short steeple over the front door. It was a design I hadn't seen before. Intrigued by the odd exterior, I guessed it might be worth going inside. It was small and intimate: only 12 plain pews made of blond-coloured wood on either side of the narrow aisle, matched by a simple wooden table as the altar. Behind the altar, the back wall of the sanctuary was covered by a mural showing in the foreground the risen Christ appearing to the Apostles, a good, traditional rendition. But the background was anything but traditional.

It was a scene of twilight blue reflecting on snow, ice and water. To the right of the holy imagery were a dog team and sled with driver in winter dress racing off across a snowfield toward a dark coniferous forest. To the left was another dog team pulling sled and driver across pack ice along the edge of the open sea, a rather deft attempt to place the biblical story in local context. Arms outstretched, hands pointing toward the two dog teams and drivers, Christ could be saying to his followers that even these people, making their lives in this most severe of environments far from the Holy Land, must hear the message. A Latin inscription along the bottom of the mural read "*Euntes Docete Omnes Gentes.*" In English in the upper right corner was inscribed "Going teach ye all nations." Inuktitut (the language of the Inuit) in the upper left corner declared the same, I presume. The overall effect was very pleasing in its concept, colour and artistry, and its message of inclusion.

Jewels of religious art are expected in the urban cathedrals and ancient village churches of Europe. But I have found equally remarkable, if less artistically sophisticated, amalgams of traditional Euro-Christian imagery and distinctly non-European imagery in remote outposts of Christianity. In Kenya, right on the Equator, on Christmas Eve, my wife and I were delighted by a crèche next to a roadside chapel. It was a nearly full-size stable with life-size figures of the Holy Family and the traditional cast of livestock and visitors, all in what we've come to assume was the plain and fancy dress of the Middle East at the time of Christ. In stark contrast, outside the stable on both sides were life-size wooden figures of Maasai warriors in full ceremonial adornment, complete with spears and shields, standing at attention as though guarding the stable and its precious residents. Like the Arctic mural in this church, the Kenyan crèche connected the biblical to the local.

It has become a minor hobby of mine to visit churches wherever I go, especially Catholic churches, which tend to greater artistic expression in their interiors. Yet I had not expected to find a jewel here in Churchill.

∞

I am attracted to churches for more than their art and architecture – not just Christian churches, but religious shrines of any culture – perhaps for the same reason I'm fascinated by the intricate patterns of plumage on ducks and sparrows. They defy utilitarian explanation, yet they are beautiful and inspiring. Cultural evolution, too, can create exquisite excess. Sometimes gargantuan, sometimes gaudy, sometimes austere, sometimes simply elegant, these places of religious devotion reach beyond the normal in our lives. They give witness to that distinctively human self-awareness, that consciousness of forces beyond what we can control, of Truth given to us rather than by us. Humans are not just another animal, after all. There is something very special about us.

Charles Darwin painstakingly detailed natural histories of animals and plants, and he proposed and tested hypotheses about nature, yielding many complex ideas and conclusions. The most controversial is that *humans are animals*. For the past 150 years, Darwin's stunning idea has been used in two ways. One is to lower our view of human nature to the level of animal nature, to draw conclusions about ourselves from what we know about animals. The reductionist extreme of this interpretation of Darwin includes B. F. Skinner's stimulus-response approach to human psychology. The other is to elevate our regard for "higher" animals, because they are so similar to humans. The activist extreme in this opposite direction includes People for the Ethical Treatment of Animals (PETA). Both extremes are appalling in their disregard for reality. Darwin's insight is best served by a mature balance of the two interpretations. I tend to tip the balance toward elevated regard for animals, because I see in animals something of the Divine, as I do in people.

I have studied the human social sciences – anthropology, sociology, psychology, economics and here I would count even history – against the backdrop of my elevated regard for animals. I have more or less searched for confirming continuities from animal nature to human nature. I have to agree, reluctantly, that human beings are indeed special. Our species is animal in origin, but clearly we have become something much more than any other animal.

We are not just more complex and accomplished, having much bigger brains, much greater capacity for problem-solving, much greater use and manufacture of tools, much more complex social arrangements, and so on. Simpler forms or precursors of all these features exist in other animals, allowing for possibilities of gradual evolution of the greater from the lesser. Though amazingly developed, these qualities do not make us fundamentally different from other "highly evolved" animals, such as gorillas and chimps. Yet we *are* fundamentally different, even from the apes.

The true departure from animal to human nature was the advent of human language. Apes and African grey parrots have been trained to use non-vocal symbols, with distinctive shapes and colours, to receive and send complex messages resembling the syntax of human speech. This might seem to prove that human language also has its precursors among the animals, except that this language-like behaviour is not observed naturally. It requires training by humans. Clearly the potential is there, as it must have been in proto-humans before language arose. But the potential requires a boost to get over the barrier to the actual. It seems this boost occurred in about the same time and manner for all humanity, because all human languages, no matter how "primitive" the culture, are fundamentally the same in their deep structure and are fundamentally different from any other animal system of communication. Somehow our distant ancestors got "trained." How, by whom and to what purpose are matters for speculation.

My wife asserts that only human beings have souls, that in the evolution of our species there was a moment in time when God "breathed" a soul into human beings. I have found this idea both intriguing and disturbing: intriguing because it rather neatly blends my evolutionary convictions with my wife's Roman Catholic Christian convictions, which are less constricted by literal interpretation of the Bible than many Protestant Christian convictions, and disturbing because I cannot get my wife or any Christian or other religious person to give me a working definition of "soul."

To treat my wife's assertion with due respect, if only for my son's sake, I am forced to go beyond my scientistic world view, dependent as it is on precise definitions in observable terms. "Scientism" is what Huston Smith (in *Why Religion Matters*) and other intellectually respectable critics of the postmodern society call the materialist "religion" to which I was recruited as part of my secular higher education. Just when the questions become really interesting, scientism tells me to abandon the investigation for lack of "evidence." Scientism, as a path to knowledge and wisdom, is limited entirely to what its instruments of observation and paradigms of theory can detect or predict at any point in history. It cannot conceive, in its own terms, of immaterial, spiritual phenomena, so scientism simply denies that such phenomena exist. Wishing to explore further, I am forced to open myself to other possibilities, other paths to Wisdom and Truth.

Perhaps "soul" is the same as the language capacity I contend makes humans unique among animals. One notion of "soul" is that it is the part of us that communicates with God. That seems consistent with the proposition that human language is a God-given faculty. In what a physicist might call a "singularity" and a religious person would call "divine intervention," the plodding course of human evolution may have received a boost from outside the universe. With this newly bestowed "soul," humans not only obtained the capacity to listen and talk to each other, but also to communicate with God. From the self-awareness and introspection made possible by language, we may have received the capacity and propensity to become alert to the presence of God – in others and in ourselves.

This is a neat formulation. Its logical plausibility could serve to keep intellectual peace in my family. Nonetheless, it is based on a narrow and uncommon notion of what is the human soul. The lead definition of "soul" in my *Webster's* dictionary (reflecting the most common connotation) is "the immaterial essence, animating principle, or actuating cause of an individual life." This sounds rather like "something of the Divine" that I sense in both animals and people. Yet my wife's assertion that only humans have souls seems to deny my beloved animals the same essence that we have. It relegates the non-human to second-class citizenship in the kingdom of God. More troubling is that my wife's assertion keeps solid company with the wisdom of the major world religions. They focus on the God–human relationship; in that sense they are anthropocentric – human-centred. Skeptics say our religions exalt the importance of our species simply and solely because it is *our* species. They have a strong case, but it does not by itself demonstrate that humans are *not* special in the eyes of God.

I remain a scientist, and therefore a chronic skeptic in the examination of assertions about humanity, nature and God. But I have abandoned scientism as my unconsciously religious persuasion. It is too narrow, too limited by hard edges, too willing to blind itself to evidence and deafen itself to logic that attests to a universe, a Nature, and a humanity that are rich with spiritual meaning indecipherable by the methods of science. Knowledge of the spiritual world has to be sought obliquely, not head-on by the human mind. As C. S. Lewis was reported to put it, we have to sneak past the watchful dragons of our self-consciousness to get a glimpse of our quarry. For guidance on this strange path to knowledge and wisdom, I have lately and rather tentatively turned to religious method and thought. I find it does help me reflect more deeply on human and animal nature.

My regard for religion has been elevated by exposure to the rich intellectual history of Christianity. More than any other writer, C. S. Lewis has been mentor and comfort to me in the face of my profoundly secular peers who dismiss questions of religion as simply irrelevant to practical living and to making this a better world.

God's existence may be acknowledged – but with self-assurance that God plays no part in our world, that we're on our own. God is neither help nor threat. To the contrary, Lewis assures me, the wisdom offered through a religious world view is exceedingly practical. More than making the essentials of Christianity accessible to an appropriately skeptical mind, Lewis lends intellectual respectability to religious faith. He leaves no doubt that an educated, disciplined intellect, giving imagination and feeling their due as sources of spiritual knowledge, can experience leaps of faith that secular society lazily attributes to ignorance or insanity.

How is it that religion developed such a sour reputation in the eyes of so many people, especially well-educated people? One problem is the history of religious institutions – or, more specifically, of people acting in the name of a religion. I share the mixed feelings about churches and institutional religion in general. They are *human* institutions, inspired by the Divine in, around and beyond us, but behaving in distinctively human ways. Human mental chatter controls them, making them capable of deluding themselves into believing that Evil is good and Good is evil. Churches and other religious institutions have led countless people, just like me, to deeds of transcendent nobility. They have likewise led or allowed people, just like me, to commit unspeakable acts of brutality. We humans have within us, each of us, the full range of conceivable capabilities. We cannot fully separate our humanity from that of the worst among us. When less than one per cent of our genetic coding is different from that of chimpanzees, we can claim very little to distinguish ourselves from each other. Name the most infamous in history, and there, but for the grace of God, we could go (and occasionally do). Churches are human institutions with that same human range of capabilities.

The problem people have with religious history also may serve as a publicly acceptable cover for their other, more difficult problem with religion. Religion challenges our devotion to self-interest or, more generally, the notion that humanity is sufficient to achieve its own salvation. How convenient that science cannot prove (or disprove) the existence and significance of a Higher Authority. By adopting the world view of scientism, we can dismiss God's importance in our lives. We can claim that God and religion are delusional remnants of an earlier, adolescent era of human cultural evolution. Or we can be more guarded, allowing that God exists, but only by lurking ineffectually in the current gaps of our scientific knowledge, which we might presume will grow smaller and smaller until God is squeezed out of the universe altogether. With either conclusion, we are spared the inconvenience of answering to a Higher Authority.

Therefore, we can do what we want, confident that we are the most intelligent beings in an otherwise cold, purposeless universe. Unnerving to put it this way, but this prideful state of mind does not allow such honest thoughts. It focuses us on the present material world and the benefits of having the autonomy to deal with it as we think fit. At our best, Enlightenment idealism convinces us that humanity can use its autonomy to propel itself up an ever-rising, self-guided path of progress toward a truly just and pleasant society. However, Thomas Jefferson, one of the greatest progeny of the Enlightenment, gave us this caution:

> God who gave us life, gave us liberty. Can the liberties of a nation be secure when we have removed a conviction that these liberties are the gift of God?

By implication, without recognition of higher authority, there is no purpose in our lives other than what we choose for ourselves. There is no moral authority beyond what humans invent for themselves. What looks to us like the path of Progress can as easily go down as up.

∞

I turned my back to the altar and started down the aisle, touching the smooth, blond wooden back of each pew. At the last one, I enjoyed the feel of my hand sliding along the full length of the pew. At the far end, I turned again to the altar and studied the little church. I imagined it filled with people and all the sights and sounds of the Mass. My wife would love this, I thought. She has been thrilled by the little churches, lovingly appointed and scrupulously maintained, that we have stumbled upon in our travels. One in the Alps above Zermatt with a magnificent view of the Matterhorn. Another on the island of Bora Bora, through which wafted moist tropical air. Another in the cool Usambara Mountains of Tanzania, with elegant wood panelling on the ceiling. Another on the Sussex Downs of England, build of flint and smelling of eight centuries. I wished she could be with me to share this gem, too. Even my son would be fascinated by the unusual mural behind the altar. That scene of North Woods and Arctic ice would be the striking memory we would relive together over the years.

I turned to go. I stopped at the door and took in the sight of the whole interior of the church, one last time, I thought. But the mural drew my eyes, then my whole body back up the aisle to the front pew, where I sat down to look long and hard at the central human figure in the mural. The artist sees in this human being something beyond the human. That something in the painted eyes seems to look at something inside of me and speak to it. At the same time, it looks beyond me in this small building, beyond the blue sky and clouds that I can see and out into the deep, black universe. The eyes seem to say that it is all right, not to fear, that I am forgiven my ignorant arrogance just as I lovingly forgive my son for claiming to know what he does not know at all. But the eyes also project a challenge to follow him – forgiveness will be on his terms, not mine.

Perhaps recoiling from this challenge, I remember from "Desiderata,"

> Beyond a wholesome discipline, be gentle with yourself. You are a child of the universe, no less than the trees and the stars; you have a right to be here. And whether or not it is clear to you, no doubt the universe is unfolding as it should. Therefore be at peace with God, whatever you conceive Him to be.

How reassuring when I found this whole "prayer" framed on the wall of the bedroom to which I was assigned in an English farmhouse in 1978. The first step on my adult road to religion, "Desiderata" became for me a devotional committed to memory for meditative review in quiet interludes. Like so many people, I thought this prayer was written in the 1600s and discovered in a Baltimore church. It spoke so clearly to my modern sensibilities, yet it had the moral authority of enduring wisdom. However, there had been a misunderstanding. Only after two decades did I learn the truth, that "Desiderata" was written in 1927 by Max Ehrmann in Terre Haute, Indiana. I still love this comforting guide to intentional living, but now I know that it is not an ancient affirmation of modern sensibilities but a modern affirmation of the post-Christian world view that barely acknowledges the existence, much less authority of God.

About the same time I learned the truth about "Desiderata," I finally read and reread the four Gospels of the New Testament, and I was shocked. To hear even devout Christians describe Jesus, you would think this man the ultimate guru of love, forgiveness, peace on earth and goodwill toward all. Certainly Jesus was all this, but I was shocked to discover how hard-edged and unyielding was the Son of Man in his moral challenge to the social and moral order of the Jews of Roman-occupied Palestine. This was a cosmic confrontation between a loving but insistent God and God's errant people. Jesus comforted the afflicted and afflicted the comfortable. He insisted on adherence to principles of thought and behaviour, even though mortals could not hope to fully comply. There would be forgiveness for this human failure, given that certain conditions were met. The people had better get with the program before the end of Time, when the "goats" would be separated from the "sheep" and sent off to their eternal destinies, not of this world. This stern program was patiently explained and illustrated by Jesus as he spoke in mind-bending parables, flouted social customs, performed impossible deeds and left everyone wondering who the heck Jesus *was* – a wise man, a prophet, the Messiah?

Then Jesus astounded even his most ardent followers by freely accepting a shockingly brutal death by crucifixion (surely the most appalling form of execution ever conceived for regular use by a "rational" government), only to rise from his tomb and appear selectively to some of his followers, but still a rather large number of witnesses. His dramatic final departure from this world was followed soon after by a visitation of the Holy Spirit upon the Apostles of Jesus. The Spirit empowered them to follow Jesus' mandate to risk life and limb as needed to spread God's news, not just to the Jews but to all people of the world.

Wow! Unbelievable!

Exactly. Why should we believe these inconsistent and poorly documented accounts of the life, death and resurrection of Jesus, committed to papyrus well after the facts, when memories were subject to confusion by passage of time and subsequent events? Certainly a comparison of the four Gospels and the Acts of the Apostles could lead the reader to conclude that some historical revisionism was practised by the writers, whoever they were. At the very least, there would have been errors in what the Gospel writers remembered or heard once or more times removed from the eyewitnesses. There is enough room for doubt to allow those who would rather not believe to dismiss the Gospel accounts as nothing more than propagandistic legends.

The problem for this dismissive view is that the total body of work in these accounts, anchored by a few events verified by disinterested writers of the time, provides documentation as good as or better than historians normally have demanded to construct their histories of ancient times. Moreover, would anyone making up stories to advance a personal agenda of some sort choose to relate such fantastic events, such puzzling quotes, such an impossibly demanding program for salvation? It would be too unbelievable. There were also too many other witnesses to allow one or a few to hijack the story for their own purposes. And finally, we can be sure something very unusual and profoundly life-altering must have happened in Palestine to commit so many people to stand firm in declaring their belief in Jesus Christ in the face of certain persecution and even tortured death at the hands of the brutal Romans abetted by very agitated Jewish authorities.

C. S. Lewis writes that Jesus left us with just two choices in deciding who he was. Either he was the Son of God, or he was a lunatic. There was no middle ground to stand on. No possibility to consign him comfortably to the ranks of inspired gurus. If so, I must reluctantly choose the Son of God, because I cannot call Jesus a lunatic. It would not fit with the historical accounts and subsequent behaviour of the followers of Jesus. If I accept that he was the Son of God, the Incarnation of God's Word, then I have to accept that the primacy of the God–man relationship is no simple product of anthropocentric bias. Animals are distinctly different from humans in the eyes of God.

I struggle with all this. I have no trouble believing in God, because I intuit God's presence in nature. My principal struggle is to accept the incarnation of God as a humble human being. I am open to the possibility, because it makes sense that an involved Deity would send the chosen species instructions for following the way to knowledge of the Deity. However, to paraphrase St. Paul, the cross is a major stumbling block for me. I cannot make heads or tails of St. Paul's vision of Jesus as the sacrificial lamb whose undeserved death opens the way to salvation for humanity, by redeeming us from sin, reconciling our species to God. Nonetheless, to be intellectually honest with myself, I cannot simply dismiss all this either. I have to reckon seriously with Jesus as both a Son of Man and the Son of God.

But where does the rest of nature, God's creation, fit into this fantastic picture?

I will have to keep reading and thinking on this problem of understanding. At some point, I suspect I'll come to see this problem not as a matter of understanding, but of letting go to faith. As Lewis advises, I'll have to sneak past my watchful dragons of skepticism and intellectual pride to catch a glimpse of the truth, just as in the act of looking for birds I find myself watching their Creator. Yet birds and nature do not speak to me of the special relationship between God and our human species. It is the Christian story of God sharing our humanity to show us the way to right relationship with God, and each other, that affirms God's special interest in humanity.

That is what I was thinking as I sat in the pew, feeling its smooth, hard wood at my back. Finding God in a church building is still a new endeavour for me. I cannot see the sky. How can I see God?

Jesus is staring into me and at the same time out beyond the edge of the universe and telling me not to forget the kinship of the two, the kinship of us all, because the all-encompassing Eternal also dwells in each of us. The kingdom of God is within us, each of us.

A flash! as of a strobe – intense, riveting, clear, momentary, filling the mind's eye even as the image fades to a dark orb wandering across the consciousness, then gone. It is an apprehension. It eludes the very language that enables me to become self-aware, to explore interior reality, where God seems to wait with bemused, eternal patience for my moment of recognition.

My response cannot be described as fear or awe but as gratitude for a parent's loving concern – which I can feel deeply now that I, too, am a parent. I am filled with a mystical sense of meaning. What we see daily obscures a reality beyond, but it reflects that reality. For this briefest of moments, I see more clearly than my rational brain can register that the Eternal, what I call God, is in everything around me. It is in me as it is in that human being pictured above the altar. We humans become special animals in God's eyes when we feel God's presence in our lives and the lives around us and gratefully acknowledge this gift.

In the pew, lost in these thoughts, my brain seemed to waken to the danger of being swept away in my own contemplation. My soul, whatever that might be, could fall gently, like a feather, into self-absorption – as much a sin as any that cuts us off from God. I had to get out of this wonderful but human-contrived sanctuary and reconnect to the mundane natural world, where I could more clearly see the daily reflection of the Eternal. Churches uplift me, they recalibrate my consciousness, but inside them, I cannot see the sky.

∞

I stepped outside and took a deep breath in the warm sunshine. Without pausing to ruminate further, I walked next door to a small, single-storey blue house belonging to the Catholic Diocese of Churchill. It was the Eskimo Museum. Inside I found one very large room filled with glass cases tastefully displaying artifacts of Inuit life. There were implements of everyday traditional life – clothing, cooking utensils, hunting and fishing tools, kayaks, sleds, harnesses. The displays included stuffed specimens of the animals important to the Inuit – polar bear, arctic fox, walrus, seals and others. There were carvings of animals and hunters, depicting the dangers of their combat, and carvings of unknown but clearly spiritual significance. There were more modern, exquisitely artistic carvings in soapstone and walrus ivory. And many old photographs on the walls, showing just how gritty were the lives of the Inuit, with the same feel as old photos of mining camps or logging operations in 19th-century California.

I quickly reviewed all this and thought it interesting, but what really caught my attention were two maps. One showed the boundaries of the Diocese of Churchill (not the Archdiocese, mind you). It stretches far to the north to include all the districts of Keewatin and Franklin, virtually the whole of the Canadian Arctic Archipelago, an area roughly one third the size of the Lower 48 of the United States! I was amazed by the thought of this tiny church next door being the "cathedral" for such a vast region. Not that Catholics are such a minority here. The only other notable church in town was the Anglican, equally tiny but far less well tended. No, this map of the diocese just reflected how nearly empty of human souls the North really is.

There are many more communities identified on the map than I would have guessed beforehand, but none of them even approaches Churchill's town-size population. Eskimos did not, could not, live in communities of any size, not as hunter-gatherers of the Arctic. There are no more than 30,000 of them in Canada even today, I estimate. With the map were some print articles that set my mind to imagining circuit-riding priests setting out from Churchill for months of travelling laboriously, perilously between the rare concentrations of Inuit people, ministering to their spiritual lives and observing their traditional lives. The priests of this diocese must have been adventurer-anthropologists, collecting experiences, stories, images and artifacts of these people and accumulating such a treasure chest of items that a museum seemed the logical next step to honour their flock for what they were, even as these priests tried to persuade them of the merits of a different way to be.

That would be the kinder, gentler version of Arctic history. Others would say the priests set out to systematically destroy Inuit culture. With the sanction of a government policy of "assimilation," the Catholic church, and other Canadian churches, took Inuit children away from their homes to place them in faraway schools that taught only the language and ways of the white Canadian world, cutting them off from their families, their culture and their heritage. The personal suffering and long-term psychological effects must have been enormous. "Re-education camps," the North Vietnamese might have called these schools, but the comparison would be grossly unfair. The intentions were probably good in the context of the times, even if monumentally wrong-headed and counterproductive in hindsight.

I heard this ugly side of the story from a Canadian graduate student at Cornell. He had just graduated from Queen's University in Kingston, Ontario, and was considered a genius by his classmates. So I listened carefully when he took exception to a remark I made about Canada having a relatively good record of treatment of its native peoples. I had been taking a course in applied anthropology, for which I had written an in-depth paper on the fate of Aborigines at the hands of Europeans moving into and dominating Australia. I had done some comparison with the treatment of Native people at the hands of similar European settlers in North America, New Zealand and South Africa, and had concluded that the Native peoples of Canada had fared relatively well (that is, a smaller proportion of their population was butchered or displaced through warfare or treachery). My friend could offer no additional evidence to what my cursory research had found, but he was determined to show that his nation should hang its head in shame. I thought his insistent *mea culpa* for Canada lent a strangely fashionable elegance to the whole notion of collective guilt. In a reactive and perverse sort of American one-upmanship, I assured him that Canada's burden of guilt could not hold a candle to the guilt we Americans should feel for our historic misdeeds.

What conflicting emotions and motives had driven the creation of this unique Eskimo Museum?

The other map was of the new nation-within-a-nation, Nunavut, which in April 1999 would become a semi-autonomous territory of Canada, governed by its mostly Inuit residents from a government seat at Iqaluit on Baffin Island. Nunavut covers almost the same area as the Diocese of Churchill, but excludes Churchill and all other parts of Manitoba. It is administratively carved from the Arctic territories – all of Keewatin and Franklin and a minor part of Mackenzie. It does not include the greater watershed of the Mackenzie River, which is mostly forested and peopled by non-Inuit Aboriginals and white Canadians – ecologically and ethnically distinct from Nunavut.

I supposed some inspirational Inuit leaders had caught the federal government at a historic moment, after the rise of guilty sympathy among Canadian opinion leaders and before the full bloom of public resentment of the financial burden of subsidizing not only the very existence of these remote outposts but also the elaboration of their machinery of self-government. The right thing to do, surely, but at such cost? Can Canada afford, others ask, *not* to maintain a population and government apparatus in its frozen

North, even if by Inuit proxy? Such may be the conflicting emotions and motives in this unique new "nation."

I wondered at the impacts of Nunavut on the Inuit and on Churchill. There was no prideful mention of it by the young men I'd met. There was no local newspaper that I could find, not even a newsletter by or for Churchillians, so I could not gauge sentiment that way. I would later ask a couple of white Canadian residents what effect the creation of Nunavut might have on their town. It had already lost the administrative offices for Keewatin District to Rankin Inlet. There was some talk of the health clinic moving north as well. But I got little reaction or depth of feeling, just a sort of verbal shrug. Perhaps Churchill is secure in its status as gateway to Nunavut, even located outside the new nation – by virtue of the lack of options. Discovery of the map of the Diocese of Churchill opened my eyes to its status as gateway to a different, exotic world of humanity, just as it is to the exotic world of Arctic tundra and ice.

I was intrigued by the idea of being on the frontier of a vast and nearly empty Arctic nation, with so many unique features, even a recently invented script for its Inuit language.

I examined the books and postcards and artwork for sale by the Museum, hoping for something in tune with this theme of Arctic nationhood. Nothing acknowledged the advent of a new nation-within-a-nation except the lone map, which was not for sale. And nothing captured my own experience of Churchill in June. The polar bear and other large mammals that I hadn't seen, and would not likely see, were the dominant themes of Inuit art. Winter scenes and polar bears dominated Churchill's postcard imagery, reflecting the real attraction for most people seeking this destination.

I wandered out into the sunshine again and down the Museum steps. I looked back at the church with some new perspective on this little "cathedral." I thought it might be time to forgive the perversions created by the distinctively human chatter of our terribly flawed institutions, and time, I hoped for my son, to look forward. Each life is a new beginning, a fresh start in the confrontation of Good and Evil.

Looking at the steeple of the odd little church, I thought again of my mystical moment in the front pew. Such experiences are very brief for me and usually occur in the natural world, where the Eternal seems more visible to my mind's eye. In churches, ironically, I tend to be more rational than mystical as I try to figure my way through the paradoxes. I often attend Catholic mass with my wife and my son. My love for them, mingled with respect for spiritual feeling, leads me to want to understand and even believe. But it is difficult.

It is one thing to admit the plausibility of the Christian story, as I now do. It is quite another to hold it to be Truth. I cannot yet let go of the possibility that the story is *not* true, in all its particulars at least. People born to the faith don't comprehend how difficult it is to make the leap from "implausible" to "plausible." It is painful to abandon intellectual pride enough to vault the chasm between the two states of mind. Still teetering precariously on the far edge of the chasm, I need time to regain my footing and balance. I must marvel a while at my feat before moving on, away from the chasm, perhaps striding forward toward accepting the details of the story one by one.

Is there a way to reconcile the liturgy of the Mass with my "naturalistic" world view? It seems to be a stretch. The words are spoken so literally. They reflect an anthropocentric culture in which nature is walled off from God and humanity. Only the Christ and his bishops and priests can offer a bridge from the material to the spiritual world. This seems too human.

My wife assures me that I try too hard, that Catholics treat all this with great subtlety and nuance. Roman Catholicism embraces a great variety of spiritual experience and thought, even within a rigid doctrinal framework: yet another paradox to sort out. There is also an authenticity in this church, because of the historical continuity from the Apostles to the present leaders. Continuity has enabled accumulation of the fruits of contemplation, an evolution of spirituality, as a succession of people have found union with God and have inspired others to follow them toward that union.

It takes great patience and goodwill to see through the disturbing history and ongoing rigidity of this and other religions to appreciate the glorious evolution in human experience of the spiritual world. It is to be admired and respected. It inspires me to find personal meaning in the Mass. I understand the Trinity as multiple dimensions of the Eternal – as God the origin of all, as the human manifestation of God, and as God the Spirit that animates all things in the universe. We wanted to murder God in Jesus, but found that God cannot be killed. We sin by willfully cutting ourselves off from the life of Spirit. Replacing this lifeline to God with our own mental chatter, often dressed up as Reason, we plunge into the hell of our own making. But the spirit of God cannot be denied its life within us. We have the option to allow this spirit to fortify us and to use our free will to return and rise above that hell. Like the moon reflecting the sun, we can turn our souls toward God and let them reflect the divine light outward and inward.

I still cannot bring myself to say the Nicene Creed with others in the congregation, much less join them in holy communion. But I feel fellowship with them as they seek union with God through the consecrated bread and wine: "Lord, I am not worthy to receive you, but only say the word and I shall be healed." I feel uplifted by the fellowship of people taking time from busy lives to do this in memory of Jesus, the human being who embodies the divine way for us all. I feel they are joining me in recognizing and honouring the pre-eminence of God.

All these awkward words and symbols are the creations of people, though they may have been truly inspired by God in some mystical way. My elite peers who scorn religion see only these mnemonic devices and miss the meaning of religious observance, just as they look at the daily sky and fail to see beyond to the universe. They do not realize that some, certainly not all, of these people who attend religious services are looking beyond to something greater, more important than themselves. Humbled in prayer, each is personally aware of a spiritual kinship with God and all God's creation. If only for a moment each, their eyes return the loving gaze of God.

Is this blind faith, unencumbered by supporting logic and evidence? Perhaps, but it seems possible to be rationally irrational. We all seem to yield to a blind faith in something. For the post-Enlightenment cultural elite, it is blind faith in the validity of human reason. The danger lies in stopping there. If we believe only in the self-sufficiency of the human species, without reference to anything outside of ourselves and what we can control, then we have no anchor to keep us from drifting off in the fog of our collective mental chatter.

In that fog, we create ideologies to solve social problems, right historical wrongs, and create all-encompassing explanations – nationalism, communism, capitalism, socialism, secular humanism, all the theologies and philosophies. Such "complete" systems of thought have incredible power over their adherents. It is a pity their often noble origins are easily contorted. Ideology can be used to justify and reinforce all manner of human weakness – hatred, obsession, greed, fear – descending too often into warfare, terrorism, murder, rape, extreme sexual perversion, child abuse and molestation, infanticide, slavery, genocide, physical and psychological torture of entire classes of people. Lazy indifference and self-absorption allow us to tolerate the antecedents and underpinnings of these evils.

What is the antidote or restraint to such personal and collective annihilation, if not consciousness of our personal and collective spiritual kinship with God and thus each other? Is this spiritual kinship the essence of the Moral Authority beyond human invention? My blind faith is that this must be so. The problem is to bring this Moral Authority down into the daily routine of life. Who among us is allowed to interpret this eternal morality for our mundane world?

Who better than those whose eyes have most clearly seen God, those whose beings most nearly personify God? Without equating them, I regard Moses, the Buddha, Jesus, Mohammed, and others before and after as showing the Way mandated for human beings to follow. Religious institutions built in their wake have served to remind billions of people of their message and the eternal Moral Authority from which it came. Not surprisingly, their individual messages, in their essence, are very similar, reflecting a common origin in full awareness of the Eternal. When we abandon these religious institutions, but more especially our reverence for the messages their messengers have brought to us, we are alone with our mental chatter and perched precariously on a terrible, slippery slope.

Still, I ask, what is the relevance of this Moral Authority to nature? How do they relate to each other?

☙

I left the church and the museum and ambled past the offices of the Royal Canadian Mounted Police, the Royal Bank of Canada and Canada Post: all very utilitarian, looking quite new and surrounded by the dominant landscaping motif – naked, gravelly ground. I walked down a street toward the Highway, noting on each side the closely packed row of small boxy houses of nearly identical design but painted various subdued colours – gray-blue or dark green or dark reddish-brown. The lack of municipal attention to landscaping had not deterred all homeowners. Here and there a tiny yard had a tasteful arrangement of rocks with perhaps a small evergreen or two struggling to survive.

An unusual feature of many houses was an uncovered, elevated entry porch reached from the ground by wooden steps; a small, detached toolshed-like structure stood on the outer edge of the porch, with a small roof slanting away from the house and a door facing the door into the house. This porch-and-shed arrangement, which I'd never seen before, was so common here that I presumed it to be an adaptation to the harsh winters, but I couldn't imagine what purpose it might serve. The shed was not big enough to house a small vehicle, like a snowmobile, nor did it seem the right size and shape to store firewood. I wanted to ask someone, but the right moment never came. I suppose I was reluctant to ask for fear of appearing to be the naive tourist that I was. Later I learned, from someone who knows Alaska, that these sheds were probably outhouses! The permafrost makes sewer systems and connections expensive, if not impossible.

From the Highway, I was surprised to notice for the first time that Churchill had a central square. It was a wide parade ground, with an evident but largely unsuccessful attempt to get some grass to grow like a lawn. It sloped gently up from the Highway to the massive black Town Centre, flanked by the large red-brown Royal Bank building on one side and the sky-blue Royal Canadian Legion hall on the other. On the Highway, the warehouse-like Northern store anchored one corner of the square, and the rather small Chamber of Commerce information kiosk defined the other corner. Between the two and facing the Highway was a lovely sculpture – a dark-green polar bear playing with a nearly grown cub. They appeared to be made of bronze, resting on a block of granite. With better landscaping, this whimsical centrepiece of the town could be a real treasure, but the whole setting had the forlorn charm of a vacant lot.

Across the Highway and a little way beyond the central square was a small stand-alone building housing Northern Images. Through the screen door, I found the very small front room jammed with a great quantity and variety of Inuit art. The white Canadian shopkeeper was engrossed in conversation with a white Canadian couple in their 50s. That left me to browse the inventory for many minutes while eavesdropping. The couple, from Penticton, British Columbia, were aficionados of Inuit art, and had their own collection of rare Dorset pieces. The store offered paintings, jewellery, weavings, clothing and black soapstone carvings. Most everything was very expensive, so I was not inclined to buy, unless I came across something that really caught my fancy.

I was drawn to the black soapstone figures of bears, seals, walruses and whales, because I had heard about these in particular, and now I had met one of the carvers. The price labels identified the individual carvers and their home villages. George Noah had several pieces here, of distinctive style. I liked his work better than the others on display. His seemed a cruder style, less polished than the others, but I liked his choice of animal subjects and the playful way he posed them. Even so, I couldn't bring myself to buy his or any other soapstone piece. I have several African and some Native American carvings, mostly in wood, and one light-coloured soapstone, picked up during many trips. My first thought had been that an Inuit piece might be a nice addition. But these soapstone carvings seemed too featurelessly smooth and bulky for my taste. I couldn't get excited about paying more than a hundred dollars and then lugging one of these all the way back to California perhaps only to decide that it wasn't all that attractive. I turned my attention to the many more affordable trinket-type items, hoping to find some little presents for my wife and son. After a while, but still spared the shopkeeper's attention by the talkative B.C. couple, I slipped out of the store without making a purchase.

I decided to try the Arctic Trading Company just across the Highway and a couple of blocks toward the Port, almost to my hotel. It was in an interesting American West saloon–style building with boardwalk and all. I entered and was surprised to see behind the counter the tall, interesting-looking waitress from my first meal at the Churchill Motel Restaurant. And she clearly recognized me, too. She smiled warmly and said hello. I told her I remembered her from the restaurant and guessed that she must be working more than one job. She said she worked three jobs. I wanted to, but I didn't, use the opportunity to ask her more about herself – like what brought her to Churchill and how long ago – and about Churchill – what does she think about this new Nunavut nation, and what are those sheds on people's porches. There was no one else in the store, and I was in no hurry. I had a feeling that she would have been pleased to chat. Perhaps because I found her attractive, I hesitated – as though I might be opening a door I shouldn't go through. I felt pretty bold for having referred to seeing her before. But when she asked if there was anything in particular I was looking for, I said, "No, I'd just like to look around."

The Arctic Trading Company had the feel of an old-style emporium or variety store. It was much bigger inside than the Northern Images store, divided into sub-rooms, all just as packed with merchandise. There were Inuit carvings and other artwork here as well, though not as broad a selection. But there was a whole lot more in the way of clothing and miscellaneous household goods and souvenir items. I focused on buying a sweatshirt or T-shirt for my son. I made it a project to examine all the designs and styles. Lots of polar bears and wolves and walruses, but I wanted something that could also serve me as a souvenir of *my* experience whenever I saw my son wearing it. Perhaps a gull or a sandpiper or a Gray Jay. I finally found a very pleasing, rather abstract rendition of Canada Geese flying over water and spruces, which certainly reflected my experience. I asked the young woman for advice on size for a seven-year-old, found the right size and colour of T-shirt and made my purchase. I also bought a small sticker sign of fluorescent orange colour with the words "Polar Bear Alert – STOP – Don't Walk in This Area." Just the thing for a small boy's room.

∞

I ended up at the Churchill Motel Restaurant for dinner. It was crowded again, but I got the same pleasant table by the window. Arctic char was the dinner special – probably the same shipment by air yesterday from Chesterfield Inlet. I happily ordered the special and relaxed with a beer and Leonard Nathan's book.

Afterward I was off to Cape Merry, driving the blue truck for the first time today. It was pleasant weather still, mostly cloudy now and cooling down, but little wind. The long hours of lovely oblique evening light had already settled in by seven o'clock.

I stopped along the way, where the road to the Cape comes closest to the shore of the bay. I had stopped here on my first evening and hiked a bit to get close enough to photograph the ice blocks jammed against the shore. It was a spectacular scene, brooding in wind-blown fog. This evening was very different, not only because of the weather but because there was an expanse of open blue water between the shore and the ice. This was not due to a higher tide. The water reached the same rock as before, but the ice was no longer jammed against the rock; it was many metres offshore. Again, I jumped to the conclusion that these warm days in the 70s Fahrenheit had melted huge blocks of ice. I had to document this remarkable phenomenon with another round of photos from the same vantage point.

Even as I took the photos, I started on another hypothesis. Maybe the southwest wind of the past three days was the real agent of change, not the warmth. Light as the wind was, it had been directly and steadily blowing offshore and could have gradually pushed the ice blocks farther out into the bay. That would be a lot of weight shifting about! I wasn't sure which cause was more remarkable, the melting or the shifting. It was hard to believe that even both working together could make such a difference in the scene before me.

I drove on to the parking area at the end of the road, where there was a Parks Canada information kiosk. The maple leaf flag flapped languidly in the light breeze above the large sign warning of polar bears and giving the phone number to call to report a sighting or problem. A pay phone stood right next to the sign. Wooden stairs and a short boardwalk led up and onto the outcropping rocks ground smooth and fluted by massive, moving ice of the recent past. This field of strange rock had many cracks, channels and hollows filled with spongy vegetation and pools of water interrupting the smooth flow of rock from the kiosk to the tip of Cape Merry itself, perhaps half a kilometre. It looked at first like an easy walk, but in fact it was a challenging hike across broken terrain.

As I set out for the Cape, I saw a man, short, broad in the shoulders, with a moustache and one of those British driving caps that golfers used to wear, the crown pulled forward and fixed over the visor. With him was a small boy who reminded me of my son. They were walking from the other side of the Artillery Battery, a small fort of low stone walls and two old cannons facing out on the Churchill River. They stepped carefully while examining the ground. From a good 10 metres away, the man called to me, "There's a huge moth here!" I stopped in surprise and looked over in time to see something the size of a large rodent dash away from their feet. My impulse was to join them, but their absorption with the moth seemed complete. It was an alert, not an invitation. I continued on with a simple "Yes, I saw it!"

I had to stop again soon after to survey the lay of the rocky land and mentally map my route. I zigged and zagged, climbed up, jumped down, skirted clear pools and stepped lightly across soft ground. I emerged from a hollow onto a tableland of planed rock surfaces in time to see in the near distance a spaniel-sized brown mammal loping away. It had to cross a distance over the barren rock, sufficient to allow a good long look through the binoculars before it disappeared into a hollow of its own. I took a moment to recognize it as a hare. The ears were upright but rather short relative to the large, compact body. But the legs were long enough in the rear to elevate its rump slightly above its forequarters, creating the distinctive loping gait of a hare in no great hurry. The white rump and white legs, as well as its size, told me I was watching an Arctic hare. I hadn't expected the species to be so large, nor out here on the rocky edge of the ocean.

I headed toward where the hare had disappeared, in case it might give me another look. It was soon obvious that I couldn't hope to follow in the maze of crevices in the rocks. The hare was gone, but I wasn't disappointed. In fact, I was elated by this sighting of a mammal distinctly of the Arctic. From the beginning of the trip, I knew that seeing any large mammals would be a bonus, depending on good luck. Of course, I did my best to give luck a hand, keeping my eyes sharpened for an arctic hare, an arctic fox, a caribou, a beluga, perhaps even a polar bear. Not counting the distant seals on the ice and the unexpected but familiar muskrat and red squirrels, this was my first lucky chance to see one of the Arctic mammals on my hope-to-see list.

I could have called it an evening and felt well rewarded, but I had a particular mission. I wanted to take advantage of this warm evening to carefully survey the ice-clogged river mouth for signs of beluga and jaegers – with the real possibility of a rare gull or two. I was also drawn to the tip of Cape Merry by the majesty of the ice on parade. There, at the edge of the terrestrial world, alone with the elemental rock, water, sky, wind and ice, I could be anywhere in the high Arctic. The declining sun cast cold light on all as it passed behind thickening streamers of cloud. The invisible moon withdrew the tide, pulling enormous ice floes downriver into Hudson Bay in unhurried, grand, implacable procession.

There was nothing in view to mark the arrival of humans except the low, dark wall of the 18th-century Prince of Wales' Fort on the far shore. And there was little evidence of the arrival of life, except the rock lichens and the gulls and terns riding the ice floes and the eider ducks floating in between. Like me, the birds could be visitors from a different world, with no intention or capability of permanence.

I approached as close as possible to where the rocks sloped into the water and I could still maintain some elevation for a good view over the ice floes. I extended the legs of the tripod and scope and set up on a level table of rock. The many birds close enough for binocular identification were the species rapidly becoming the "usual suspects" out here – Arctic Terns, Herring Gulls, Ring-billed Gulls, Bonaparte's Gulls, Common Eiders and a few Red-breasted Mergansers and Oldsquaw. Now it was time to work on the dark specks in the distance and hope that a whale might surprise me.

Some specks were darker than others, and to these I paid special attention. I was in determined pursuit of my first jaeger

– "hunter" in German. I was hunting the hunter. Earlier that day, I reread the chapter on jaegers in Kenn Kaufman's *Advanced Birding*. There are three species in North America, and they are easily confused by someone unfamiliar with the group. It is for groups of species like these that I highly value Kaufman's book. He emphasizes differences in body shapes and proportions, which are less variable by age and season than colour, pattern and lengths of feathers. If you look at the pictures of jaegers in standard bird guides, you think they can be distinguished by their "characteristic" central tail feathers. Not so, unless you see the species together and fairly close up. So I was using the scope to examine dark specks for shape and proportional size of head and body and tail. The dark specks were sitting on steadily moving ice floes often passing behind blocks of fast ice. One ice floe collapsed with a dull boom, disintegrating into many small pieces and scaring my speck into flight to another perch beyond my view. This was a challenge for the birder in me.

By now I had my eyes trained on three suspected-jaeger specks sitting on floe ice and receding slowly into the distance, out to sea. While I was becoming confident that they were jaegers, I began to despair of identifying them to species. Then one took off in rapid direct flight. Soon it was in hot pursuit of an Arctic Tern, twisting and turning with amazing speed and agility for a gull-sized bird. I had read that jaegers target the terns in the tern breeding season, when male terns are carrying small fish to show off and feed to their mates. The jaeger will chase the tern until it drops the fish to avoid being pecked by the jaeger's long, hooked beak. The jaeger snaps up the fish in free fall. What a way to make a living!

This chase behaviour was sufficient to confirm the bird as a jaeger. While flying, the bird showed enough of its tail to convince me it was a Parasitic Jaeger. Confidence in that identification was bolstered by its shape and by the knowledge from Bonnie's book that by far the most commonly seen jaeger in the area is the Parasitic Jaeger. I'm not sure why it is called "parasitic": presumably not because of "nest parasitism" (laying eggs in the nests of other species, which mistakenly raise the offspring of the parasitic species); probably because of the harassing-and-stealing behaviour I'd just witnessed. If jaegers depend on the terns to do at least some fishing for them, it made sense that I hadn't seen any jaegers until now. The Winnipeg birders had told me on my first day that the terns had just arrived, so the jaegers would naturally follow the terns' schedule with a few days of lag time.

I'm usually at a loss to explain to non-birders the emotional significance of seeing a long-sought species. But some are easier to explain than others. Jaegers are a type unto themselves – an unusual way of life, a seldom-seen dweller in exotic reaches of the Earth, an intriguing name. They are unusual looking, even beautiful in their fierce way. To see a jaeger, even once, is a birder's dream.

How good a look did I get? Not great. I was hungry for a better look and kept watching the jaegers for another half hour. There were a few more one-sided dogfights with terns and some social interaction between the jaegers on the floe ice, enough to further confirm my identification, but they remained far out on the river. I was resigned to not seeing them well, but in no way was I unhappy. I had seen Parasitic Jaegers, all right, and had observed them doing their thing.

Contentment was mine as I relaxed and absorbed this otherworld scene of rock and water, cloud and ice. I had hunted and caught the hunter. Now I could just sit for a while and digest the experience, observing the slow ending of a very fine subarctic day.

7

On the Water
June 10

Pacific Loon

It was another leisurely morning. My boat trip wouldn't begin until 11 o'clock. I was to report for transport to the boat from a house across the road from my hotel, right behind where I had parked my truck. I could walk door to door in two minutes. Around nine o'clock I came down the stairs from my loft and peeked out between the still-closed curtains to check what the weather had in store for me on the water.

The sky was the colour of lead, a lowering ceiling of thick, rain-filled clouds. It looked cold, but there was little wind. I could deal with a cold rain if the wind would give us a break. I had wanted a change of weather more in keeping with my Arctic expectations. Here it was! But I hadn't expected to be out on the water in it. I was mentally committed now and that was that. Still, the weather added an edge of apprehension to the adventure.

I considered how best to dress, remembering a boat trip from San Francisco out to the Farallon Islands and beyond, most of a day on the open ocean, for whale and seabird watching. That was mid-October, when the Pacific Ocean off California was supposed to be at its annual warmest, and I wore almost every article of winter clothing I had in my possession. Still, I was just plain COLD!

I would wear my lighter Polartec jacket with undershirt, long-sleeved shirt and light wool sweater underneath, and then suit up with my hooded Gore-Tex rain pullover once we reached the boat. I would also carry my ski jacket along in case I needed to do a swap with the lighter jacket. The outstanding problem was my legs. I didn't have rain pants. But I had discovered earlier in the year, while birding in January wind and drizzle, that I could wear my baggy khaki pants over tighter blue jeans and be comfortably warm and dry around the legs all day long. So that's what I would do. I would also wear my fur-lined leather gloves and thick wool ski cap.

I was ready for the day, whatever it would bring.

A couple of minutes before eleven o'clock, I arrived at the appointed house. I was surprised to find the blue-and-white Bluebird (a.k.a. "school") bus, with "Churchill Wilderness Encounter" painted on the sides, parked in front of the sign reading "Sea North Tours." Puzzled, I walked past the bus and into the driveway, where there were three people standing, waiting, two of them looking at least as bundled up as I was. I nodded and joined them, stiffly. After a moment, I recognized the third, more lightly dressed one as the short, broad-shouldered man with the British driving cap whom I had encountered last evening at Cape Merry. He seemed to be in charge, so I went up to him and asked, "Are you Mike?"

"No, I'm Paul. Mike is down at the boat." He explained that he would take the group down in the bus to the boat once we were all assembled. I asked about the connection of the Churchill Wilderness Encounter bus to Sea North Tours. It seemed they work together pretty closely. One for the land, the other for the water, with a bus and some of their clients in common.

Paul directed me into a side door of the house. Inside was a tiny standing area in front of a small counter, behind which a middle-aged, friendly woman with glasses was seated. There was a kitchen or utility room behind her. I assumed she was Mike's wife, taking the money for the tour. I gave her my name, and she found it on the paper in front of her.

"I owe you $49, right?"

"Yes, that's right." I gave her a Canadian $50 bill, and she gave me back a loonie, the Canadian $1 coin with a loon's image on one side and the Queen on the other. Pocketing the coin with thanks, I stepped back outside. It had started to rain lightly. Paul came up to me with hands stuck in his pockets against the chill and wet, clad only in a short-sleeved shirt and vest.

"Weren't you out at Cape Merry yesterday evening?" Paul asked with inviting interest.

"Yes, I remember you, too. You called my attention to a huge moth. If you hadn't told me what it was, I would have guessed it was some sort of rodent dashing away from you." He made me feel like conversing.

"I'd never seen such a big moth! My son and I were out there at the Cape looking for Harlequin Ducks, and we just stumbled on this thing sitting right on the path."

Sensing that I was in the presence of someone who knew his birds, I changed the subject. "Is Cape Merry a particularly good place to look for Harlequin Ducks? Did you see any?"

Paul laughed in a wonderfully encouraging way. "No! But if they're around, you usually see the Harlequins right in close to the rocks there. What did you see out there? Anything unusual?"

I told him about the Arctic hare and the Parasitic Jaegers. He nodded and smiled approvingly.

"Do you know the birds around here pretty well?" I asked.

"Oh, yeah. I'm a what you might call an 'avid' birder." There was a twinkle in Paul's eyes. So I started asking him about the local birds. He knew a lot without being overwhelming.

"Would you expect to see Bohemian Waxwings this time of year?" I probed tentatively.

"Oh, sure – at Twin Lakes. They're not always easy to find. I saw some a few days ago out there." I told him of my failed attempt to find them there. He directed me to a clump of poplars ("aspens" to me).

"You know where the burn area is?"

"Yes, I was there."

"Okay, so you saw there are lots of bulldozer cuts made when they were fighting the fire last year. It gets pretty confusing, but you follow the real road that goes west through the burn for about 2 kilometres and you come to a large pond and a grove of poplars that were spared by the fire for some reason. The waxwings like poplars. I've seen them in those trees reliably several years now."

"Great! I'll go out there and try again." I was grateful for this intelligence. Immediately, I knew that Twin Lakes would be my destination tomorrow, my last full day of birding. I had the Twin Lakes area in mind anyway, and this news served to confirm the plan.

I went on to ask about other animals, like caribou – where and when to look and the likelihood of seeing them.

"You can see them anywhere, anytime – usually very early in the morning. Just a couple of days ago, a single caribou was standing right out in the middle of the Highway out by the airport."

I filed that information away and turned my interest to Paul himself; I found out that he helps Mike with his boat trips but also runs his own tour operation. It was his van I saw out at Twin Lakes and his partner with a Japanese couple as walking clients. I asked about the high-powered rifle his partner was carrying.

"Is the rifle just for effect or is there a real threat that requires a rifle?" I asked.

"Oh, sure! Polar bears can show up anywhere any time of year. It's not likely you'd see a polar bear this time of year, especially that far inland, but it's been known to happen." Paul was quite serious.

I fell silent for a solemn moment, realizing my own vulnerability when out by myself, but it was a fleeting moment. I don't know why, but I wasn't bothered by the thought of running into a polar bear when my truck was only a speck in the distance. I should be so lucky, I thought. I guess my mind was figuring the odds were too slim to worry about.

I got to the standard questions. Paul was from somewhere near Winnipeg and had been knocking around the Canadian Arctic for many years. Among other jobs, he had worked for the Northern stores, including a stint as store manager in Resolute. That took my breath away. "Wow, you were Way Up There!" Paul agreed with a big laugh and led me to believe that Churchill was easy duty by comparison. Resolute is nearly 75°N, close to the North Magnetic Pole and much farther from Churchill than Winnipeg is. What a location for a retail outlet!

Before I could inquire about life in Resolute, others had arrived and paid, and it was time to get on the bus and for Paul to become our guide and driver. With binoculars around my neck, camera in its case on my belt, and ski jacket and rain pullover bundled under my arm, I climbed aboard and squeezed into a kid-size bench seat. There wasn't enough legroom to sit straight ahead, so I squeezed in sideways with my back to the window and an awkward smile facing my fellow passengers. Paul closed the door the way the school-bus drivers of my youth used to do, pulling the chrome handle toward him, and we were off for the Port and the Churchill River.

I recognized the couple from Penticton, B.C., whom I'd seen in the Northern Images shop yesterday afternoon. They boarded the bus last, attending to a tall but unsteady bent-over elderly man. I realized this might be the man they had been talking about with the shopkeeper yesterday. I gathered they had picked him up in Thompson and brought him with them to Churchill on a sentimental journey to visit the haunts of his robust adulthood. The shopkeeper seemed to know the man as well. The couple had mentioned a date with their friend later that afternoon, because he wanted them to see "his dogs" (possibly the sled dogs I'd seen on my second day here). On the bus, Paul bantered with him as though he, too, knew the elderly man.

Also on the bus were two more couples about my age and three young adults, a guy and two gals, all in their 20s. As we travelled, they talked, and I mostly listened. I learned that one of the couples was from Michigan. Everyone else seemed to be Canadian. The young people were nursing staff from the health centre in Churchill, all from Winnipeg or nearby, and all had arrived to start work in January or February. This would be their first outing on the river, probably because it had been too cold and the river too frozen until the last few days. One of the young women had an angular, olive, strikingly attractive face framed by straight black hair. I decided after a few thoughtful glances that she must be Aboriginal. Her distinctly Anglo female companion was not as pretty but considerably less shy and easier to engage in conversation.

The bus passed by the train station, the flatbed rail cars with semi-truck trailers still on top waiting for onward shipping to the North, and the huge white "tundra buggies" parked for the summer, some undergoing repairs. One of my companions explained to the others that in winter the longest of these long white vehicles, looking like mobile homes on giant rubber tires, would be rolled out onto the frozen tundra where the polar bears hang out, and hooked together like a train to create a hotel on the tundra, to which other, smaller tundra buggies would ferry tourists for overnight or longer stays among the polar bears. I was amazed that the polar bear viewing industry had developed to such a level of comfort and convenience. October was the month to come: a good time as well to observe the aurora borealis. It sounds tempting – great white bears prowling the snowy landscape illuminated by the pulsing, dancing Northern Lights. I had seen a very memorable display of the aurora borealis from my home in Connecticut in the early 1960s, very rare that far south. The prospect of seeing again this weird, enchanting phenomenon made the idea of visiting Churchill in the winter almost attractive. The bears by themselves wouldn't be enough to bring me, but if the idea excited my wife and son, and I could be guaranteed to see the Northern Lights again, I might be persuaded. Maybe.

We rolled past the grain elevator complex on the left and the Granary Ponds on the right and down a road to the north end of the Port, which is off limits to the general public. The bus approached a cove with a pebble-and-cobblestone beach, and we came to a stop alongside the steel boat I recognized from the Sea North Tours brochure. The problem was that the boat was hauled up on a boat trailer, waiting for Coast Guard inspection, we were told. Where was our boat for the day, I wondered. The advertised boat had a cabin in which one could shelter from the rain, if need be. The only alternative in sight was a black Zodiac inflatable raft fitted with a large outboard motor, pulled up to the shore next to a man in a rain slicker, wool fisherman's hat, and high rubber boots, standing expectantly. I didn't like the look of this. An image formed in my mind of being engulfed by freezing sea spray as we bounced across the water clinging precariously to this oversized life raft. But what to do? No doubt the same imaginings had seized the others; nonetheless, they were getting off the bus after Paul announced, "Here we are!"

The boatman approached the bus as we dismounted. Paul introduced us to Mike. He immediately and warmly greeted the elderly man as "John." It was clear that John was a local celebrity, a long-time Churchillian returning briefly from reluctant exile to civilization. In the manner of a man feeling compelled to joviality, John repeatedly teased Paul and Mike about their long hair, which flowed over their collars from behind their ears and from under their caps. Mike responded that they needed the extra warmth, and besides, there's no barber in Churchill! I wondered, with a bit of shock, if that were true. Could be.

Mike, probably sensing the apprehension of the group, explained that we would be using the Zodiac instead of the big boat. He took care to reassure us that the Zodiac was a very sturdy vessel, made of several layers of the same kind of material used to make bulletproof vests for police officers; no punctures by ice floes were to be feared. He told us that he had two Zodiacs, which cost a remarkable $20,000 each, even without the very large outboard engine. Furthermore, the Zodiac was more manoeuvrable among the ice floes and to be preferred until the ice was mostly gone from the river. I was reassured. In fact, Mike's very face and demeanour were hugely reassuring. I've seldom encountered a man who so immediately elicited trust, even allegiance. He had shy, attractive eyes and an easy, confident voice: a calm, professional presence, in command without commanding. I would have no trouble getting into that Zodiac with Mike operating the outboard in the rear.

Mike and Paul led us over to a shed near the shore, between the dry-docked boat and the beached Zodiac. Mike pulled out rain slickers and life vests, all bright orange. I was the only one who already had a rain pullover; mine was ocean blue and soon covered by the orange vest except for the arms and hood. Everyone else was completely orange, except Paul and Mike. We moved tentatively over to the Zodiac, which Paul and Mike proceeded to wrestle and push out into the water, requiring a jump up and over the shallow water between the beach and the raft. Feeling like I'd done this many times before, I was the first one up and in and made my way to the rear. The others quickly followed, until it came time for John to board. At best, he was very unsteady on his feet. Simply crossing the cobbly beach was a chore that required the balancing assistance of his two companions. There was no option but for him to be cradled by Paul and Mike, both relatively strong and young, 40 at most, and lifted into the raft as they splashed ankle-deep in the water. Paul had only sneakers on, but he seemed cheerfully accustomed to having cold wet feet.

Mike came aboard and rearranged the seating order a bit to assure balance for the raft. It was clear that he could take only 12 people, including himself. I ended up seated to Mike's left as he stood at the outboard tiller-throttle. Paul pushed us off, and we glided gently backward out into the cove. Mike instructed us not to stand up without permission. Then he summarized his plan for the next two hours: up the river a ways to check out the area where he had seen two or three beluga whales the day before, then back down the river, out into the bay, around the Prince of Wales' Fort and into a bay of Hudson Bay just to the west of the river mouth. I hadn't realized that we would get out onto Hudson Bay itself. I was pleased.

Mike started up the outboard motor – a well-muffled purr – and turned us in a graceful arc to head out of the cove. Like ships at anchor, big blocks of eroded fast ice stood high above us as we cruised by and into the wide river. We rode low, only a foot above the water line. This new perspective made the distance to the far shore seem greater than ever. The rain had paused, and the water surface was blessedly smooth, a dark, lustrous gray, like a polished steel deck. The sky was a low, pearl-gray deck of clouds. Only the thin line of the far shore marked the end of one deck and the start of the other. What would have been a dreary scene was saved by the dozens of ice floes, like bright, white jewels scattered across the length and breadth of the vast river.

We sat on the round tube sides of the Zodiac. Lean too far back and in you go! My point-and-shoot camera was on my belt in its case over my right back pocket and inches above the water. Several times during the two-hour voyage I carefully removed the camera for a photo and even more carefully replaced it. The accumulated layers of clothing and life vest made it nearly impossible to look over and down at the camera case, so I had to feel the way back into the case.

I enjoyed the sensation of smooth movement through the water. It was comfortably familiar from all the long hours of crew rowing on Lake Waramaug in Connecticut. Rowing was the only organized sport I took seriously in school. I loved it – but April and even May days in the middle of a good-sized New England lake were too often cold and windy. When even a little wind roughed up the water's surface, it could be grim to try rowing a crew shell with long sweep oars in exact unison with three others. But when the water was like the surface of the river today and when the crew was "clicking" together, the sensation of surge and glide, surge and glide was euphoric. Canoeing on lakes and rivers in central Québec, the rhythmic dip-pull-recover with the paddle could create the same glorious feeling. Even sitting in a slowly cruising boat with a powerful engine gives the feeling of effortless gliding when the water is as smooth as it was this day on the river.

Mike headed us upriver to where he'd seen belugas the day before. He was careful to point out that he saw them only at some distance. Very likely they were not ones that know his boat and so would not let us approach closely. As the days wore further into June, there would be more and more of the white whales coming into the Churchill River. At the peak, there would be up to 3,000 of them in the river, where the females would give birth. But it was early in the season for them, so we could not count on seeing any and most probably not up close.

He asked us to let him know if there was anything in particular we would like to see in addition to the belugas. He would try to accommodate. I asked if he knew the birds pretty well. Not really, he said, only a few of the bigger ones.

"Would you know a jaeger if you saw one?" I asked.

He thought he would. "We often see jaegers out here."

I pronounced the name with a "j" sound, but Mike pronounced it with a "y" sound. Normally I do, too. But I had been thinking to myself that I had no recollection of hearing any reliable source person pronounce it for me. Maybe I was guessing wrong all these years. Choosing the proper German pronunciation is not the same as pronouncing it the way most North American birders would do. It would not be the first time that I had guessed wrong. I asked Mike if the "y" sound was the way he heard most people pronounce the name of the bird. He said yes, he thought so. He pointed out that it was a German word, so it made sense that it should be pronounced "YAY-ger." I agreed.

In this exchange, Mike conversed with the self-effacing modesty of a man whose formal education might be far less than you would expect from his intelligence and breadth of knowledge. This intuition was reinforced later when one of us asked him about the food eaten by belugas. He named an abundant fish, the capelin, as a mainstay of their diet. Someone asked how capelin is spelled. Given the local importance of this fish species, it surprised me when Mike indicated with barely perceptible embarrassment that he didn't know. Having seen the name more than once in Bonnie's book, I knew how to spell it, but I kept quiet. I have an excellent memory for the spelling of words I've seen written down. Some people have a poor memory for spelling. I didn't want to be a smart aleck. This was Mike's show, not mine.

I asked Mike the standard questions. With the noise of the outboard and our proximity to each other, we could have an almost private conversation. He told me he had grown up in Windsor, Ontario, across the river from Detroit. He didn't volunteer many details, but I gathered that after high school he had taken off for a life of bumming around Canada, kicking around from place to place, job to job. He had been in Churchill for about 16 years, and doing the boat tours for about 12.

There was something about this guy that didn't quite fit my image of a local boatman. I could not believe he was working for the money to buy beer and watch television. From a total insufficiency of information, I conjured a personal history and personality for this shy, sensitive, wise-seeming man. I imagined him growing up in a middle-class family with high expectations for their son. A family like my own. He struggled in school with a learning disability, maybe dyslexia, that belied his considerable natural intelligence. His sensitivity to the disappointment of parents and friends in his poor academic performance led him to reject the conventional life and escape to the road as soon as he was free from school. He had found in Churchill a place where he could be himself among others with similarly checkered careers, where he could be judged by his character more than his resume. He had an abiding fascination for this world totally different from the one he grew up in. In short, my version of Mike was a classic figure of the frontier.

I later added to this preposterous musing when I saw the name M. Macri under the photos in the brochures of Sea North Tours and Churchill Wilderness Encounter – very good wildlife photography, including belugas coming right up to the Sea North tour boat. This made me think of Mike as a self-taught photographer of the subarctic, an occupation in keeping with his intelligence and sensitivity, a passion that filled the long frozen months when boating was out of the question. Clearly Mike had intrigued me without giving me enough information, so I filled in the spaces and romanticized our boatman.

Mike warned us that the raft would lift up rather dramatically when he cranked up the speed, which he proceeded to do, so we could make better time now that we were clear of the Port area and the fast-ice obstacle course. Indeed, the raft lifted up, first in the bow to put us at an alarming angle, then in the stern. It was like the raft had transformed into a hovercraft skimming over the water surface. Jump to light speed, Commander. It was exciting!

It didn't take long to get upriver about as far as the Hydro Station. The river was even wider at that point, perhaps a couple of kilometres or more. Mike transformed us back into a slow glider, and I started scanning with my binoculars for whatever I could find. But the woman from Michigan, seated at my left, saw the first beluga. It was well in the distance. Mike headed us toward it, picking up speed only slightly. Soon we all had seen it – a flash of dull white back as the beluga rolled up and forward and down. Having no noticeable dorsal fin, it is a small whale, more the size of a large porpoise. It broke the water surface for only about a second. Not much of a view and quite far away, but there was still something magical about seeing a whale. The popular appeal of whales mystifies me, given how few of us ever see one, and when we do, we see so little, so briefly. But I could sense the excitement of my companions, a feeling of success in this outing, which I shared.

Mike was not satisfied. He gave slow chase to the whale, but he recognized quickly that it wanted nothing to do with us and gave us the underwater slip. He commented that these first belugas of the season are usually not the ones from this river. They don't know his boat like the ones that are born here and return annually. The residents will come right up to the boat, he said wistfully. "What a wonderful experience that must be," I said. He made no comment, but I could tell his relationship with the belugas was very special to him. I resigned myself to missing that experience, another tradeoff I'd made by coming so early in the season. For me, any sighting of a beluga was an unexpected treat. The children's song "Baby Beluga" and its line "a little white whale on the go" drifted through my brain and made me think of how much my son and my wife would love to see these belugas up close and personal. I asked if these non-residents were stopping off en route to their own natal river, such as the Nelson River to the south. Mike thought it was likely, but he made no attempt to present himself as an expert on the species. He simply knew the belugas that belonged to his river, and that was enough for him, I suspect.

I took up the scan with the binoculars again and found a cluster of ducks toward the far shore. Mike could see I was studying something and asked what I had. I told him, and he said, "Let's give you a closer look." With nothing better to do at this point, he was ready to indulge whatever natural history interests his group of the moment might have. We lifted up into hovercraft mode again and were soon close enough for me to make an identification. "What are they?" asked Mike. "Looks like American Mergansers, plus some Surf Scoters and Common Eiders." I first pronounced the name "MERgansers" and then quickly said, "or merGANsers, however it's pronounced." I've heard it both ways. I've been trying to learn from others which is the preferred version. Mike knew exactly what I was talking about, but he didn't repeat the name. He would remain neutral on pronunciation. Others asked what we were looking at, so I repeated the identifications. Silence. Mike could tell he would lose his group if he indulged me too much. If the ducks had been something a little more exciting, he might have persisted. Actually, the American Mergansers were a good find, an addition to my list for the week. But Mike quickly got us moving again, this time back downriver.

He turned our attention to the increasing numbers of ice floes as the river narrowed toward its mouth. We approached one closely and circled around it. Mike pointed out how clean it was compared to the fast ice nearer the Port. It was roughly the shape of an anvil, its top the brightest opaque white. But the interior, which we could see under the anvil's overhang, was a beautifully translucent blue. I would have gone right in under the overhang to peer deeply into this other-worldly glow. Mike fortunately knew better to keep a distance. Just then the ice floe collapsed with a dull crack and boom, sending a shock wave under us and out across the river's expanse. What was one moment a giant chunk of ice about eight feet high above the water was the next moment a ruin of many smaller chunks floating low in the water.

We sat in stunned silence, realizing the falling overhang would have crushed us. It became very clear how dangerous it could be to get too close to these frozen behemoths as they began their early summer disintegration. Now the dull thuds I'd been hearing from the river over the past few days took on more personal meaning.

Mike commented that the ice floes could partially collapse like this one and, having their centre of gravity suddenly shifted, roll completely over. I asked if such a sudden upending of an ice floe ever endangered boats. He said he had never seen it damage a boat, but he didn't rule out the possibility.

After studying the floating shards of ice a while longer, we headed downriver again, carefully skirting the increasingly large and numerous chunks of floe ice. Back into hovercraft mode, we passed the Port facility and headed into the narrow passage between Cape Merry on our starboard side and Prince of Wales' Fort on the port side. Here we slowed to a fast glide again. I could sense that Mike was becoming more vigilant and cautious. I was feeling very relaxed and enjoying the scene. I remarked to Mike that it was pleasant out on the water today – cool but little wind, no rain at the moment. He agreed, seeming to appreciate the comment. Nice that at least one of his customers was enjoying himself.

John, the elder, clearly was not enjoying himself. He seemed to be tiring and unaccountably leaning back, threatening to fall out of the boat. His male companion from Penticton struggled to keep him from going overboard by placing his arm and shoulder behind his back and applying his own strength to counterbalance John's considerable weight. Yet John persisted in leaning back, seemingly unaware of his peril, and his devoted friend kept urging him to lean forward and pushed him from behind toward the boat's interior. Mike was noticing these goings-on, and soon some of the rest of us were visibly concerned. Mike took no action, because the Penticton man seemed to be doing all right. I was concerned for him, however, wondering how long he could keep John propped up. Occasionally, John seemed to recover his equilibrium, giving the younger man a bit of a break for a few minutes at a time, but the trip had become a major chore for both.

Once it was clear that John would not soon be going into the water, I nonchalantly but quietly asked Mike how long a person could last in this water. I was expecting him to say something like three minutes, but instead he indicated that people had been fished out, still alive, after as long as 20 minutes.

The sky was darkening as we entered Hudson Bay itself. We were hemmed in pretty tightly by the ice floes now. There was no change in the water surface, no wave action or ocean swell to speak of. But the air became noticeably colder, as though someone had opened the refrigerator door. Mike acknowledged my comment on the change, as though it was normal. We were seeing Common Eiders in good numbers, up close. The males were striking in their black and white breeding plumage against the dark-gray water.

On the Water: June 10

We were close enough to see clearly the light wash of pastel green on their white necks. Mike admired their hardiness. He described the conditions they could tolerate during winter on the open bay – 40-foot waves and temperatures far below zero Celsius. Tough ducks! Protected by the real thing, eiderdown.

We headed west around the point on which stood the Prince of Wales' Fort. Soon Mike had to slow and then stop. The ice was becoming too much. We were blocked in that direction. He turned us around and headed east past Cape Merry and to the bay side of the town. Soon we were just offshore from the long black structure of the Town Centre. Here we were among big blocks of fast ice with expanses of open calm water between. It was a less menacing place to be in a small inflatable boat.

Mike pointed out how this fast ice stood well above the currently lowering water line, revealing melted caves and pits below the high water mark. The ice contained a great deal of embedded dirt, showing that it had formed near the shore, where there was a good deal of gravel and sand mixed in with the water at freezing time. He reminded us that the fresh water from the river is less dense than the sea water of the bay, so it rides up and over the sea water and also freezes first and floats to the top as ice. Only later does the sea water freeze below. The tops of sea ice blocks can be melted for drinking water. Just as it freezes first, the fresh water on top thaws last. So the ice below the water line melts faster, undermining the block of ice from underneath. Protruding as they do at lower tide, the fast ice blocks often look like fat toadstools, wider at the top than below, where tidal and wave and thawing action have eaten away at the ice.

Mike said we might find Harlequin Ducks right along the shore. He manoeuvered the raft to cruise along the rocky shore back toward Cape Merry. A few minutes of this revealed no Harlequin Ducks, but we were treated to a couple of Parasitic Jaegers giving aerial chase to Arctic Terns carrying fish. Mike confirmed my identification of the evening before. At least he confirmed that they were jaegers, and he described the routine of the chase, leading to the terns dropping their prizes for the jaegers to snatch up before the fish hit the water. This time I was able to get the binoculars on the jaegers at much closer range and confirm for myself that they were indeed *Parasitic* Jaegers. I passed this certainty on to Mike and told him I'd read they were the most commonly seen around here. He nodded.

He moved the raft back out into the deeper bay and headed for the mouth of the river. As we cruised slowly, we started to see seals popping their heads up nearby to have a look at us. Mike spent several minutes trying to give us all good looks at the seals. It was not easy. "There's one" in front of us. But it was down before most of us could look forward. "There's one" behind us. But it was gone before most could turn back. The seals were single, not in groups, and they could pop up on any side of us.

I questioned Mike about the different species in the area and how he could distinguish them. He clearly felt more knowledgeable about sea mammals than sea birds. Here we were seeing mainly harbour seals, he said. I was surprised that they were so dark. Among them, Mike thought he'd seen one or two ringed seals. Their heads have a more salt-and-pepper colouration, and are smaller, not easily told from the harbour seal at a distance. He confirmed that the bearded seal is rarer, also quite different, much larger, and looks like a walrus with its long, prominent whiskers.

I realized then that the two species of seal I'd seen lying on the ice a few days before must have been ringed and harbour (not bearded) seals. I also realized how easy it is to jump to the wrong conclusion when working from only one source of information about species identification. Always learning! Which is what keeps me looking at the same species over and over, to get a better fix on characteristics and differences between them. I wished I could have had a good look at the head of a ringed seal to compare with the harbour seal in this area. But Mike saw no more of them.

We rounded Cape Merry and could immediately feel the current of the outgoing tide slow our forward progress into the mouth of the river. Belugas! There – not far off! Two of them. We could see their smooth white backs very clearly as they broke the surface in regular cadence, slowly working their way into the river. Mike fell in with them, running parallel and a little behind. We drew gradually closer. The whales and our boat had to manoeuvre around the outgoing ice floes. I thought I could hear the whales exhale once or twice, but we were a little too far off for me to be sure. I could not make out the shapes of their bulbous foreheads. In fact, I could see little except their backs, making me even more wistful for the experience of having them come right up to the boat. Mike concluded that these belugas were also just visitors, perhaps coming up the river for the fishing, and certainly keeping their distance from his Zodiac. We kept up with them for several minutes, then they dove.

Mike sped a little ahead to where he anticipated the belugas would surface again and then cut the engine speed just enough to stay in place against the current. We waited. Ice floes massive and small glided past in majestic silence. Irregular groans and crunching thuds reminded us of their passage. We waited. The *kip*-ping cries of the flying terns went unnoticed. Comments from Bonaparte's and Ring-billed Gulls hitching rides out to sea went unanswered. There! There they were again! Mike had positioned us well. He knew his animals, and he knew his river.

He was feeling good, at home. He opened up and spoke without prompting about the belugas. He told us a little about their life cycle, how their skin turns a pale yellow shortly after they arrive in the home river. These belugas hadn't turned yellow yet, probably because they weren't home yet. I think he said the fresh water starts them sloughing their outer layer of skin, a moult from which they emerge an immaculate white. They have their babies in the river, and possibly mate there as well, starting the cycle again for the following year.

Funny that I don't fully remember the details of what Mike said then. My wife laughs at my inability to remember the blow-by-blow of conversations. It is a standing joke, and I laugh along with her. She asks, "So what did he say?" And I respond, "Well, I can't remember the *exact* words, but it was something like...." She looks at me, rolls her eyes and smiles that smile of mixed irritation and love. And I feel half irritated and three quarters sad when I cannot remember such details, unless I've seen them written down. Even, it seems, when the topic involves one of my great loves – animals. Brains are incredible filters, so selective. Each of us is tuned to different channels, selecting for slightly different details. It amazes me that I can recognize so many bird calls and songs, so many dates of events, so many relationships among people, places and things, and then I sometimes cannot recall people's names, even people I may know pretty well, much less what they say to me. Perhaps I am concentrating too much on the meaning behind the words to fully record the words themselves. So I'd like to think.

The belugas dove again, and Mike repeated the manoeuvre, speeding ahead and then holding position in the current. As we waited, he asked tentatively, as though he was a little reluctant to find out, "What do *you* do back home in California?" The question was hardly unexpected, but it took me by surprise nonetheless. I hadn't had to tell anyone what I do for a living in so many gloriously anonymous days that I felt for a moment that I had to wrench myself back into a lost world of the past. I often feel awkward about the question when I'm out of daily practice, out of the daily routine of doing what I do.

"I run a non-profit international development organization," I said. "We provide financial and educational services to groups of very poor women in developing countries." Mike nodded. I looked at him. He seemed unable to comment. Perhaps I had somehow made it clear that my world was impossibly different from his. Or perhaps I had come across as one of *those* people, the kind whom he had moved to Churchill to get away from. Perhaps I simply was expecting too much. I felt sad. For whatever reason, the possibility of real connection seemed lost.

John began to lean heavily to starboard again, despite his companion's heroic efforts. As we were coming to the end of the promised two hours anyway, Mike gave up on the belugas and headed back for the Port, in hovercraft mode again. My spirits lifted, too. Despite fairly limited luck in sighting interesting birds and mammals, it had been a good outing overall. As we came into sight of our beach, Mike shifted to a slow glide and then stopped us dead in the water. He stood as tall as he could to survey the scene. "The ice has moved in and blocked our approach to the beach," he announced. "We'll have to go to the other beach. I'll call Paul and have him bring the bus around." He unholstered his cellular phone and made the call.

The other beach was nearby. As Mike headed toward it, we fell into conversation about the Ross's Gull. He told me their numbers had been steadily declining for several years. He knew the details, because this species had assumed special importance in elevating natural-history tourism to Churchill to a new high – outside the polar bear season, that is. The nesting of this beautiful and rare Siberian gull in North America was exciting by itself, but in addition because it continued to nest year after year and its colony had grown to several nesting pairs. What's more, the colony was right outside accessible Churchill, where birders could come and observe with relative ease.

Small, isolated colonies are highly vulnerable to random events of bad luck. Last year, Mike said, only three birds returned to the colony. One of the nesting pair had a mid-air collision with a power line and nearly severed its wing. It is a tribute to the importance of the species to local birders that this accident was witnessed. More than that, the bird was packed off to Winnipeg on a special mercy flight in an unsuccessful effort to save its life. If the remaining two should return this year, it seemed unlikely they would successfully nest, even if they happened to be of opposite sex and not too closely related.

Mike concluded by saying, "It looks like you'll have to make your next trip to Siberia to see the Ross's Gull."

"I think I'll pass on that," I replied, smiling, but feeling a little embarrassed to be categorized as a rich, go-anywhere birder in search of the rarities. But I knew Mike meant nothing by it. And, after all, I had come all the way to Churchill to see birds, so he was not far off the mark.

When the alternate beach came into view, Paul and the bus were there waiting. Mike shut down the outboard and let us glide in. Paul waded out to intercept the bow and pull us up securely onto the cobblestones. Mike moved forward and jumped down from the raft. He and Paul gave each of us a hand as we dismounted onto the loose stones at the water's edge. Finally, only John and his companions remained in the raft. It was agony to watch the struggle to get John up, much less off the boat. John wasn't joking any more. His companions from Penticton managed to get him seated on the bow and then turn him around with his legs over the side so that Mike and Paul could cradle him again. They carried him a few metres across the mushy, unstable cobbles, then set him down and propped him up as he struggled forward step by shaky step for the rest of the difficult walk to the bus. The distance between boat and bus was much greater than at the other beach.

On the Water: June 10

It couldn't be helped, due to the width of the cobbly beach. The rest of us waited respectfully near the bus.

Just before I got on the bus, Paul came up to me and said, "There was a report of a Long-tailed Jaeger at the Akudlik marshes."

"When was that?" I asked with keen interest.

"Just about an hour ago," Paul replied. I knew where I was going that afternoon. I thanked Paul warmly for the hot tip. He smiled broadly and climbed into the driver's seat.

Mike came on board only to say goodbye to John and his friends. He was staying behind to tend to the boat. As he got off the bus, we all barely had the chance to say "thank you" for the great trip on the water. Mike was gone.

∞

I had a light lunch from my supplies in the hotel room. I could see from my window that the clouds were thickening again and the wind was up. Akudlik marshes would be cold and blustery, but what of it? It was about time I felt the elements – the morning on the water had been surprisingly pleasant.

And feel the elements I did! I walked out on the same dike as I had on my first day, between ponds toward the big lake, Isabelle. I was dressed warmly enough for the temperature, which was somewhere between 5° and 10°C (40s F), wearing the same outfit as for the boat trip. But now the wind fiercely pulsed out of the northwest. Even with the hood of my Gore-Tex rain parka up and over my wool cap pulled as low as it would go over my ears and face, the wind chill was not to be suffered directly for long. I walked with my side to the wind, with scope on tripod over my shoulder toward the wind, keeping my hooded face to the southeast as I scanned the water and sky for gulls, terns and jaegers. Blasts of wind forced me to stop and brace to keep my balance. Enough cold air stung my face to make me stop occasionally and turn my back full to the wind, letting my face recover for a minute.

Wanting to be complete in my survey of the marshes and lakes, I turned several times into the wind to look to the north and west. I could tolerate it for only a few seconds at a time. The wind seemed to prevent my breathing, and my face quickly went raw, then numb. There was no way I could hold the binoculars steady to look at the pair of Pacific Loons huddled near their nest, wisely or luckily placed on the shore in the lee of any wind from the northern quadrants. I could use the binoculars toward the south and east, but the scope was out of the question in any direction. There wasn't much to look at anyway. The same pair of Oldsquaw lingered on the downwind side of the dike, close in and not eager to move away as I walked past them. Some ever-hardy scaup drakes and ducks floated in a small group farther out on the open water. Everyone else was hunkered down to wait out the storm. Only a few Herring Gulls or Ring-billed Gulls shot across the sky, riding the wind. What was I doing out here? I soldiered on to the end of the first dike, from where I scanned the big lake, just to verify that I would not be seeing a Long-tailed Jaeger today.

I retreated directly to the truck and savoured the warmth of the cab. As I let my face warm and regain feeling, I idly scanned the nearby lake with my binoculars, but mostly relaxed and drank in the view of open water, wetland and low, heavy clouds sliding downwind. The truck rocked with the buffeting wind. In retrospect from my metal and glass shelter, I was pleased to have been out in the subarctic "spring" weather. I had experienced it. Only for a short while, perhaps 20 or 30 minutes, but longer would have served no purpose. I had been dressed warmly enough to survive, if I'd had to, but only if I had followed the birds' example by hunkering down and waiting.

On the Water: June 10

With most of an afternoon still ahead, I drove around to the other side of Lake Isabelle, to a pullout observation area along the road to the airport. Through the windshield, I scanned the open water and sky beyond, again to verify that I hadn't missed something obvious. I hadn't. My duty done, I drove back into town, my destination being the Eskimo Museum. It seemed like a good place to shelter and learn at the same time.

Just as I pulled up to the blue museum house next to the tan-coloured church, a squall line of cloud, wind and rain swept across the town from the northwest, preceded by a blast of dust, sand and debris from the raw dirt streets and open lots of the town. It was too late even to make a dash up the few steps and through the door of the museum. I'd have to wait – like the birds – for the squall to pass.

∞

I watched the tremendous energy of Nature sweep between my windshield and the door of the museum. I thought of the gulls swept downwind, unable to turn into it, going with its flow to who knows where. And of the loons huddled behind their feeble windbreak, not knowing when or even whether the storm would let them venture out again. I imagined their unconscious faith in this divine energy shaping their evolution. It is faith in a genetically encoded wisdom, challenged by personal fear when this energy unaccountably bundles itself into a violent burst across the face of their world. If they adhere to their faith rather than succumb to their fear, they greatly enhance their chances for survival, for contributing to the next generation of loons.

The church nearby faded in and out of sight through the horizontal dirt and rain, reminding me of yesterday's meditation in the pew. The divine energy that was manifest in the painter's benign image of Jesus looked today like a dangerous squall. Is this energy *for* us or *against* us? "Neither" and "both" seem equally suitable answers. The divine energy is *in* us but not *of* us. It gives us life, but if we are in the wrong place at the wrong time, it will snuff us out. Our genetic wisdom is a part of that energy. It tries to keep us out of harm's way as other parts of the divine energy pursue different missions, sometimes contrary to ours. Even so, sooner or later, we will be transformed in death into yet another manifestation of this divine energy that yesterday I called God.

I wondered to myself once again, how can it be that this messy, self-destructive state of affairs is intentional, much less good? Woody Allen's nature as a big, nasty "restaurant" mocks the joy I find in the natural order. Yet Christianity and other religions assure me there is a moral order in the universe, governed by moral law given by a moral law giver. Certainly there is order, conforming to laws susceptible to mathematical description, conceivably established by divine design, that yield a chaotic, quantum mechanical sort of predictability that supports the physics and chemistry of the universe.

A *moral* order, however, implies contrasting Good and Evil in the affairs of the universe, that there is a choice between ways that are right and ways that are wrong. In the world view of science-as-religion, such choice is inconceivable. There is no possibility that these governing laws can be violated. If they are broken by an unpredicted event, our mathematical description is presumed faulty and soon amended to embrace the unforeseen. If the questionable event is far beyond the boundaries of what we currently "know" of the universe, the reality of the unforeseen is simply denied. In contrast, a God-centred yet scientifically sophisticated world view would agree there is no choice but to follow the rules given by God, because God has offered the universe no other way to conduct its affairs. A choice has been made by God – the laws governing the universe determine the "right" way chosen by God.

The universe is fully obedient to the will of God, but the laws may be broken by the lawgiver – when God chooses to intervene from outside the universe.

It seems, however, that there is more than one way to be obedient to the will of God. The universe and each of its component parts can still take a "random walk" within the confines of the God-given laws. The number of possible paths to follow is almost infinite, and they diverge spectacularly over the expanse of Time (itself a product of the universal laws). Allowance for random "choice" is part of the moral order of the universe. So, any of the paths allowed by law, though followed only by chance, is the "right" way. Some paths lead to star and galaxy formation, some to clouds of gas, some to dark energy, some to black holes. The law-abiding result we see now is not a tranquil universe, a cosmic Garden of Eden, but a violent, ordered chaos of matter and energy, of stars and galaxies that form and grow and age and explode and consume each other and die. It is as though God, as the Divine Watchmaker, set the governing laws and the initial conditions of the universe, then let it play itself out like improvisational theatre on the cosmic stage. The actors, however, do not freely choose their next steps. The "choice" is made at random. Randomness itself is likely an intentional creation. Thus, the cosmic chaos we see is by divine design, and therefore *moral* in the sense of being right in the eyes of God.

The universe probably needed a divine boost over the physical-chemical barriers to self-organizing, self-maintaining, self-reproducing life. Billions of years of random walking in the universe set the stage on at least one minor planet of the Milky Way galaxy for this divine intervention to happen. With no further outside assistance, it is possible that protein synthesis controlled by genetic coding shaped by natural selection in response to chance and necessity took life from there to what we know now on earth.

Though it heads down many, many incredible paths, development of life on earth has followed the universal laws as surely as the stars and the galaxies of the universe. Again, in the sense of being right in the eyes of God, in compliance with God-given laws, there is a *moral* order in life on earth.

Here is the major problem I see for us individual living beings. Moral as it may be, the moral order does not make this earth a nice neighbourhood in which to raise kids. The more sentient life forms find it downright awful at times, with all the suffering and death we have to face. The natural world may be in tune with the universe, and thus good in the eyes of God the Divine Watchmaker, but it looks pretty bad at the species and individual level. My earlier musing on the right conduct for the Blackpoll Warbler seems to point toward unconscious flow with the evolved genetic wisdom of the species. I still think that's the right answer – for Blackpoll. Yet this genetic wisdom has been forged in the terrible waste and suffering of little Blackpoll lives that lead to the natural selection that shapes the genetic code of the Blackpoll species. For a different species, the genetic wisdom might be different and even contradictory. Evolutionary change has gone down myriad paths to generate different species that play different, often conflicting, roles in the ecosystem. What seems good for one species may be bad for another, depending on its role, as in predator and prey.

The squall by now was abating. Though it was still blowing and rainy, I could have made a dash for the museum door. But my mental chatter held me captive. I stayed put in the comfort of my driver's seat and continued to explore the implications of this line of thought.

Yesterday's question came back to me: what is the relevance of the Moral Authority regarding human behaviour to the moral order of nature? The major religions, being anthropocentric, deal almost exclusively with the Moral Authority, and say very little about nature and even less about how the two might fit together. How can laws governing the universe lead to a natural order that is both right in the eyes of God and so cruel to its individual inhabitants, when, in stark contrast, the Moral Authority, God's Word incarnate, enjoins at least the human species to expunge such cruelty in our internal affairs – not just because this is what is best for our species, but because this is the divine way, God's way, that we should aspire to follow? How does the detached Watchmaker, satisfied with a smoothly functioning but cold, impersonal universe that chews up individual beings like so much fuel for the Machine, square with the God waiting patiently, lovingly inside each of us for our individual moments of recognition and gratitude?

At the level of individual lives, the moral order of nature seems to be highly relativistic – what's good for one of us is bad for another – and often terribly cruel. Yet it is in the individual life that we sense the presence of God. It is the individual who makes the choices that can be either good or bad, consistent with the genetic wisdom of the species, in tune with the universe, obedient to the will of God – or not. Animals generally make their choices unconsciously, instinctively, according to the genetic wisdom of the species. Some would say this is not choice at all. However, more complex animals are also genetically programmed to learn from experience and base decisions on what they know from learning. Some even learn extensively by watching each other, especially older kin. These are the conditions that allow for cultural evolution to emerge as a complement to genetic evolution. Learned choice complements and can even override instinctive choice. These seem to be the pre-conditions that set the stage for another divine boost from outside the universe – for humans to be ready to receive the gift of language and self-reflection and consciousness.

There is a suggestion somewhere out there in the world of books I've read that the whole evolution of the universe and of life should be taken as a divine construction project to create a sentient being capable of keeping company with God, a creature able to sense God's presence and love and to respond with gratitude and love. This seems at first like a silly notion, since God is so unlikely to be anything like a human being, much less lonely for companionship. Yet we can think about God only through metaphors, and this one may be useful for exploring the paradox of God the satisfied Watchmaker versus God waiting patiently for our individual moments of recognition.

Perhaps God could not have created the human species without several billion years of improvisational theatre we call cosmic and biological evolution. Once in motion, even God had to let the play run its course, only signalling the players occasionally to interject a new storyline, to give their play a little boost. But God is constantly watching the play with fascination and whatever feelings we can imagine God to experience. Perhaps that is how the creative process works. We may misconceive how much control the Creator can have over the creation and still be creative.

How ironic that most of those who believe in God and most of those who reject God's existence both tend to conceive of God as controlling everything all the time and also caring about individual lives. Conceiving of God as the rational, omniscient and omnipotent Controller, they can only choose to be puzzled but faithful or to be disillusioned about the possibility of God when inexplicably irrational events happen. The notion that God is intentionally interacting with, rather than controlling, creation allows for omniscience and omnipotence and also the divine wisdom to use these powers indirectly to foster creation. The notion allows for imperfections to arise and grow, elaborate and even turn against the divine intent. It allows for evil to emerge within the created system, the undesirable but perhaps inevitable consequence of a creative process dependent on an element of randomness in the system – a kind of free will.

With this understanding, I must also acknowledge that God's improvisational theatre continues. Billions of years of cosmic and biological evolution more than likely have not reached an end point in the human species as it is now. Before I object to God's "using" all these other creatures to develop and favour our special species as God's companion, I'd better realize that contemporary humans may only be the featured player of the current act in an ongoing play. God knows how this play is unfolding!

I am certain the loons, huddled against the blasting wind and rain, do not know. All they can depend on is the wisdom of their species built into their genetic coding, a creation of God's creation. Their faith in this wisdom gives them a chance to survive the storm.

∞

Once inside the museum, I discovered I was one of three spending indoor time productively in study of the Eskimo, or Inuit. Also present was the same Anglo lady at the desk in the back. She reminded me of a school teacher or librarian, one of the more severe-looking kind. Yet, she was engaged in helpful conversation with one of the other two visitors.

I was hopeful that she might give me the local scoop on Nunavut – what led to it, what it might mean for the future of Churchill. I had asked Mike the latter question and got a disinterested shrug and "I don't know." No expansion on that. Waiting my turn to catch the "school teacher's" attention, I browsed again through the displays of photographs and artifacts of Inuit life. I was impressed as before with the grittiness of the traditional life. In its graceful way, the impact of the whole museum could be described understandably as a glorification of an inglorious existence. But on further examination and reflection, I saw no attempt to glorify. Only an honest and respectful reporting of the evidence of the not-so-distant past. I admired the sincerity.

But the Eskimo Museum is what most museums are – about the past, not the present, much less the future. Other than the maps I had discovered the day before, and these were not for sale, I found no literature at all about Nunavut itself, only books about Inuit art and traditional life and a few tour guides, one of which talked about the scant accommodations for visitors to the Inuit communities of the far North. As before, I found the picture postcards focused on winter scenes and animals I hadn't seen. I was becoming discouraged.

Still the conversation went on. As I overheard bits and pieces, I lost confidence that the woman at the desk would be helpful to me. I even began to think she might think me impertinent to ask such questions as I wanted to ask. Who knows why? That's the way my brain was operating at the moment. Perhaps I was losing the battle with shyness. I always have to get up my courage to ask articulate questions. When I do, I usually feel rewarded. I'm not sure why, in this case, I didn't think the result would be worth the risk to my fragile self-esteem. If she had taken notice of me hovering around the merchandise and asked if she could help me, I might have overcome my shyness and asked my questions, and probably would have learned a great deal. But the other conversation went on. Feeling increasingly awkward, I gave in to my weakness and left as unnoticed as I had entered.

∞

The storm had passed by the time I emerged from the museum. There was only a light misting rain, due to stop soon. The wind was down. The sky was brightening. Nonetheless, I decided to do some reading in the comfort of my hotel room before an early dinner. I wanted to save my energy for another evening outing to Cape Merry and a walk around the Granary Ponds and along the river. As I drove and then walked back to the Aurora Inn, I wondered how the loons and the gulls were doing, whether they had heeded their genetic wisdom and whether it had saved them once again.

I fell into imaginary conversation with my son as a young man thinking for himself about our human genetic wisdom and what good it does us now that we have moved way beyond the geography and living patterns for which our genetic evolution has adapted us. To my surprise, he wants to know my opinion.

"What good to *us*, then, is that unconscious faith that serves the loons and gulls so well?"

"Still essential for our daily survival, I'm sure." I answer with no hesitation, but then I have to choose my thoughts and words very carefully. "No doubt it serves us even more by equipping us with capacity for cultural evolution, allowing supple adaptation to new places and ways of life. We have the benefit of a cultural wisdom, a more conscious, more adaptable guide to protect us. But it is also less reliable than our genetic wisdom, because it is easily twisted out of harmony with the divine energy by Reason, our mental chatter, our inner voices. We humans have too many choices and chances to deviate from our genetic wisdom – free will." (If only I could be so articulate in real time!)

He presses me harder. "So, we're the only animals that can deviate from their genetic wisdom?"

I rise to my son's challenge with a bird example, of course. "Even in species like Blackpoll, individuals can follow other paths. Not every Blackpoll can or wants to march lockstep with the dictates of what is best for leaving lots of healthy offspring. I think back on my year-round visits to Bodega Bay, for the purpose of observing the annual rhythms, the months of abundance and absence of the common species. Even during the peak breeding season for shorebirds, when Marbled Godwits should be far away in the interior of the continent in step with their genetic wisdom, there they are – tens if not hundreds of perfectly healthy-looking Marbled Godwits probing the mudflats. And not just godwits – there are loafers of many different shorebird species. Maybe they are all immature, not yet of breeding age. But I figure that some of them decided not to play the usual game of their species, not this year, anyway. Something inside wanted to spend the season on the coast in leisurely pursuit of mud-dwelling organisms."

"How is this possible when natural selection is set so hard against such deviance?" My son is taking his biology courses a bit more seriously, I see.

"Excellent question," I assure him. "Yet there they are!" I know this flip answer won't satisfy him, so I dig deeper to offer this speculation.

"Let's see. We know that natural selection has also favoured the bizarre complications of sexual reproduction, which occasionally but dependably generates deviants from the favoured norm. The reason seems to be that the 'norm' currently favoured by natural selection may soon fall out of favour – as climate changes, for example. To evolve in response to change requires the species to have on hand at least a few deviants who can survive, even thrive, in the new conditions. Generations later, these successful deviants become the new norm. The loafers on the coast appear to be a bunch of irresponsible mudflat bums, but they may at the same time be the species' insurance against disaster on the interior breeding grounds. Deviance from the genetic wisdom of a species could very well be a protected part of that same genetic wisdom."

He is not as impressed as I am by this adept answer. My son smiles and asks, "How about deviance from the *cultural* wisdom of humans?" He is pushing me and enjoying it a little too much. I'll have to dance around the political implications of this one.

"Well, we know that despite often harsh 'selection' by cultures against their deviants, deviance still persists and provides grist for the mill of cultural evolution. Especially in our youth," I look at him pointedly, "many of us long to innovate, create, push the envelope, and break the bonds of social prescription. Individual humans can and do abandon one form of cultural wisdom for another entirely different one, as in a religious conversion. More often, they simply refuse to participate in the mainstream of their culture and find society with fellow deviants." I thought of some of his friends, especially that one with the nose ring and the tattoo on his shaved head.

That thought was just too scary! Anyway, I could no longer keep up the mental game with my imagined older son. Where my line of thought was going I had to focus hard to keep the logical thread from tangling. The question of right conduct was emerging again.

Culture is easily contorted by our human mental chatter into something far removed from any divine intentions. For that reason alone, I cannot propose going with the flow of cultural wisdom as any credible sort of universal code of conduct. We must go to a deeper understanding of the reality underlying both genetic and cultural wisdoms and build directly on that truth.

In the depth of our unconscious cultural wisdom seems to be a mystical intimation that we are one with God, this energy. Occasionally, we become conscious that we are packets of divine energy – produced by, consuming, producing and being consumed by other packets of energy, in an interminable round of transformations. Like bubbles on the surface of boiling water, our individual divine energy packets emerge, divide, collide and subside into the ultimate Source.

What are we to make of this understanding? How do we let it shape our lives? How does it affect faith in our genetic and cultural wisdoms? We could struggle to protect our transitory energy packets as long as we can, even at the expense of others. We might try to escape the round of producing and consuming by seeking liberation in permanent union with the Source. We could go with the flow of our cultural and genetic wisdom. How does one translate understanding of divine reality into conduct of daily life?

Much of the postmodern, post-Christian notion of morality is focused on the importance of human rights – our collective and individual obligations to honour and assure the rights of others. Who grants us rights? What makes a right universal and beyond repeal by human agency (as is everywhere implied in the modern discussion of human rights)? The traditional answer, that God is the bestower of rights to humanity, has more power and clarity than the modern alternatives. But it also calls into question the creation of a laundry list of specific rights. More likely, the many human needs that ought to be honoured or served by our societies are derivatives of a few fundamental, God-given rights.

I'll go way out on a limb and assert that the most basic human right is to have options. God gave us free will to exercise for good or ill. The specific rights protected now by international conventions and national laws are specific applications of the right of every human being to have options without impinging unnecessarily on the options of others. It is said that no other animals on earth received this dubious gift. William Barclay, in his commentary on St. Paul's letter to the Romans, asserts:

> Before man there stands a choice. It has to be so. Without choice there can be no goodness, and without choice there can be no love. A coerced goodness is not real goodness; and a coerced love is not love at all.

I do believe that what allows humans to freely choose to love and to be good – or not – comes to us through the gift of language and, more to the point, the self-awareness that becomes possible with language. Having such options is the most fundamental and distinctively human right, which God may have granted us for the purpose of fostering a new surge of creativity in the universe, beyond what can be generated by the randomness factor already built into the system. It is an advance over randomness, because human choice can be exercised in awareness of and even interaction with God. In this sense, God can now have a companion in the creative process.

It's also very problematic to have this right.

Parents get a tiny sense of God's perspective as they raise children. One of my cousins captured the conundrum of parenthood perfectly when he tried to prepare me for the birth of my son. My cousin said, "For the first year or two, you work hard to teach them to walk and to talk. Then after that, you're always telling them to sit down and shut up." And without much effect! Parenting helps us share in God's consternation with humanity and its exercise of free will, its most fundamental human right, as I am proposing.

In the Christian perspective, God got fed up several times and tried to set things right, even to the point of manifesting as a human being just like us in order to show us the way forward, to make it clear how free will is supposed to be used. Yet God never exercised a creator's power to force us, like remote-controlled automata, to do it right. In this and most other traditional religious perspectives, God clearly intends that we have options and make our own choices. In fact, we seem to be given free will for the divine purpose of demonstrating that we can restrain our will in line with the higher will. A very curious way to run a universe. As has been said by wiser people, "For those who believe, no explanation is necessary; for those who do not believe, no explanation is possible."

∞

I returned to the restaurant where I ate on my first evening in Churchill, the one attached to the Arctic Trading Company on the main street. I was disappointed, not by the quality of the food, which was again very good, but by the terribly slow service. They had a lot of customers, true, but not nearly as many as the Churchill Motel Restaurant the night before. There evidently was some breakdown of the system in the kitchen, and the two waitresses seemed inexperienced. I usually take such delays with good humour. I like to give service people a break when they are struggling. I had my book by Leonard Nathan, nearly finished, and a wildlife magazine, but after nearly half an hour without even getting a beer, I was feeling ignored and growing irritable. I couldn't concentrate on reading anymore. I found myself studying the movements of the waitresses and plotting my intervention. Being by myself is usually no problem, but this time I felt it keenly. I was self-consciously waiting, feeling conspicuously alone. Let's move it! Can I get some service here? Not that I said these things out loud, being either too gentlemanly or too shy.

The weather was improving, even inviting, though still cold. I was getting anxious about wasting the best part of the evening. Finally I was served. After practically forcing the waitress to let me pay up, I was a free man at last. The ordeal had taken an hour and a half. Now I walked up the street to get my gear into the truck and be off to Cape Merry. My immediate objective was to check for Harlequin Ducks on and around the rocks along the shore. The greater goal was to take another look at the mouth of the river with new eyes, informed by my trip on the water today. As I drove out, the clouds dissolved into streaks of stratus. The sun broke through and suffused the winter-bleached grasses and orange lichens on the great rocks around the Port with a warm glow of evening light. My favourite time of day. I loved being out in it.

I didn't see Harlequin Ducks, but I had low expectations. It's worth a shot, I thought. What I most enjoyed was watching the river and its ice floes on their way out to the bay again. I didn't stay long, though. I chose instead to focus on the Granary Ponds, to visit with my "old friends." And to see if anything new and unusual had shown up as a result of the storm blowing through.

I walked among the Granary Ponds, getting reacquainted with a blissful sense of well-being. I now knew this place and its regulars – the Red-necked Phalaropes, the Stilt Sandpipers, the colony of Arctic Terns, the many gulls and ducks, the White-crowned and Savannah Sparrows, the singing Waterthrush, the Yellow Warblers, and my special favourite, the Horned Grebe, in all his breeding finery, solitary on his willow-rimmed pond. It felt so much like home now that I was inclined to play host to others. I was not the only birder working the ponds this evening, and unaccountably I felt like talking to the others. One was a 30ish woman on her own with a very long lens on a substantial tripod. She was stalking photo images in my line of walking; I did not go out of my way to intercept her. But as I approached, she withdrew steadily without making eye contact. She seemed to want nothing to do with humans at all – at least not me, not now. I could respect that, and I did.

Farther on I encountered a trio of birders, also young adults. The two men were stalking birds with cameras and were very engrossed at different parts of one pond. The woman was standing watching from some distance. Her binoculars gave her the appearance of a birder, not merely a go-along spectator. I diverted from my path to join her for a moment or two. I came up beside her, not too close, and asked, "Have you all just arrived?"

She gave me a slightly startled, sideways glance. "Yesterday," she replied.

"I've only been here since Saturday," I went on. "This spot is one of my favourites." She chose not to respond to that. We looked out over the pond for a moment. I raised my binoculars to check out a bird, and while doing this, I asked, "Are you finding some interesting birds?"

"It's been pretty good," she said perfunctorily. I could tell this conversation was not meant to be. Resigned, I lowered my binoculars and left her with "Well, enjoy your evening here." She chose not to respond. Alas! I finally get myself up to being sociable and then go unrewarded. We birders are a funny lot – just like most human beings, but even more difficult, I think.

I ended up on the railroad embankment along the river, at the south end of the Port facility. As I was setting up my scope to scan the distant water and ice floes, Bonnie drove up in her signature blue-and-white van with a small group of birders. They set themselves up with scopes a few metres away, but took no notice of me. I had the benefit of overhearing their conversation about what they were seeing, which served to confirm my own increasingly confident identifications.

Then I heard Bonnie say, "There are some Snow Buntings among the rocks down there." She was pointing south along the river shore. "Since it's pretty late for them now, you'll want to take a look. This may be your only chance." This first day for her new group might be the last day for the buntings before they continued on to their breeding grounds farther north. I hadn't seen Snow Buntings since my first day, so I was interested and trained my equipment in their direction. I caught a good glimpse, but only as they flew on to some rocks farther away to the south.

Here again I had the opportunity to introduce myself to Bonnie. I really wanted to connect with her somehow, to thank her for her great book, perhaps. It had been my excellent guide to the area, my main source of information. More than that, one gets to know a person through her writing – sort of. I wanted to interact a bit to get a better sense of her as a person. She seemed the same with this group as with the other – knowledgeable, helpful, enthusiastic. As I was gathering the courage to make my move, searching for an opening pretext to speak, Bonnie herded the group back into the van. Soon they were off, probably eager to get out to Cape Merry.

I wasn't doing very well today connecting with my fellow human packets of divine energy!

I picked up the scope, slung it over my shoulder and headed south along the grassy railroad track, the same one the grain trains follow into the Port facility behind me. Ahead about 200 metres lay the train station for passengers and non-grain freight. The evening sun shone over my right shoulder, at the low angle of the 9 p.m. position for this date and latitude. The sky was mostly pale blue now, with lavender-gray bands of cloud stacked above the southern horizon. The dry grass of last year still stood in erect clusters, reflecting the golden light. The many small houses of the part of Churchill between the tracks and the river were like a jumble of brick-red, tan and white toy blocks. The river itself was royal blue, wide, stretching south to join the clouds on the horizon, giving sharp contrast to the hundreds of ice floes glinting pure white on the deep-blue water.

I walked on into this magical scene until I came to a substantial stream from the Granary Ponds exiting through a culvert under the tracks and into the main river. Here I caught up with the Snow Buntings. There were two or three males in full breeding plumage, and several females, poking around among the stones at the edge of the side stream. I'd never seen the full breeding plumage before. The males were literally picture perfect, as in the bird book

– pure white like tiny, stubby gulls with jet-black backs and some black in the wings and tail. Tiny compared with gulls, but good-sized for a finch. I sat down on the railroad embankment, set up the scope and watched these Snow Buntings foraging as long as I could. I must have been there up to half an hour. When I wasn't peering through the scope at these Arctic micro-beauties, I could scan the Arctic macro-beauty of the evening scenery. It matched memories of magazine photos of the North Slope, of Baffin Island, of Patagonia, of Tierra del Fuego, of South Georgia Island. I could have been just about anywhere in the high latitudes of the summer hemisphere.

∞

Watching the social interactions in this small flock of Snow Buntings, I drifted into thoughts about the social life of animals. Mostly they come together for safety in numbers as they travel and forage for food. Many eyes see predators sooner. Yet animals close together means more competition for food and other things of value, such as safe resting places and mates. Social life is useful, and a social animal feels uncomfortable on its own. But there can be lots of conflict. Needing to contain aggression so the group can stay together, animal groups like this flock of Snow Buntings are often organized in social hierarchies or pecking orders, in which each one learns who must yield to whom in any dispute. Social life is not meant to be pleasant, just useful. Even those on top of the pecking order sometimes have to work with grim determination just to stay on top.

There isn't much similarity between the simple flocking behaviour of birds and our own exceedingly complex social lives. It's easier to identify with animals that are born, live and die in social groups like ours, especially like the hunter-gatherer groups of our prehistory, in which the vast majority of human genetic evolution has occurred. Beyond the primates most like us are many social examples in a remarkable variety of creatures – bees, ants and termites, naked mole-rats and prairie dogs, dwarf mongooses and coatis, elephants and porpoises, and on and on. Observation and theory about social life reveal a major tension between co-operation and competition among group members, affecting genetic evolution of social skills.

In the 1970s, evolutionary theorists started talking, in almost anthropomorphic language, about animals deceiving each other with false social signals – lies. At the time, I found this line of thinking profoundly unappealing, not so much because it was unfounded but because it sullied animals with some of the same vices I'd come to loathe in people. Yet field research evidence has mounted to show that animals do cheat and lie in social encounters. There are sneaky characters who take advantage of others' gullibility. They invite co-operation by signalling a promise to co-operate in return. Then, after getting what they want, they don't give back as promised, sometimes with dire consequences for the deceived party. So the ability to detect deceit, to pick up on even the subtle lies, has evolved as a countermeasure. There's even evidence, in primates at least, that detected liars may be punished by other group members, by exclusion from the group's activities and protection, for example.

Evolution of complex social skills appears to be part of a broader evolutionary "war game," in which social (and evolutionary) advantage is gained sometimes by aiding, sometimes by deceiving, sometimes by trusting in others, sometimes by distrust. Sounds familiar.

The guiding rule of this evolutionary game is self-interest. Social behaviour in animals evolves when it is in the self-interest of the individual animal, when it enhances the opportunity to pass its genes on to the next generation. Therefore, theorists have been puzzled and intrigued by the multiplying reports of altruistic behaviour in animals, when individuals increase risk to themselves by aiding others.

The most obvious and widespread example is parental care and protection. All the great cost and risk to the parents is directed to the benefit of their dependent offspring. But parenting is so closely bound to one's genetic self-interest that it is seldom included in the question of altruism. The most commonly reported form of animal altruism is alarm-calling by a great variety of birds and many mammals. The animal sees an approaching predator, but instead of fleeing silently without attracting unnecessary attention to itself, it lets out a cry of alarm that alerts others nearby to the threat to their lives, at the risk of drawing the predator's attention to the one sounding the alarm. Some bird and mammal vocalizations seem to have evolved for the specific purpose of alerting others to danger; they are used only in response to predators on their own species. A few species, such as vervet monkeys in Africa, have more than one alarm call: one to signal the approach of an aerial predator (which causes the vervets to descend hastily from the treetops), and another for a predator on the ground (which causes the vervets to vault into the trees from the ground).

Theory and evidence indicate that alarm calls may evolve through a modified form of self-interest, called kin selection. The assumption is that closely related kin are nearby and able to benefit from the warning call. By helping kin, an animal is indirectly helping its own genetic coding to pass on to the next generation, because a certain proportion of the genes of kin are identical to one's own genes. Even if the caller is killed by the predator, several of its kin are likely to survive and learn to be more wary. The closer the kin, the greater the benefit to the self-sacrificing animal, because it shares more genes in common with the surviving kin.

Distant kin and even unrelated animals may benefit as well from the altruistic act of potential self-sacrifice. Saving their lives does little or nothing for the genetic future of the animal sounding the alarm. That appears to be acceptable, because most animals giving an alarm call are not killed; the risk to self may be rather low while the benefits to any close kin within earshot are considerable. Still, field research has shown that alarm-calling is often done selectively. For example, when an animal has recently migrated to a new area where there are no close kin nearby, the animal is likely to remain silent when it sees predators.

Thus, even apparently altruistic behaviour in animals can be explained without abandoning the ruling principle of self-interest. The power of this extended notion of self-interest in animal social behaviour has tempted some scientists to try explaining all human behaviour in the same terms. The exercise seems reasonable, because so much of what we do socially (including our economic lives) is motivated by pure self-interest.

But even kin selection cannot explain our distinctive capacity for transcendence of self-interest in our treatment of others totally unrelated to our genetic heritage. Such transcendence may be distressingly uncommon, but at some level, I believe most of us agree with what St. Paul wrote to his fractious friends in Corinth – that we, all of us, whether we live in Canada or Cambodia, are parts of one mystical body. Each part plays some vital role in the whole, and therefore no part is more important than any other, and harm to any one part causes harm to all of us.

The body analogy is imperfect, because in this era of infatuation with the power of self-interest as fuel for the magic of the marketplace, we may be tempted to the false conclusion that we help others only to help ourselves. This is a misunderstanding of the mystical nature of this body. We know this body, but it is unknowable; we sense it, yet it is insensible; it is beyond detection by our science, but it is no less present in our lives than the gravity that is everywhere, in everything. We feel the bond with others we've never met and never will meet. It gives us our life, and, if we let it, it gives us our moral purpose, part of which is an obligation to each other that extends to all humanity, not just family or even friends. The word "obligation" doesn't play well in our self-centred, pleasure-seeking culture. But the world religions teach that profound, lasting happiness is not about pleasure. It comes to those who are internally balanced and aligned with the moral purpose we are given by that mystical body.

For Christians, the mystical body is Jesus Christ, "one in being" with God, through whom "all things were made." Humanity a couple of thousand years ago, having used the gift of free will mainly to drift off into the fog of its own mental chatter, had mostly ignored its distinctive capacity for transcendence. The species was much in need of another divine intervention to save us from the sin of pure self-interest. The message of God's manifestation as human being is that we can and must move beyond the animal level of social behaviour. The special favour of God for our species places on us a special obligation to break the rule of self-interest in the evolutionary war game – to transcend our animal selves. We have the capacity, therefore the choice – unlike animals, who rarely if ever have this option for transcendence. Given choice, we can also sin against God by choosing to ignore the gifts or misuse them in favour of our pure self-interest at the expense of our fellow beings.

Transcendence of self-interest is the source of all charity and self-sacrifice for those we do not know. But what of our relationships with friends and family? In these long-lasting relationships, it seems to me, self-interest cannot be fully transcended. To maintain years of intimacy, we have to get as well as give. We have to get at least the reward of feeling good when we are sharing experiences with friends or family. The flow of rewards cannot be all in one direction if the relationship is to last. Self-interest has to be honoured in dynamic tension with the interests of others.

Yesterday I was feeling defensive about not engaging more enthusiastically in human contact, what I myself labelled "the most precious and meaningful experience of our social species." Since human social life arose for the same reasons and with the same unpleasantries as for other social animals, there seems to be a contradiction here. What is so precious and meaningful about being social? Is it not as mixed a blessing for us as it is for other social animals?

Social life can be hard work, even for those who say they love it. I have only to review my social scorecard for the day to see it's difficult, even when I'm in the mood to be sociable. People often do not respond as I wish they would. Maybe my social skills need some work. Perhaps my timing is off, my interactive style a bit offensive. Or my expectations are too high. Maybe a little, but even so, it's not all my problem. Many of us find it difficult to meet new people. I think everyone finds it a challenge to develop safety, much less intimacy, in relationships with others. I think we're all a little anxious – some of us more anxious than others – about what can come from a social encounter. We're on edge, like a chimp nervously approaching a higher-ranking member of the troop. When we try to socialize, we risk rejection, even ridicule, damage to our egos, possibly even to our bodies. We can do much psychological, if not physical, harm to each other in our social lives. People learn to be wary.

It's a wonder that we ever get past our wariness to have more than superficially useful relations with each other. Some of us don't, but most do, and we're grateful for it. If we've had a satisfying relationship with a parent or two, with a sibling or three, with a childhood friend or more, we find ourselves seeking such intimate solidarity the rest of our lives, despite the risks in the seeking. The ability to feel such compelling satisfaction from a relationship with a fellow human being is probably yet another consequence of our evolutionary history. As a social species, we feel driven to seek companionship, in spite of the wariness fostered by negative experience.

The Snow Buntings continued their search for food among the rocks at the river's edge, some carefully staying out of the way of others. Each looked up regularly for predators and the reassurance of each other's company. I wondered if they felt a bond, even a loyalty, that kept them together rather than splitting off to join others passing by. Individual animals get attached to each other, no doubt. Social life is more than a mere convenience for many social animals, as it certainly is for us. The bond of shared experience builds a sense of companionship enough to keep them together, for a while at least. Is it too much to say they're "friends"?

What does it take to become friends? Some of these buntings may be mates from last year's breeding season or siblings sticking together in migration and on the wintering grounds. Or they may have been thrown together by chance en route, grateful to find others of their kind. Like backpacking youths facing the common rigours of penny-pinching tourism, perhaps they are finding fellowship on the route going north, fellowship born initially of chance meeting, but reinforced by common need for each other to stay alive and pursue their individual destinies. Shared experience in overcoming common challenges glues them together as "friends."

I thought back on the deeper, longer-lasting friendships I've developed. First, there was my family of kin, thrown together by pure chance for all I knew as a child, but sticking together through thick and thin, because alternatives were not options. The companionship of shared experience led to attachment, and love grew.

On the Water: June 10

For all the distances and difficulties, they are still my family. To my surprise, my father and mother and brother and sisters are not only my oldest friends, they are among those most likely to resurface in my life over and over again, despite the feuds and hurts and long separations. We cannot walk away from each other forever, at least not in our minds, even in this modern society of families spread over a continent, if not the globe. Our irrefutable kinship creates a glue we might as well call "friendship."

As I ventured beyond my family, I was thrown together with little, then bigger friends by the chance of our being neighbours, of being in the same school trying to find fun and self-esteem on the playground, of facing the challenge of the same teachers and the same opponents on the playing fields. The common adversity and joy of childhood glued us together as friends. In a more traditional society, where children rarely moved away from their native communities, we would still be as inescapably friends as our kin. But modern life pulls us apart, and not even kinship is there to help reunite friends. It takes extraordinary luck or determination to keep these early friendships alive.

So as young adults wandering the "real world," we find our friends as we can. The ones we care about most deeply are the people we found common cause with at work, on the road, in any circumstance throwing us together in shared experience. But we know we cannot hang on to these people in our lives. They move on. They marry and have children and move into new worlds of experience beyond ours. Their ambitions and careers force them to move to new cities, states or provinces, even across the ocean. I was lucky enough to marry one of these people I care deeply about and build a life with her and our child. We've found new friends through the common experience of raising children. But just as circumstances threw them together with us, circumstances will pull them or us away. We know we cannot hang on to these friends forever. They move on, and so do we.

The measure of a person is not so much in the ability to make friends as in the will to keep them. Friends require investment of time and energy; they place joyful (and sometimes not so joyful) obligations on us, and we on them. It is difficult, even if joyful, work to stay in touch with friends who have moved on. If we take friendships seriously, we know we can maintain just a few beyond our family and work relationships. In this modern life of busyness, we dare not engage new friends lightly. It makes sense, then, that many of us are a bit aloof. We find ourselves mutually bypassing intriguing possibilities, as I did with Paul and Mike and Bonnie, and others did with me today. As I did with Victor, the Weir Guy I had dinner with on the train. He probably would have been my soulmate through a long summer and fall of construction work if fate had thrown me in with that crew. We missed an opportunity to enrich each other's lives.

I felt alone and sad.

Then I let myself see again the royal-blue Churchill River sprinkled with sparkling ice floes and the sky streaked with pale lavender clouds and the pure-white Snow Buntings with jet-black wings and the clumps of dry grass golden in the cool subarctic evening sun. The Divine in all these is a constant, dependable source of companionship to those who can allow themselves to *be* with them. In the end, we are each, human or non-human, alone with this divine energy. But for those born as social beings and now on our way back to the Source of all this wonderful world, the few friends we find and keep help make the journey precious and meaningful.

8

"A Waxwing!"
June 11

This morning I was in the truck and rolling by 5 o'clock. I could tell I had succeeded in being the first person on the road. The length of a whole block of the main street in front of the Churchill Motel was covered by Ring-billed Gulls, about 50 of them standing there looking at each other. They seemed so at ease I hesitated to disturb their roost, but I was in a hurry to get on the Highway and out to Twin Lakes before anyone else. I figured only the first person down the road had a chance to see caribou or other large mammals that are shy of humans. So I turned left onto the main street and headed for the gulls. They obligingly lifted off in a cloud of graceful, unhurried wings. I passed by, keeping an eye on the rearview mirror to see if they would settle back on the road. They didn't, but dispersed in various directions. It must have been time for them to start their day anyway. I was their alarm clock.

No power walkers today. No Whimbrel on the high wire, either. It was too early. But the sun was already several degrees above the horizon. Not that I could see the sun. It was a solid overcast day, temperature near the freezing point, and little wind to speak of. I was thankful. This was just about perfect for my purpose.

I enjoyed my steady, fast progress along the Highway, gently rocking and rolling with the paved surface. Past the Akudlik marshes and lakes, past the airport and the once again spectacular view of the frozen ocean, past the dump, past the turnoff to Bird Cove, past the Canadian rocket and through the still-sleeping launch-site compound, and then south on the gravel road toward Twin Lakes. No sightings yet, except several Canada Geese and ducks in the roadside tundra along the way. I was in travel mode and not looking all that diligently yet.

Once on the gravel I began to concentrate on the roadside vegetation, keeping a sharp eye out for a Northern Shrike or a Northern Hawk-Owl sitting atop a spruce – and, of course, any sign of the elusive Bohemian Waxwing. Most likely any large mammals would have to be standing on or crossing the road for me to see them from the truck. I travelled more slowly now because of the gravel and to reduce the noise of the tires. My eyes strained forward as I rounded each curve and topped each rise, hoping to catch a glimpse of a caribou or an Arctic fox at a distance, before my sudden appearance propelled it into flight.

I retraced the now-familiar route, stopping briefly on the first rise to listen – Harris's Sparrow and Blackpoll Warblers again, also the Hermit Thrush in the distance and the Ruby-crowned Kinglet close by. Then down and up to the second rise and down again toward the expanse of tundra before the Twin Lakes plateau. As the tundra plain came into view through the last of the spruce trees, I was thinking that this would be the most likely spot to see the caribou. Still, I was amazed when three of them walked casually onto the road ahead! Three caribou on the road. They paused to look. I braked to a stop as quietly as I could and looked back through the binoculars.

"Okay – caribou!" I exulted to myself. "Thank you very much! Wonderful!" I was still some 50 metres away, but my view through the binoculars was very good. The light angle was perfect. One of them had the beginnings of antlers (1 to 2 feet long). The other two had none yet. They weren't much bigger than deer, with heavier "hammer" heads, rectangular and large for the body. They continued to stand and look. I turned off the engine to reduce noise. Still on the downslope, I was able to let the truck roll slowly forward toward them. They let me get within 30 metres. I could really study them now. Their colour was a dirty gray-brown. They were in various stages of uneven moult from their much thicker winter coats. Patches of the winter fur clung to various parts of them, giving them an oddly ragged appearance. As I continued to roll closer still, they became slightly alarmed, trotted off the road and splashed across the wet tundra. I switched on the engine and quickly moved up to where I could follow them with the binoculars. They trotted and splashed only about 40 to 50 metres from the road, then settled down to browse among the hummocks. I watched them as long as they were in view. After a few minutes they had browsed away from me and gradually disappeared behind the sparse tamarack and spruce dotting the tundra.

I sat back and felt wonderful. Seeing caribou is somehow special, almost like a sign reading "You are now entering the watershed of the Arctic Ocean." This accurately describes most of Canada, but seeing caribou is like stepping into a novel of the far North or an adventurer's tale of Arctic exploration. Caribou are the most important land animal for human survival in the far North. The hunting pressure is what keeps them elusive, even out of the hunting season. Only a sighting of muskox or wolves or polar bears would surpass seeing caribou. All of these were conceivable but highly unlikely here. I still had hope for an Arctic fox; visitors to Churchill do see them crossing the road or in open areas at odd hours of the day. Maybe today. But the caribou were special, a symbol of the tundra, the bison of the North. Somehow, my personal experience of the Arctic now felt complete. I had seen tundra with caribou on it.

I continued to sit a while, enjoying the view over the tundra. Nearby a male Willow Ptarmigan flew up with white wings to the top of a lone spruce and uttered its call. It is a beautiful bird even in mid-moult from the pure white of winter to the mottled brown of summer. I could even see the patch of bright-red bare skin, the "comb," over its eye. I also witnessed a Northern Harrier chasing a Short-eared Owl. They compete in the hunt for rodents in the marshy tundra, both by day. It would be tough to be a strictly nocturnal animal at this latitude.

Finally I moved on, remembering my remaining, less comprehensible goal – to see a Bohemian Waxwing. Crossing the tundra, I stopped a few times briefly to admire a Hudsonian Godwit stalking a shallow pool, to listen to the lovely song of Smith's Longspur and get another look, to compare the song again to the singing American Tree Sparrow, and to marvel once more at the ubiquity of American Robins, Common Redpolls and Canada Geese.

At last I drove up into the boreal forest of the Twin Lakes area. Blackpolls forced out their song along the way. Bypassing the turn into Cook Street I made a beeline for the burn area. At the spot where I could see both the East and West lakes, a snowshoe hare dashed off the road into the thick vegetation. It was the colour and size of an unusually large cottontail rabbit, still a lot smaller than the Arctic hare. It wasn't a good look, but it was exciting to see another mammal characteristic of the North. I arrived at the turnoff toward the burn area and drove in past the spot where I'd seen the Spruce Grouse displaying for me, and to the edge of the burn itself. Now it was time for a long walk through a charred world of black tree trunks and ashen ground.

It was just before six o'clock. The air was cold enough for my ski jacket and wool hat. Immediately I was struck by the acrid smell of burned wood, like an old campfire. The sky was thinly overcast, enough to cool the rays of the low sun. It would be a while before the day would warm up. I set out at a brisk pace, expecting to see little in this forest of burnt sticks for the next kilometre or more. But I was wrong.

Peek! sounded a woodpecker's call nearby. Then *tap-tap-tap* and the sound of dry bark breaking, and again *tap-tap*. I froze. Could it be a Three-toed Woodpecker? I was still labouring under the impression that this species ought to be very hard to find. Nonetheless, there was the black-and-white ladder on the back of an otherwise black-looking bird clinging to the base of a black pole that had once been a mature white spruce. It was a female – no yellow beret. Couldn't be the same bird I'd seen before, a yellow-crowned male.

I watched as she chipped away at the bark. With a sharp sideways flick of her chisel beak, she sent a large chunk of bark flying, unveiling a patch of light-yellow dead wood. Then she flew a good distance through the black sticks and settled low toward the ground beyond my line of sight. I left the vehicle track to follow across the blackened ground. The acrid smell became pungent with each footfall. I could see that the fire had been hot enough here to carbonize or vaporize all organic matter in the soil. Before I could locate my bird, I found another one low on a burned tree. I was incredulous as I identified a male Black-backed Woodpecker. A close cousin to the Three-toed, it lacks only the ladder back. This one is even rarer, unexpected here. It, too, was launching chunks of bark to the right, then left, then right, like chips off a woodsman's ax. I watched intently, fascinated by his behaviour and amazed at my phenomenal luck in seeing both of the "black" woodpeckers of the North – in one spot.

I began to notice that many other black poles around me for several metres had multiple patches of exposed deadwood, especially near the ground. Clearly the woodpeckers had been busy here for some time. This guy flew off to where I could not follow, but as I returned to the track and continued toward my destination, I saw two more Three-toed Woodpeckers, a male and another female, and more areas where many black tree trunks had lots of light-yellow patches within six feet of the ground. Far from being burned out by last year's forest fire, these birds seemed to be thriving on the dead trees, presumably as insects began to work away at them. Nature doesn't take long to renew itself. From disaster and death, new life rises again.

∞

For a few minutes, walking and thinking, I pondered the deeper meaning of this dependable resurrection. From fire's searing heat, from winter's freezing cold, from drought's dusty desiccation, life recoils into death, yet soon re-emerges with dazzling vitality. I think again of packets of divine energy, like bubbles formed on the surface of the invisible Source. The white spruce are burned – death to the packets but not to the Source, which promptly forms new packets of life from the same energy, transformed. Have the trees really died? Yes. Has the forest died? No.

Individuals die but live on through their species. Species are extinguished but live on through the bio-communities they once lived in and contributed to. Death and destruction are everywhere, all the time, but so is life, because the Source is inexhaustible. Resurrection is a commonplace. It is dependable. We take it for granted.

But what of our own lives and deaths? Why do we despair in the face of death when there is so much evidence that our divine energy will live on? My life will be resurrected in a new life. But it will not be *my* life – at least it will not *feel* like my life anymore.

"A Waxwing!": June 11

Why do I cling so to *my* experience of that life? The evolutionary explanation is easy: genes that don't make us cling to our individual lives are not likely to be passed on to the next generation. Okay – but why is it that way? I ask this if only because I know my son will ask *me*! Lying within the question "Why do we have to die?" is another, deeper question: "Why are we so afraid of dying?"

It occurs to me that each divine energy packet has emerged with a particular assignment from God the Source. It goes with the assignment that the packet, the individual, must take its own life seriously enough to see the assignment through, even without knowing the objective. There must be a primordial imperative to live. That is the common bond of all the packets of divine energy – to live their assignments as long as possible. In fulfillment of what, only God knows.

Think of the implications. The energy of God propels each of us, dwells in every one of us, and so we, each of us, must regard everyone and ourselves as we would regard God – with the respect, gratitude, honesty, humility and service that Jesus called "love," modelled on the affectionate love between spouses, kinsmen and friends. His hard prescription for right conduct is that all thought and action be guided infallibly by this regard for God in each of us. He applied this commandment right across our species, regardless of our version of cultural wisdom or any deviance from it.

The consequences of living by this Christian code of right conduct have been explored and ignored in the multiple histories of Christian and other cultures. True violence has been done to the code as our mental chatter has figured all sorts of ways to turn it upside down and call it right side up. But this Golden Rule is as simple to understand as it is hard to apply. Because God dwells within a person, we should regard that person as we would regard God, which should be as we regard ourselves. We lose the compass for right conduct only if we have no reverential regard for God.

Hard to apply! Imagine a man who denies his share of God within, and try to treat him, nonetheless, as though God dwells within him. How much harder it would be if he had killed my brother or raped my wife! My society, my culture must call for severe sanctions against such behaviour in order to maintain safety and civility. But the universal code from Jesus requires that we treat this perpetrator of terrible acts as though God dwells within him, as though he is one with the rest of us, worthy of our love, and potentially redeemable.

To turn my natural grief and anger into personal violence in kind would be to break the code and challenge the divine reality itself. Yet sanctions are needed to protect society, even as society must allow this man to seek redemption. We as a society must apply these sanctions with deep regret and humility, because this man is one with us and with God: "There but for the grace of God go I."

Hard to apply! Especially when we follow the implications into even darker recesses of human experience. How should we deal with those who commit suicide, euthanasia, infanticide or abortion? In each case, a divine packet of energy is snuffed out like the flame of a candle, popped like a bubble on the surface of the boiling Source – by the choice of a human being, in violation of the most obvious corollary of the universal code "Thou shalt not kill." Societies and cultures often choose to tolerate these acts when there are special circumstances: the deep despair of a mentally ill woman drives her to take her own life; a doctor and a daughter of an elderly man who is terminally ill and in constant, severe pain finally are persuaded to help him end his life; a young woman gives birth to a hydrocephalic infant forever doomed to be a "vegetable" and in tears she smothers her baby; the parents of a 12-year-old girl who has been raped and made pregnant by her own uncle arrange for their daughter to have an abortion.

It is excruciating to condemn the people trapped in these awful cases, but it is in the interest of civil society that such acts are rare, not commonplace. Whether legal or illegal according to the society, these acts may be tolerable "in the eyes of God" if committed with profound regret and deeply felt respect for the life taken, in keeping with the universal code. Without such regret and respect, these acts are clear violations of the code and therefore intolerable in any circumstances.

Hard to apply! I have fallen into a trap set by my own mental chatter. I realize I must apply the universal code beyond even the ragged boundaries of humanity, if I insist on believing that Blackpoll is as much a packet of divine energy as I am. I do believe that. I see God in an animal as much as in my wife, my son, and myself. We are all creatures of God. Not just divinely created. God, the divine energy, dwells within.

My son has already asked me at the dinner table, "Since you love animals so much, Daddy, why do you eat them?" He was six, and I was stumped. I had to tell him, "I really don't know. I wish we didn't eat animals." It seemed little consolation that eating animals is part of the genetic and cultural wisdoms he and I have inherited from our ancestors.

I have often toyed with the idea of becoming a vegetarian. Aside from the practical difficulties in a meat-eating family and culture, I come up against the logical problem of drawing the line between animals whose killing, for food or whatever reason, I will not condone and those that are okay to kill, such as mosquitoes and ants. What is the distinction? They are all packets of the divine energy. For that matter, so are plants and even micro-organisms. That some are cute like a family pet and some are not, that some are beneficial to humans and some are serious, even dangerous pests, that some I feel very squeamish about killing and some I don't: none of these distinctions are real in the divine perspective.

They are real only to people. But therein is the question. How to live a human life in harmony with the divine reality?

I couldn't say if it would stand the test of another day with a different mood, but for that moment amid the burned forest, I could see the parallel between the awful circumstances of regretfully and respectfully having to take a human life and the circumstances of killing animals for food or in self-defence – or, for that matter, killing plants for food, fibre, lumber, and so on.

I remembered stories of traditional hunters revering the animals they hunted – once they made a kill, they would reverently thank the spirit of the killed animal, even apologize for taking its life so that they, the hunting family, could live. In my society, we're barely aware of the lives taken so that we might live. In fact, it is a daily carnage! How much of this is needed? How would we know, since we are so removed physically and mentally from the killing? What a different perspective we would have if we had to be physically, mentally and spiritually present at each death of an animal or plant for our sake.

How much more carefully we would move among our fellow packets of divine energy if we were truly mindful of their share in God! We would take their shares only with sincere regret and respect, in line with the universal code of right conduct, the Golden Rule.

I wondered if I could truly resolve to be as mindful every day of the divinity around me as I was at this moment in the blackened landscape of a forest destroyed yet slowly returning to life.

My thoughts returned to resurrection. The Resurrection. Into a world of packets of life struggling to stay alive, of human beings unable to imagine any experience of the divine energy other than its embodiment in the physical and mental lives they know in the here and now, into this world comes a person and a set of events that seem to suspend all the rules of the universe. Only a suspension of disbelief can accommodate the life, death and resurrection of Jesus Christ as recorded and interpreted by Christians. As yet, I cannot fully suspend my disbelief, but a charitable Christian friend says that at least I am asking the right questions. I do not doubt Christ because of the inconsistent acts of his followers. I do not doubt Jesus because his messages are so difficult to understand and follow. I just doubt the biophysics of the Resurrection.

Yet the earth is filled with life, death and resurrection. Why so much doubt about this one event? Granted, we can explain most of the mundane resurrections we witness in terms of the rules we perceive at work daily in the universe. But we do not and may never fully understand the Source. Is it inconceivable that the Resurrection is that exception, a singularity, that proves the rule – that the fate of the divine energy in us is not bounded by the experiential packets we call our lives?

∞

My contemplation was disrupted by a Lesser Yellowlegs passing overhead in a display flight from the surrounding tundra. Its piercing cries rang across the black landscape. It seemed too improbable to hear shorebirds flying over this burned forest, almost comically incongruous. I shook my head and smiled. Farther on, a flash of white-on-gray attracted my eye to a bird zooming off through the treetops. I immediately thought Northern Mockingbird. Couldn't be! But improbable things *were* happening this morning. No, more likely a – whoa! a Northern Shrike! I studied the options for giving chase, conscious of how easy it would be to get lost if I struck out cross country in pursuit. I noticed a side trail that looked like it had been made by the firefighters last year. I could follow that in the general direction of the bird's flight. So I did, for several minutes, stopping frequently to scan for any movement in the trees. Nothing. I gave up, disappointed that I'd missed such an opportunity, but I wasn't about to complain about bad luck. I returned to the main vehicle track.

Some 40 minutes into my meandering, stop-and-start walking, I came upon a large pond. The track paralleled the length of one shore. All the trees and willows rimming the pond had survived the fire. The opposite shore appeared to be an extensive willow swamp projecting a long way back into intact spruce woodland. Recalling Paul's directions, I figured that the stand of poplars would be at the far end. En route, I heard the unmistakable yelping-yodelling calls of a Pied-billed Grebe, so familiar from home but an unusual find here. Always a pleasure to hear this engaging bird, now in the Canadian wilderness declaring this as his pond.

The vehicle track led away from the pond's shore. I began to doubt I'd find the poplars. Then the track curved right to follow around the end of the pond. Sure enough, there were the poplars, a grove of some 30 to 40 mature trees, their distinctive heart-shaped leaves quaking in the light, cold breeze. I was delighted. At last I might see those darned Bohemian Waxwings. I walked in among the poplars for several minutes, listening intently. Nothing. So I settled down to wait nearby, confident that if a flock of waxwings were to fly in I'd hear them calling as they came. I had all day, if necessary. I found a good seat on the trunk of a tree toppled by a firefighting bulldozer, and I waited, listening and watching.

And I waited.

And waited. There was surprisingly little bird activity of any kind. The cold air kept my nose running, but even that was a pleasant reminder that I was out of doors, far from civilization, in the subarctic no less, pursuing a lifelong passion for nature. I didn't mind the wait. Eventually, a pair of Boreal Chickadees showed up, foraging in the low branches and ground cover, talking to each other in their nasal accents, unaware of my presence. The patience to sit still and wait for animals to come close on their own is often rewarded by real-life performances unaffected by the audience. But it's hard to sit still for long. The squeaky-door-hinge call of a Rusty Blackbird beckoned me to the edge of the pond, where I got a good look at a dull-black male with a striking yellow-white eye.

I returned to my perch on the log and waited again. This time a pair of Yellow-rumped Warblers came on stage to do their show. Their white throats declared their membership in the "Myrtle" subspecies of the eastern half of North America, unlike the yellow-throated "Audubon" subspecies I know from Arizona and California winters. The *chit* call is the same, though. I could identify that in my sleep. Yet I enjoy seeing them every time. I was lured off my log again by a rather complicated song pattern, an unknown warbler, maybe a Tennessee. It came from an extensive patch of thick spruce and boggy vegetation I couldn't penetrate. So I worked the edges, looking for some movement. I had no sooner mobilized the search than the song stopped. No movement to be seen. Nothing to go on. It was as good as gone.

After nearly a half hour had gone by and no waxwings had appeared, I thought it better to retrace my steps to the truck and try Cook Street down to the West Lake for a while and then come back here later for a second try. It was now 7:30 a.m. I hiked quickly back through the burned forest, sniffed the acrid smell again, and saw the Northern Shrike en route. It was in the same general area. It flew at treetop level, showing the flashes of white in the wings and rump, and then perched for a minute, giving a typical up-and-down pump of the tail and letting me confirm my identification. Not getting a good look, I manoeuvred for a better one, but then it was gone again. Enough to add Northern Shrike to the list, but not enough to feel the deep sense of satisfaction when I see an interesting bird really well.

∞

Soon I was parking the truck in the same spot along Cook Street as I had three days before, near the old quarry. I had a plan. It was time for a mid-morning snack. I stuffed a whole cinnamon-raisin bagel in my pants pocket to eat along the way through the forest to the lakeside cottage. I figured I was likely to have company. I had hardly left the quarry area and entered the magical forest with its thick beds of reindeer moss/lichen when I was intercepted by one of the local busybodies.

The Gray Jay silently sailed on fixed wings through the trees – like a slow, feathered arrow on target. I think I could feel it coming before seeing it. It landed with a light click of scaly bird claws on a branch a little below my eye level, 2 metres off. Without looking long at it, I pulled out the bagel and sat in the middle of the vehicle track, spongy with spruce needles. I was busy unwrapping the plastic bag and pulling out the bagel. The jay bounced quickly to another branch, then swooped to a low tree across the track, nervously pumping its body up and down, cocking its head to look at me with one shiny black eye, then cocking again to use the other eye, then back again. It dashed back across the track to the first tree and emitted a raucous rattle and whoop.

I started eating, first breaking off a small piece and tossing it to the ground about a metre in front of me. The jay hesitated only a moment and then was standing beside it, looking at me, then the bagel bit, then me. Next moment the bagel bit was in its beak, tossed back and swallowed. The jay looked at me intently, staying put on the ground. I tossed it another bit. No hesitation this time. It made three high jay-hops, grabbed the second piece and flew up to a branch before tossing that one back. Again the raucous noise.

I took a second bite and tossed another piece on the ground, this time closer to my feet. Another hesitation, but the jay was now a few inches from my toes. As it grabbed and gobbled the food, two more identically fluffy gray-and-white arrows glided through the trees and landed close by. Soon they, too, were on the ground grabbing bits of bagel. Once they'd all gotten a taste, the competition for each piece became intense – some noisy squabbling, but nothing combative. The first jay to arrive remained the boldest and had its way before the others. One of the other two seemed nearly equal in courage and dominance, but the third jay was timid and submissive by comparison. All were bold enough to take bagel off the tops of my shoes! I threw out three pieces at a time to restore an equitable peace.

I then offered a piece in my outstretched hand to no one in particular. The first jay hopped toward me, looked and retreated a moment. I looked away purposely. At once I felt the jay standing on my fingers, hardly any weight at all. I looked sideways in time to see it grab the bagel and fly to a branch almost within my reach. I quickly offered another piece to see if the other two might be so bold. The number two jay hopped forward, hesitated, and I looked away but watched sidelong. It hopped up on my hand, grabbed and fled in the span of a heartbeat. The number three could not be persuaded by my third offer in the hand, but soon the number one was there again, not as hurried this time. Then number two made another dashing grab. Meanwhile I kept number three eating at my feet.

Three more birds had joined us, lurking in the trees some distance off, as if waiting to be introduced. They were very different, completely the colour of dark soot or slate, but the same "cute" look – large, rounded heads, big black shiny eyes, and short beaks. They were juvenile Gray Jays, the same size as the presumed parents, differing only in their very dark body colour and the light-gray, not black, beaks with yellow "gapes" in the corners of the mouth.

Soon they were on the ground begging from the grown-ups with fluttering wings, open mouths and high-pitched squeaking.

The adults didn't look quite so cute as they dashed at the young birds with harsh squawks and flashing wings, attempting to drive them off – unsuccessfully. A bird doesn't grow to adulthood by being easily chased off by its exasperated parents. Nonetheless, the adults never gave in. I took pity on the juveniles by busying all three grown-ups with their own morsels, then tossing a bit of bagel in front of each young bird. All three looked interested but hesitated too long and were pre-empted. After a couple more tries, one of them picked up a bagel bit with a raisin in it and gobbled it. It stood there for a moment looking thoughtful. Then it went through the open-mouthed motions of regurgitation. Up and out came the raisin. Pitooey! I guess the young are universally reluctant to try anything new to eat.

By now I'd concluded I was entertaining a family of Gray Jays. That might seem pretty obvious, but you seldom know for sure. I figured the two boldest birds were the parents of the other four, the shy one in adult plumage probably an offspring from last year's nesting season. The other three were almost certainly the result of this spring's nesting. Perhaps the older sibling had helped its parents feed the younger siblings – a non-parent helper at the nest, as has been observed in other jay species. Complex family groups were the subject of my own field research decades ago on round-tailed ground squirrels in the Sonoran Desert of Arizona. I didn't find anything as unusual or interesting as nest helpers, but social systems of animals (including humans) have remained a lifelong interest. It is a special treat to discover a "complex" family of Gray Jays on my own. It made me feel almost like a field biology researcher again, without all the tedium of research. Just a snack break.

Gradually I became aware of a seventh bird, not at all the same species. A female Pine Grosbeak had approached on the ground through the undergrowth and was now feeding in the middle of the vehicle track just beyond the bustle of jays. Perhaps the bustle and noise was what attracted her, at first curious and then thinking it must be safe if the jays were having a party. The grosbeak made no attempt to join the competition for bagel bits. She foraged calmly a few metres away on the track. While the jays waited impatiently, I studied her with the binoculars. She was a large finch, having black wings and tail with contrasting white wing-bars and a plump ashy-gray body. The crown, sides and back of her head, and her rump as well, were washed with a most unusual greenish-brownish yellow, something between olive and ochre. Hard to describe, other than as "the colour of a female Pine Grosbeak." An unusually beautiful bird when seen up close.

It had been my intention to eat much of the bagel myself. So far, two thirds of it had gone mostly to the jay family. I didn't want to make them sick with too much human food. With my knees up and elbows resting on them, I set out to eat the rest of the bagel. I took a bite and held the remainder in my hand up near my left shoulder. Number One (safe to presume) landed on my shoulder and grabbed at the bagel. I held on tightly, examining the bird's round face through the reading portion of my bifocal lenses. Its shiny black eye looked back at me with implacable determination. It persisted in tearing off a small chunk and scrambled to the nearest branch. Delighted by its audacity, I took another bite and returned the bagel to its resting position near my face. Would Number One try again? Within 10 seconds, I felt the claws grabbing my shoulder. This time I didn't hold on tight enough when it gave the bagel a good yank. Number One had the whole of the remaining bagel and was flying fast through the trees and out of sight. It knew it had pulled off a great robbery and needed to make a getaway.

For the briefest moment, I was cross. Then I laughed, startling the other jays, who had been watching all this very closely. I showed them my empty hands and said, "Sorry guys. Back to your nuts and berries!" Gradually and reluctantly they slipped away one by one into the forest. The party was over. But the Pine Grosbeak kept on foraging, closer now that the jays were gone. I watched her through the binoculars again, admiring her subtle hues. Then something seemed to cross her mind, and she, too, was gone. Perhaps it didn't seem so safe after the jays had left. Birds recognize the safety found in numbers – at least when the other birds aren't trying to steal the food.

I hoped Number One would share his prize with the others, but remembering that unblinking gaze up close, I sincerely doubted it.

∞

I gathered myself up and carried on along the track, finding peace in every step and smiling at the forest around me. It now seemed even more magical than before. At the lakeside, I sat for some length of time on the deck of the tiny cabin, reflecting on the morning so far. The terns and gulls were there again, *kip*-ping and *kee-ahr*-ing. The Oldsquaw drake needlessly fled from me with an *ooh-wah*. Reassuringly familiar sounds by now. I could have lain down and drifted off to sleep, had it not been so cold.

My thoughts went back to the family of Gray Jays and then my erstwhile career as a field student of kinship among animals. I felt wistful, a longing for what I originally had thought a career of field study would be – spending weeks or months in places like this, having experiences like this morning. It was a boyish dream. But I know people who have made such dreams come true. At least they *seem* to have made them come true, becoming wildlife writers and photographers, natural history tour guides, conservation biologists working for various government and private agencies and universities. I met many of them in East Africa in the 1970s. I could have joined them, if I had wanted it badly enough. I anticipate my son asking someday with youthful impatience, "Why didn't you?" Given the enjoyment I feel in nature, why didn't I make it a way of life when the opportunity presented itself?

Like any happy vacationer, I was really just asking myself how to make the feeling last. I know what will take my son years and a few keen disappointments to learn. If the dream were to come true, it wouldn't be a vacation anymore. It would be work – real life. There would be onerous tasks as important as the fun ones. There would be difficult people to deal with as well as the reasonable, pleasant ones. There would be enjoyment and satisfaction, but also risks and anxieties and crises. There would be serious setbacks and challenges to test one's resolve to keep on going.

For me personally, something higher than the "ups" of field biology is needed to keep me going through the "downs." It could be the sheer necessity of feeding my family. It could also be something bigger – a purpose that contributes in some small way to a better world. Something more important than my own happiness and fulfillment has to be there to make it worthwhile. I must have a purpose that drives me through the resistance of the everyday world. I would find it hard to settle for "just a job" to earn enough money to make ends meet and enough social status to make me feel good about myself.

In other words, the purpose that drives me has to take me beyond myself and even my family. It has to reflect the obligation imposed by my awareness of being part of that mystical body (of Christ, says the Christian) that connects me to all other people. Even more, I believe the mystical body extends outward to embrace all God's creatures. Humans must have first consideration, because I am one, but more important because of our favoured status with God, our potential for communion with God. However, animals and, more generally, nature are also special creatures of

God; a life devoted to their welfare is no less noble service to the mystical body.

I have to conclude that the purpose I found in my potential career as a field biologist was not "big" enough to get past the routines and people and anxieties and probable setbacks I'd have to deal with in that line of work. More than anything, I suppose, the subculture of field biology researchers bothered me. The animals being studied were seldom honoured with the respect and reverence they deserve, in my view. I'm certain that many, if not most, field biologists are attracted to their line of work by such respect and reverence, but the professional indoctrination to the field frowns on its expression. In fact, the study animals are spoken of and too often treated as mere instruments of the trade, tools to be used and discarded as convenience dictates in pursuit of a career goal. I fell into this pattern of thought, but I'd like to think I never abandoned my regard for the animals I worked with. Perhaps for this reason, I never became fully comfortable with the majority of my professional colleagues and the purposes that drove them.

The alternative wildlife career would have been conservation education and advocacy, in which loving animals and nature for their spiritual value is more openly admitted and encouraged. This is a very much more social profession than wildlife research, not as well suited to my social reluctance, but so is my current line of work in the poverty-fighting world of international development. More significant, I believe, is again the subculture of conservationists, tending toward an unreasonable disregard for human needs, bordering often on misanthropy – a deplorable sort of elitist presumption of intellectual and moral superiority over the ignorant and selfish mass of humanity. I found it too difficult to respect such a narrow view of God's creation.

Once I had a good fix on what my potential career in biology would probably be like, what I would probably be like, and what good it and I would likely do for the world, I made some conscious and difficult choices, landing me where I am now. It's not at all a bad place to be. I like what I am and what I'm doing for a living. I respect and generally enjoy my colleagues at work. In addition to the real service it provides to people with far fewer options in life than I have, the work brings me some real personal satisfaction and some honour among my professional peers, as well as remuneration and some honour to my family. At the same time, the magic that nature holds for me is enhanced rather than diminished by the precious little time I have to spend in it.

Wrapped in this cocoon of thought as I sat staring at the lake, it came to me that perhaps the trouble I was having in connecting with people like Bonnie and Mike and even Paul is that I see myself as their colleague. They are neither biology researchers nor conservation ideologues, but they make their living by knowing the wildlife of their area, as I know the wildlife in my home area. I want them to regard me as one of them, not as a paying client, a novice to be brought along for the ride. But long ago I chose not to be one of them, for whatever reason. I can't have it both ways. I'm either in or out of that way of life. I'm not a professional naturalist. I've chosen to remain an amateur.

∽

I didn't go beyond the cabin this time. I left my incomplete thoughts on the deck and retraced my steps to the truck. The forest was still magical, but the jays were nowhere in sight. As I approached the quarry area, I heard a finch call and saw it fly to a distant treetop. I could barely make it out, but it was definitely a White-winged Crossbill. Just then a Chevy Suburban emerged from the other side of the quarry, entering Cook Street from the main road. The driver was a man my age or older and his passenger a respectful-looking teenage boy. They drove up to where I stood.

We exchanged warm greetings. They had seen the crossbill as they were driving in. We shared our reasons for being out here and then got down to swapping species "needed" for sightings made and their locations. I had a lot to offer, as this was my second time out here in recent days. They had just arrived in Churchill to lead an Elderhostel birding tour group. They were scouting the birding hot spots in advance of the group's arrival in Churchill the next day. This was not the man's first visit to Churchill.

As they drove on toward the lake and I carried on toward the tree where I had seen the crossbill land, a classic yellow school bus (not the blue-and-white one with "Churchill Wilderness Encounter" on the side) came lumbering awkwardly in along Cook Street. It was loaded with older folks. I waved and they waved back curiously as we passed. I stopped and looked after the bus. It came to a stop, but they didn't disembark. I surmised they were getting a briefing on the area they were about to invade. I concluded that this place was filling up with birders and I'd better get back to the burn area before that started to fill up as well. So back to the truck and off I went while they were still preparing to disembark. I felt a bit unfriendly, but I had an agenda.

To see a Bohemian Waxwing!

I parked the truck at the same spot on the edge of the burn area and quickly walked in to the pond and the grove of poplars. I saw none of the woodpeckers on the way and felt fortunate to have been here earlier in the day. It was now about 10:30 and finally beginning to warm up a little. As I approached the poplars, I heard a probable Gray-cheeked Thrush singing in the distance well beyond the grove.

Scanning the direction of the song with my binoculars – usually a fruitless effort – this time revealed the singer on a treetop. I could hardly believe it. I've never seen one of the small brown thrushes singing from a prominent perch, much less a treetop.

Expecting the bird to fly off any moment, I approached with quick steps, but halted frequently to look through the binoculars to see if I could yet pick out distinguishing features. I could tell it was a thrush, all right, and the song was different from any other than the Gray-cheeked. But I wanted to see its ashen face. Soon my way was blocked from getting any closer. I'd have to make do at a distance. The lighting was neither good nor bad. I sat down on the ground, propped my elbows on my knees and strained my eyes through the binoculars.

Well, okay. I'd say I saw the plain-gray face, no eye-ring. But without the song, I could not have been sure. That's the way it often is with these brown thrush species. Like the shrike, not a satisfying experience, but it was good enough for the list. No complaints.

I'd barely turned around to return to the poplars when I heard that same warbler song from the same spruce thicket-bog I had inspected earlier this morning, except this time I was looking in from a different angle. I found I could see into the interior by climbing up on a fallen tree trunk. The singer was pretty close, so it was worth being patient to see what could be seen. It would have to come to me, though. *Psshhh, psshhh, psshhh.* I made the silly noise with my lips to see if the warbler might want to check out the baby-bird-in-distress sound. The singing stopped. My hopes sank. But I remained super-vigilant, with binoculars up to my face, ready to pounce on the slightest movement in the foliage.

It was an idyllic scene. A small pool of dark, tannic water surrounded by low sedge grasses, backed up by shrubs and then a thick wall of spruce. Flit! There it was, the warbler. Binoculars up. I didn't need to hurry. This bird was relaxed and looking for grub on the open conifer branches. It was indeed a Tennessee Warbler, all white below, green and gray above, with a black line from the bill through the eye. Not much to look at, but just like its picture in the book. It opened wide and threw back its head to confirm its connection to the song I'd heard. Very nice! Now *that* was a satisfying experience, much more than a name on a list.

At last I arrived at the poplar grove and started for my log seat to settle down for a wait. But I never sat.

A waxwing!

At the top of one of the poplars, as predicted. But just one. I couldn't see others in the same or neighbouring trees, which puzzled me. Waxwings travel in flocks. My first concern was to position myself so the bird had a dark background of poplar leaves; this would allow me to see the colours of the Bohemian well. By range alone, it had to be a Bohemian. But I was eager to see this bird clearly. This was a lifer, and not just any lifer. Before it flew, which could be any moment, I needed to see the cinnamon colour under the tail. That would clinch it, distinguish it from the Cedar Waxwing, which has pure white undertail coverts.

Oh, how many hundreds, even thousands of Cedar Waxwings have I looked at in California to check the colour of their ... you know ... undertail coverts, hoping to discover an errant Bohemian. Here, the Cedar would be the errant one. I just had to confirm my first sighting of a Bohemian Waxwing by seeing this bird's bottom!

But the waxwing was sitting on the far side of some awkwardly placed leaves. I swayed back and forth to get views around the leaves. What was worse, the bird was sitting with its back to me and its tail down. I didn't dare to make a major move. I'd have to get lucky. The bird would have to shift its position.

"Come on, baby. Let me see you now." I muttered to myself. "Come *on*!"

And then it shifted! My heart jumped. I could see its bottom! I was stunned. I was shocked. I was incredulous. Its bottom was *white*!

Trying to be gracious in defeat, I smiled. "It's a f---ing Cedar Waxwing!" I said out loud. I smiled more broadly still. "It's a f---ing *Cedar* Waxwing!" Again out loud, this time aware that I was looking at a real rarity for the Churchill area. How utterly ironic, how ludicrous.

As if offended by my rude remarks, the Cedar Waxwing took flight and didn't stop until well beyond the far line of spruces on the other side of the pond.

"It was a f---ing Cedar Waxwing," I told myself yet again, in reluctant belief. And I smiled even more broadly. I had to enjoy this wonderful joke at my expense. As I approached completion of my 50th year, I thought I could close the book on whether there is a God who takes an interest in the lives of individual human beings – a Personal God. Now I'm not so sure. It even seems that this Personal God has a pretty good sense of humour.

∞

It is one thing to believe in God as the Creator of the universe and even as C. S. Lewis's "transcendental interferer" in the unfolding show, giving divine definition to Truth and Duty. It is quite another to believe in God as personal Saviour, as offering divine protection and consolation to individual souls. I have long rejected the latter, not as impossible but – to me – inconceivable. Yet in this moment of sharp disappointment, I felt a pang of resentment, an impulse toward defiance of some Person who was intervening, unbidden, in my life for my own good. But I was immediately disarmed by the fitting irony in the mode of intervention. I couldn't help but let spiritual calm settle into me like the warmth of hot chocolate after a bitterly cold winter walk. Relaxing of mind then body, letting go of compulsion to control and achieve, surrendering of pride in the face of far superior wisdom and power. Then feeling an ethereal embrace by a weightless cloak of loving concern.

My response was the only one possible – joyful gratitude.

The waxwing did not have to speak for me to hear clearly its message that I need to put birding, and my whole life, in a broader perspective. That it is best to let go of attachment to goals and their achievement and focus on being with the life around me. Was it a message from God coming through a bird? What better way to reach a birder? But how could that be? How preposterous to think that a force, an energy – no matter how divine – could be operating like a person, sending messages personally tailored and targeted to a human being.

Yet it's not the first time it has occurred to me that God was speaking to me through a bird. Once upon a fine English evening, I sat alone in the tiniest of ancient churches atop a hill some distance from the nearest village. I sat in the gloom in front of the old altar rail, pondering an icon of Christ in agony on the cross and trying my best to make sense of the Christian story, looking for some logic in the illogical. Outside, the June light was finally fading around 9:30 p.m. A patch of trees, a "wood" in which European Blackbirds were nesting and singing, surrounded this little church. As I was sorting out some conclusion, long since forgotten, a male Blackbird started in singing his remarkable song. It was a thrush song, not very different from the American Robin's (the Blackbird is really just an all-black American Robin in size, shape and behaviour), but different nonetheless. He phrased his song like a person in thoughtful soliloquy, almost a hesitant, extemporaneous prayer to the oncoming night. The song was timed as an inscrutable response to my proposed conclusion.

I smiled then as I thought this Blackbird could be sending me a message – from God, no less. The message I read into the song was that I was not thinking broadly enough, that I would have to look outside the little church, as well as within, for the answers I sought. The bird himself seemed to be an essential part of the answer. I allowed that God might be speaking through this bird as the only way to get the message across to me. Absurd? My wife thought so – at first – when I dared to share this idea.

For absurdity in media for sacred messages, it's hard to beat a tag on a teabag! Good Earth Teas of Santa Cruz, California, prints a different short quote or message on each tag attached to the string on each teabag. Here is one, a quote from William McGill:

> The value of persistent prayer is not that He will hear us,
> but that we will finally hear Him.

One never knows where to expect revelation! But that is exactly what this teabag tag was for me as I thought about the singing Blackbird and now this errant waxwing. It's not that God is talking to us personally, but that we are listening to God with very personal ears. We shape our own experience of the divine energy. No wonder. We each are our own packet of that divine energy. When occasionally we open our consciousness to the divine energy within ourselves, it seems to meld with the divine energy of the very universe. We seem to hear God or whatever we are willing to believe in. Yet it is a message coming from within and naturally, therefore, very personal in its construction and meaning.

There's another way to describe it, perhaps, that might make this concept more accessible to my son. I saw a movie many years ago, a sci-fi adventure under the sea (the title now forgotten). A disabled submarine had sunk to a great depth and all hands were lost. A special deep-sea submersible vessel with a small crew was sent down to investigate. Something strange had happened after the accident. The submersible crew discovered the cause; some alien being had inhabited the submarine. Was it dangerous or benign? Crew members who believed the being to be dangerous encountered a being with deadly form and behaviour. Those who believed the being to be benign encountered a harmless, even helpful being. Each member of the crew shaped the alien being in his or her own image of what this being might be. The very act of perceiving moulded the thing perceived. Their hopes or fears were fulfilled. The being was outside of them, far more powerful than they were, yet it seemed to come from within them. The divine energy? A Personal God? Mysteriously one and the same.

I had to travel all the way to Churchill, Manitoba, and out to Twin Lakes to a clump of poplars just to see a Cedar Waxwing out of place? This was a religious experience?

Well...yes.

I suppose my inner being was ready only then and there for the message this bird was to deliver.

The watchful dragons of my self-conscious intellect were rearing their ugly snouts in objection to this notion of personal messages from God – especially when such messages are delivered by birds that don't say or do anything out of the ordinary, that simply suggest a thought to my brain. What is to say this messaging is not solely me talking to myself – my mental chatter? Am I imagining a communication? I have no conclusive response. How can I know the difference between what arises solely from my mind and what emanates from a source that is both outside me and inside me?

The skeptic cites the power of suggestion, but cannot be specific as to the source of such power. If the soul is the immaterial Me that persists beyond my material life, and if my soul encompasses my rational as well as intuitive mind that persists beyond the life of my material brain and sense organs, then the mind may well be the soul's means for communication with God, or God's means to speak through my soul. Just as we don't know how, in any practical way, to distinguish the mind from the brain, we are even more at a loss to separate the mind from the soul or the soul from God.

My evidence comes from the feeling inside, which was very different from me talking to myself. It is an internal voice addressing me in a language I do not know. It needs contemplation, translation, interpretation. I intuit that it means something important. The intuition draws from a deeper well of knowledge than is available through the five senses that feed the rational mind. The deeper into the well the intuitive mind descends, the greater the opportunity to encounter God within. But the knowledge that intuition offers still requires translation to the language of the rational mind. I must interpret it for others in the terms of familiar experience that can be shared verbally. Even then, only my appearance of rational daily conduct will help me escape charges of madness.

My intellectual dragons grow especially nervous at the mere suggestion that God is not only setting rules for the whole universe, not only intervening in the unfolding play, not only admonishing humanity to adjust its collective and individual conduct, but going so far as to communicate directly to me personally with guidance that reflects intimate knowledge of all that I have been and am likely to be. It raises the disturbing possibility that God and I can join in an inseparable embrace that overrides the power of my intellect and challenges the autonomy of my soul. There is the terrible prospect that I might surrender my Self. But it would not, could not be a forced embrace by an overpowering God. It would be a truly happy union entered into freely and voluntarily. To paraphrase C. S. Lewis, from outside the universe, God reveals himself in our hearts, inside us, to influence our behaviour toward Good. If we let ourselves sneak past those dragons, we can feel this influence, and, depending on how we interpret its meaning for our lives, we can respond – or not.

∞

I walked back through the black forest of sticks as though a great burden had been lifted off my shoulders. A spring in my step, a light heart, a smile on my face. Even the acrid smell of burnt woodland seemed right. I had done what I had come to do. I had seen what there was to see. I had come to know a new world as I might know a new friend, well enough to joke and tease each other as old friends.

There truly were no more objectives, except to savour the last 24 hours of my visit. Who could know what new experiences might happen in that time? But I had no ambitions or expectations. I wanted now to focus on reviewing the familiar, enjoy the sense of (almost) belonging. My only remaining obligations were simple: pack my gear, return the trusty blue truck, and find my way to the airplane bound for Winnipeg and beyond. I was ready to leave, but in no hurry to go. It was a magnificent feeling.

I heard the Rusty Blackbird and the Pied-billed Grebe again as I walked along the shore of the pond. A Lesser Yellowlegs displayed overhead, piercing the air with its calls. Two Common Redpolls descended from the sky, buzzing and twittering into a spruce.

Up ahead, through the black sticks, I could see the same school bus parked just off the vehicle track. Its large group of birders, maybe 20 of them, had hiked up the same sidetrack I'd used to chase after the shrike early this morning. They were now returning slowly en masse. Their average age appeared to be a robust 65, except for the tall, 40ish bearded man in the lead. He was the very image of the professional naturalist, a very positive image, the young professor of ornithology. He reminded me so much of a few guys I knew in graduate school, good people whom I really liked. So I was ready to like this guy.

They reached the bus at the same time I was passing. I waved and called, "Good morning!" The leader called back, "Have you seen any Bohemian Waxwings?"

I stopped and looked at him and the rest of the group with a broad smile. "I've been looking for Bohemian Waxwings for days. I haven't seen any so far. Have you?"

"A Waxwing!": June 11

The leader left the group clustered around the door to the bus and came over to talk a bit. "No, we haven't. They seem to be scarce this year. Some years they're easy to find around here, and some years you're lucky to see any at all." I concluded that he led tours to Churchill regularly.

"I was told there'd be a good chance to find them in the stand of poplars down here at the far end of the pond." He nodded as if he knew the poplars well. I went on, "I didn't see any Bohemians ... but I *did* see a solitary Cedar Waxwing!" His eyebrows went up a little.

"That's a good find," he allowed.

"It would be tough to track it down again. It flew off a long way that way." I pointed. He nodded as though he'd take a look anyway. He seemed thankful for the information. He asked what else I had seen today. Just then a shorter man came over to join us. He also was about 40 and had a large tape recorder hanging off one shoulder. I told them both about the woodpeckers, especially the Black-backed Woodpecker. They were interested, but not as much as I was expecting. They had seen the Three-toed Woodpecker and confirmed that both species have been seen here every year, though the Black-backed is still a good find. I also mentioned the Northern Shrike in this very area. The shorter man said that they'd seen it here last year, but not yet this year.

The shorter man left us to walk down to the edge of the pond. I asked the leader which tour company this was. "Victor Emmanuel Nature Tours," he said. One of the oldest and best birding tour operators in the world, I knew. One of the graduate students whom this guy reminded me of, Steve Hilty, had gone to work for Victor Emmanuel and become one of the star guides. He also had co-authored a field guide to birds of Colombia. VENT is top-notch. My appreciation for this fellow increased. I looked from him to his clients gathered around the school bus and thought for a moment

319

what it might be like to spend days at a time shepherding such a large group around beautiful natural areas in search of birds. They seemed like pleasant, likable people – but so many! Then I thought of the accumulated training and experience this guide probably had, of the passion for birds and nature that drove him, and wondered how fulfilling he found this line of work. Perhaps he was in fact a professor of ornithology or something similar, and this tour guide gig was something he did on the side for the money and the opportunity to get away to exotic places. Perhaps he enjoyed teaching a crowd, or at least he didn't mind.

I was about to see what I could find out about this leader when a blackbird's *chack* sounded from the pond. It was the guy with the tape recorder broadcasting a recording to attract the Rusty Blackbird – one of the more artificial tricks of the trade. I guess they still "needed" that species. The leader had to go back to work. I bid him good luck, and he returned the sentiment. I waved and smiled to the group, who looked puzzled and did not respond. I turned and walked on.

No, thanks, I thought to myself. Not for me. Nope.

∞

I was still feeling light and complete as I drove the familiar truck down the familiar gravel road approaching the familiar tundra plain. I did experience a twinge of loss at the thought I might never see the Twin Lakes plateau again. But I turned my mind back to the very different world of the tundra; this patch of tundra had become my favourite. I decided to stop at every one of the six turnouts along the straight causeway across, to absorb as much of the sight, sound and feel of the tundra as I could.

Now it was midday. It was no longer cold, just pleasantly cool. But the light was "flat." There was little bird activity in evidence. And whenever I stopped with the windows rolled down, the cab of the truck quickly filled with mosquitoes. It was almost immediate. I thought the mosquitoes would need some time to pick up the whiff of carbon dioxide from this warm-blooded animal and rise from their roosts in the vegetation to go to dinner. Instead, it seemed the mosquitoes were constantly patrolling the air by the tens per cubic metre. Their response time was phenomenally short. I applied mosquito repellent spray, Cutter's, which seemed to work well. Still, just having the little beasts whining around my head and zigzagging on the inside of the windshield was annoying. I dutifully stopped at all six stops, but not for more than a minute or two each. By the time I reached the forest on the other side, I was relieved to be moving on. I thought of the poor caribou I'd seen this morning and wondered how they cope. Good grief!

I covered the ground to the launch site quickly, feeling good still. I was not in the mood to stop until I approached Bird Cove, where I decided to check out the track that goes in to the east side of the cove. Perhaps the tide would be higher now, and I'd see why the Winnipeg birders thought so highly of the location for seeing migrating shorebirds. This track turned out to be little better than the one I'd taken to the west side. And once there, I couldn't find easy foot access down to the water line. Furthermore, the tide was well out again. I didn't see much advantage in trying the cove again. It looked pretty much the same as before. I was getting tired, so I went back out to the Highway.

A very short way onward, I stopped by the side of the road for the dual purpose of eating my other bagel (sorry, jays!) and checking the tundra hummocks for the jaeger nest that Bonnie mentions in her book. The mosquitoes were practically non-existent here – because the tundra here was relatively dry? Sure enough, there they were, Parasitic Jaegers, three of them sitting on one of the tundra hummocks only about 50 metres from the Highway. I set up the scope to study them as I munched. I thought again of complex families, wondering what three jaegers at the long-used nest site might signify. They refused to be entertaining, to interact, so that I might get some ideas. They simply sat there and calmly inspected their domain.

After "lunch" I drove on, past the dump and the airport, and decided to take a detour to the town. I turned off the Highway between the airport and the Akudlik marshes and lakes and took what Bonnie's book calls the Coast Road. It goes back down to the Hudson Bay shore, from which you can look upslope and see the plane wreck called "Miss Piggy." The plane's approach to the airport had been too low and resulted in a belly flop on the big boulders. Ouch! That was many years ago. Remarkable how long ship and plane wrecks last in the subarctic.

The Coast Road went back up on the coastal ridge and along the edge of an inviting patch of tundra stretching some 50 metres to a large tundra pond. It looked relatively dry, so I decided to give the tundra one last close look. I pulled on the tall wellington boots for only the second time and splashed out across the "dry" tundra. It was fairly easy going. I got reacquainted with the great variety of diminutive plant species, to which I couldn't attach names but remembered seeing out by Landing Lake. As for birds, nothing much again, except a Canada Goose sitting on a nest and eyeing me warily with neck low, parallel to the ground, literally maintaining a low profile. I made it to the edge of the pond, skirted it for a few metres, then headed back to the truck on the other side of the nervous goose. I flushed a sandpiper, either Least or Semipalmated.

Not ready to call an end to the walk, I crossed the road and climbed up onto the huge, rounded rocks that form the crest of the coastal ridge. There I found American Pipits, as expected. I stood for a while enjoying the view out to the sea ice on one side and across the tundra and ponds to the other. I wanted to keep drinking it in! But I also was getting tired and thought a nap would be good, too.

∽

Early dinner was back at the Gypsy Café. Another great meal. I listened in on local conversation about the first World Cup soccer match, about to start this evening on the television in the restaurant. It was Brazil versus Scotland. This was a partisan crowd. The small round man and the thin bald one with glasses who worked at the café were solid for Brazil. The thin one had lived in Brazil for a few years and was knowledgeable about the makeup of the Brazilian team. They were bantering as old friends with an Anglo family having dinner there. Not surprisingly, the Anglo Canadians were rooting for Scotland, but resigned to the high probability that Scotland would lose to the superb Brazilian team. I learned that the small round man was the owner, named Tony. He and the other fellow, his cousin, were from Portugal via Montréal.

As I left the restaurant, I discovered the fascinating map of the Canadian Arctic on the wall near the door. It showed the "polar" view, placing the islands and tiny communities of the far North in the featured centre of the map and the vast majority of Canada's cities and towns on the remote periphery. An Inuit-centric view of the world, which literally turned the world map upside down. From that perspective, Nunavut made more sense as a distinct political entity. The map also highlighted Churchill's position as a key border post between the Inuit world and the rest. Face one direction, south, and the key concern is the World Cup in Paris and a game between Europeans and South Americans. Face the other direction, north, and the key concern is Nunavut and the future of the far-Northern peoples. These two almost mutually incomprehensible world views could be having dinner at adjacent tables in this odd little restaurant in this remote outpost town on

Hudson Bay. The end point of one way of life and the starting point for another. The same could be said for the ecological endings and beginnings around Churchill. For me, that map captured the special significance of Churchill.

I had told myself that I had no more objectives, but I did have a good deal of daylight left in my last full day. I wanted to use it well, expose myself to as much of this subarctic environment as I could. So I decided to drive down the Goose Creek Road and give the area south along the river another look. It was a long drive on the gravel road all the way to the Hydro Station on the river. I enjoyed the changing habitats along the way and was impressed again by the width and power of Goose Creek and its flanking expanses of willow swamp. But I saw and heard nothing new, only the now familiar. And that was good enough.

On the way back, I stopped at Akudlik junction to add the Black-backed Woodpecker and the Cedar Waxwing to the CWE Rare Bird Alert white board. No question in my mind this time that these two species belonged on the board. They were good finds. And no elaborate location descriptions this time, just "Twin Lakes burn area." Call it acculturation or going with the flow or whatever; I was playing the game by the right rules now.

I had finished writing on the board when another pickup truck pulled up beside mine. A man in his late 50s stepped out. I sensed immediately that he was not from the Churchill area and was definitely a birder. He had on a distinctively American hat, like the Budweiser hats that were popular in the '70s and that older men still fancy. Or it could have been a sport fisherman's hat, the kind that might have several fishing flies hooked on to the brim. He walked up, staring at what I was writing and said, "What did you see?" in a friendly and genuinely interested way. Without waiting for me to answer, he said, "Cedar Waxwing! That's good!"

"Not for me," I laughed. I gave him a quick, cleaned-up synopsis of my Cedar Waxwing story. He agreed that the Bohemians were scarce this year, without saying whether he had seen one. He also confirmed that the Black-backed Woodpecker was a good find.

"What have you seen that's worth adding to the board?" I asked. He already had the marker in his hand. Without answering he proceeded to write "BWT" at "Granary Ponds." I looked at this and puzzled for a moment, then asked without embarassment, "What does BWT mean?"

"Blue-winged Teal," he replied simply.

"Oh! ... I've seen them at the Granary Ponds the past few days, but I didn't know they're that unusual." I hoped I hadn't come across as trying to one-up him. He made no verbal response, but I could tell he was not put off, especially when he asked where I was from and how long I'd been in Churchill. I asked him the same and found out that he had been here for a week and would be leaving on the same plane as I would tomorrow. He was from Maryland and had been coming up to Churchill every year for the past 12 years or so.

"Gotta go," he ended.

"Perhaps I'll see you tomorrow," I offered. No response. He drove off toward the airport. I figured he must be staying with the Churchill Northern Studies Centre out at the old launch site. Very little else out that way.

∽

I drove right on through town and out to Cape Merry for a quick goodbye look. Then I returned the truck to the hotel and set out on foot for a good long walk around the Granary Ponds, ending up as usual at the south end of the Port facility. The clouds had thinned through the day and now they were covering only a portion of the southern horizon, much like yesterday evening.

I walked down the railroad tracks toward the station again and discovered the Snow Buntings in the same spot where the stream from the Granary Ponds flows into the river.

Seldom can you recreate a magical moment, but it recreated itself that evening. The same gorgeous low-angle sunlight suffused the river, the ice floes, the town and train station with hues of gold and blue, accented with whites and reds. It was not yet 10 p.m. I sat down and watched, occasionally studying the Snow Buntings and the Ruddy Turnstones that joined them. The scene seemed a reflection of the inner peace I felt.

I was tempted to try to wrap this experience up with a bow, like a souvenir to take with me. I would have my list of birds and mammals seen and the visual images and remembered pleasures to go with each check mark. The memories would be reinforced and enriched by colours and forms recorded in my photos of tundra and forest, river and ocean, rock and ice, cloud and sky. But what of the interior journey? What could I take with me from my thinking these days? I wondered if this Churchill experience was some sort of passage through a critical point in mid-life. I obviously had a lot of thoughts to sort through.

I would have enjoyed the company of a birding friend. Although it might have been more fun, it would have been a very different experience. I would have missed something even more precious and meaningful than sharing experiences with a friend. The kind of thinking I seemed compelled to do here requires the clarity of mind that comes to me only when fully alone with the natural world. I had believed the trip would be about experiencing a new world. Certainly the particulars of the northern world had been the star attraction, but they seemed even more interesting when they confirmed what is universal in the natural world. The beautiful and wonderfully varied birds had been like clues or passwords to gain entry to the mystery of this universal nature.

Another person, even a birdwatcher, would probably need different clues in a different place to find the way to understanding. We would have distracted each other from the task.

I thought with deep gratitude and love of my wife and son, who encouraged me to come and who would so much enjoy hearing about it all. What could I share with them? I felt I was far better prepared now to explain my world view to my son, in part because I had discovered that it is not so different after all from his mother's. I thought, too, of my father, who would have loved to join me on an adventure like this, but for his emphysema. And of my mother, who does not travel but whose love of nature is always within me. I wished I could share these past days with them all, or at least the feeling of this evening scene. Yet, having come and seen and felt, I knew again what I knew before I started: that this was a trip I had to take by myself.

It seemed fitting to reflect on the overall meaning of my trip. I wondered if I had gone far enough north this time. Would I have to return someday and push farther on? Or would I be able to see what I'd seen here wherever I might be from now on?

I still had no clear understanding of the meaning of life – not that I could articulate in words. I had not seen the face of God or heard a clear message from beyond. I hadn't even seen an Arctic fox or a Bohemian Waxwing! I could understand the joke of seeing the Cedar Waxwing as a message to see my life in a perspective broader than listing bird species or knowing lots of facts and theories about nature or even travelling the world to help the poor in some small way. All I seemed to have now was a surer-than-ever feeling that I am a bit player on an inconceivably grand stage, a tiny packet of the divine energy that pervades and embraces the universe. And that I have a lot of companions on that stage, human and non-human. It is by seeing the divine energy in them that I can see it in myself.

There is more.

Until this journey of the mind and spirit, I had found only cold comfort in my vague awareness of the disembodied divine in the universe. My mystical consciousness of its continual surge and transformation gave me no joy or hope, only a sense of perspective. I had not known what to do with this sense. Here, in my solitude from friends and family, I discovered once again, through animals in the wild – but this time with a sharp, incontestable clarity – a companionship with a mysteriously personal divine presence within my own indescribable soul. I felt the joyful invitation to deeper companionship.

I am still pondering my response.

Jack Kornfield poses the problem in the title of one of his books on the meditative life of the Zen Buddhist, *After the Ecstasy, the Laundry*. He writes:

> Most spiritual accounts end with illumination or enlightenment.
> But what if we ask what happens after that?
> What happens when the Zen master returns home to spouse and children?
> What happens when the Christian mystic goes shopping?
> What is life like after the ecstasy?

In other words, Kornfield continues,

> As much as our breath comes in and out,
> [spiritual life] must integrate inner knowing and outer expression.
> It is not enough to touch awakening.
> We must find ways to live its vision fully.

How can I let go of attachment to achievement and still participate in a community of striving human beings? This question describes the spiritual work yet to be done. What I could conclude from today's enlightenment was that, while it is essential to have goals and strive for them, it is better not to be so attached to their achievement that we fail to embrace the striving. In seeking the Bohemian Waxwing, I had experienced so much that was delightful in itself. I failed my goal, but I could be thankful that failure didn't blind me to the Cedar Waxwing and all the other manifestations of the Divine that were my privilege to see.

But what of my loved ones and my life itself? Can I let go of attachments and still treasure them? I suppose the only enduring attachment is to the Eternal – to God. Can I accept joyfully the invitation to union with God and still participate fully in this material world, even continue to live at all?

I began to recognize that I would need help with this spiritual work. I would have to read many books and listen to many sermons and talk with many friends and others who have been at this work for a while already. It would be a Christian way of understanding, particularly a Roman Catholic interpretation, so that my wife and son would be able to support me and offer access to their own support network. For me at this moment, it would be a big step simply to *seek* a way to live life fully while seeking union with God. Any tried-and-true way could suffice. The Christian way seems as good as any, but coming to accept Jesus Christ as my Saviour would be a challenge. By comparison, dealing with the particulars of Roman Catholic Christianity would be the least of my concerns. To be humble, to detach myself from worldly possessions, to give and receive forgiveness, to care for those in need, to give thanks in all things, and to persevere in faithfulness to the end (as listed by our parish bulletin) is a daunting program in itself. But I thought I could set these as *my* program, too.

What is the end? The purpose? The meaning? The seeking for answers must continue. But I have already had some success, I thought, in sneaking good glimpses of Truth past the watchful dragons of my prideful self-consciousness. These glimpses gave me hope of even greater success in the future. I resolved not to worry about the end. It would come in its own way and its own time. The details would have to sort themselves out. I could only have faith that sincerely seeking union with God would settle the rest.

An essential element of this spiritual journey would be the fellowship I join and keep with my companions on the universal stage, each with our share of the Divine. I recently heard science journalist Michael Guillen say that "relationships bring meaning, light and God into our lives." I concluded he was right. My wife and son have certainly shown me this truth. And my animal companions as well. While I could no longer claim the study of nature as the sufficient path to knowing the Creator of all, birdwatching would continue to be a special aid to my spiritual journey. When I cannot see the Divine in people through the fog of mental chatter and emotional action and reaction, I know that I can pick up my binoculars, take a walk through a natural area, no matter how manhandled, and dependably catch a glimpse of the Divine in the birds I see. They are available when I need them.

All these birds in all this nature had brought me to my senses. Thich Nhat Hanh writes about the "bell of mindfulness." In his practice of contemplation, Nhat Hanh rings a bell to remind himself and the people around him to return to the conscious breathing and smiling that makes them aware again of the moment in which they live – right now. Mindful of the life we have in this moment, we can see and understand the food before us, the task at hand, the people and nature in and around us, the Eternal within and beyond, and the happiness available in the here and now. Nhat Hhan lives in Europe, where church bells are heard regularly through the day. Each time a bell rings, it reminds him and his students to return to that mindfulness.

Nature is my church, and the birds are my bells of mindfulness.

∞

I could see the train for Winnipeg waiting at the station. At exactly 10 o'clock, the train pulled out and diminished slowly to the south. I watched it as long as I could, thinking of the events of my trip north. I had no desire to take the train back. I'd happily chosen to leave by plane at 11:30 a.m. the next day, if only to give myself another half day. But the train's departure symbolized the end of my visit. I got up to go, yet stood looking out on the river for many more minutes.

At last, I walked back up the tracks toward the entrance to the Port. There ahead of me was a lone birder looking out on the river through binoculars. I immediately wanted to share the week's experience, but all I could offer were the Snow Buntings – just as I wanted to share them with the Winnipeg birders on my first day, the way Bonnie had shared them with me yesterday evening.

I walked directly up to him and smiled a greeting. He gave a puzzled smile in return.

"You can see Snow Buntings just down these tracks," I told him. "They're in among the rocks at the water's edge. You see where that stream comes into the river? They're right there." I pointed.

Only then did it become clear that he could not express himself in English. He sounded Italian. Convinced that any world-travelling European could at least *understand* English, I repeated myself more slowly and in less detail. But he was puzzled by what I was saying. I suspect the key words he failed to understand were "Snow Bunting." Without that, there was no way he'd grasp the significance of my directions. I wasn't getting through to him – a fellow birder come all the way from Italy. I was suddenly and profoundly sad. The extreme difficulty of sharing with a fellow human being, even another birder, what is so personally precious and meaningful was brought again into sharp focus. Though I could recognize myself in him and feel the bond of common purpose, I would never be able to share my experience with him. Yet I felt his fellowship simply in being out there with me on the riverbank, with binoculars, looking for birds. My spirits lifted as I reckoned that he must find this evening precious and meaningful in his own way.

I could think of nothing more to say or do. I wished him a good evening and good luck. He smiled. I smiled and turned to walk back to the hotel to finish my packing. I looked over my shoulder. He still stood looking through his binoculars at the river, making no move down the tracks. I hadn't made the connection for him with the Snow Buntings, but perhaps he was making his own discoveries of birds that I had missed. In other circumstances, he and I would be friends.

∞

I finished packing a little before midnight. I felt restless. I wanted to go out again – to see how dark it was, if I could see any stars. I walked up toward the bay, around the Anglican church and onto the open ridge between the bay and the Granary Ponds. My destination was the flagpole, from which I could still see the Canadian flag flying. It was dark, but no darker than a full-moon night. I could easily see where I was going. The sky had clouded over again, obscuring the stars. I passed a young woman out walking. We warily greeted each other with "Hello" and "Good evening," each wondering what the other was doing out this late.

I stood beneath the Canadian flag and gratefully watched this remote outpost of the civilized world sleeping in the half-dark of the subarctic wilderness.

To Those Who Helped Me Believe in This Book

Who knows how many books have been denied to the reading public by the self-doubt of their authors? This is a safeguard against embarrassment – it has great "adaptive value," says the evolutionist – but it also presumes the author can truly judge the worth of the work. The more personal the story, the less the author can be the judge. Others must read and react. They should be the judges who sink or float the project.

If my wife, Christine M. Dodson, had not loved this book in its earliest form, and all its subsequent revisions, I would have set aside any further thought of seeking affirmation. To Chris, this book owes its very existence.

Since happily married authors cannot fully trust in their spouses' objectivity, I still had grave misgivings as I sent out copies to family and friends. The reactions were mixed. I would not have predicted who would tell me how much they enjoyed my writing and who would respond with ambiguous silence. Without the supportive words and active encouragement of Rosemary Dodson, Dave Dunford, Walter Boyce, Ian Deshmukh, Nanny Carder, Marilyn Aucutt, Janice Pulliam, Chuck Dodson, Russell Davis and Charlie Dunford, this project would have remained on my shelf as a journal of my week's vacation in Canada. They saw both its value and its potential for better.

They emboldened me to share the book with co-workers, and I was rewarded by more enthusiasm from Kathleen Stack, Ellen Vor der Bruegge, Claire Thomas, Joan Dickey, Robb Davis and Vicki Denman. Claire persuaded me that seeking to publish your own writing is not just an act of self-aggrandizement, but the fulfillment of a duty to share your inspiration.

The first version of the book made me keenly aware of both my nascent spirituality and my profound ignorance of true religious inquiry. I set out in search of understanding with a visit to the Rev. Richard Blinn, S.J., who convinced me that you can be both intellectual and religious – I still marvel at his patience with my naïveté. My Mennonite colleague, Robb Davis, took it upon himself to school me in the moral and political implications of Christianity. Vincent DiCarlo shared his library and his even more impressive Roman Catholic intellect. My Methodist friend, Bill Buchanan, shared his own interpretation of faith and introduced me to C. S. Lewis. Professors Maria Jaoudi and Harry Smith supplied books and ideas on the margins of the Christian world view and beyond. Without all this guidance, I would never have penetrated my self-imposed barriers to spirituality.

Having revised the book to deepen its spiritual meaning and broaden its appeal, I faced the nearly impossible task of finding someone in some publishing house whom I could intrigue enough to read such an odd book as this one. I approached published authors for advice and was rewarded by the interest and kindness of a few. Leonard Nathan was especially thoughtful and helpful. Barbara Kingsolver (a workplace acquaintance from many years before) and Pete Dunne (a noted author on birding) offered me some critical pointers about the publishing challenge.

For all the interest and encouragement, I am embarrassed to say that I lost heart for two years or more, until my dear friend Ellen Vor der Bruegge sent the second version of the book to her old friend Marie Connors, a birder and a literature professor at the University of California, Irvine. It was Marie's enthusiasm and encouragement and professional advice that finally gave me the sense of confidence and determination to create a good synopsis and send it directly to several smaller publishing houses.

Still, I felt resigned to going through the motions to fulfill my obligation to the source of my inspiration – perhaps the source of all inspiration. I almost looked forward to the day when I had finished ticking off the names of the publishers as they sent back their polite and not-so-polite letters of lack of interest, so that I could say that my duty was finally done. But I was surprised by one (and only one) expression of interest in seeing the full manuscript. Within a month, I was asked to call Kevin Burns of Novalis to hear his reaction to the book. He clearly "got" what I was trying to do and was intrigued. But, he said, I would have to do a lot more work on it before he could seriously consider adding this odd book to the Novalis list. Then he proceeded to tell me what he thought the book needed, without telling me how to do it. If I could figure out the how, he said, he would like to see the revised, expanded version.

I found Kevin's advice and challenge empowering and invigorating. I rewrote and expanded the book within four months while holding down a more-than-full-time job and participating in a busy family. Again, it was my wife's love and her deep respect for this project that allowed me to do it at all, and so quickly. Kevin's reaction to my new version made me believe in this book at last – enough so that his further prodding to add a bit more here and there was easy to respond to, and happily. I also found the excellent editing of the final, final version by Suzanne Nussey and Anne Louise Mahoney a remarkably pleasant experience. Novalis even asked my talented friend Robin Mouat to do the chapter illustrations. I marvel at the slim likelihood of finding such a good fit between a book and a publisher. Just a matter of good, dumb luck? I doubt it.

It is now up to the readers of this book to judge its value. But its value to me has been deepened and broadened immeasurably by the support of so many thoughtful, wonderful people. I now fulfill the original purpose of this project, stated on the first page, by offering this value to my wife, Chris Dodson, and my son, Jeremy Dunford, to both of whom I dedicate this book. May they treasure this book almost as much as I treasure them.